HIGH SCHOOL ASTROLOGY

A TEXTBOOK OF AGELESS WISDOM

WRITTEN AND ILLUSTRATED BY ARISA VICTOR AS

GRANNY RAINBOW

Second Edition
ISBN 978-0-9818977-5-2

Over the Rainbow Productions

Ageless Wisdom for the Young and Young-at-Heart

www.GrannyRainbow.com

www.lvx.org

**Published by
Fraternity of the Hidden Light
2009**

DEDICATION

For all young people,
with great love and respect.
You are the hope of our future
and our teachers of today.

We will make it on this planet
because of youth and truth and love.

Buckminster Fuller

MISSION
STATEMENT

Granny Rainbow and Friends
support young people's natural spirituality. We invite
the young and young-at-heart to journey
together on the Path of Light into the
Aquarian Age of Peace.
We live by and teach the timeless truths of
Ageless Wisdom, honoring the divinity of every living
being. We are spiritual, not religious.
We serve Mother Earth
with utmost
devotion.

Granny Rainbow trained for ten years in the Builders of the Adytum Mystery School of Holy Qabalah and Sacred Tarot. She has been a professional occultist since 1968. In 1979 she was ordained as a Priestess of Isis, and in 1987 she founded a Temple of Isis (the ancient Earth Mother and Mistress of Magic). Besides counseling clients, she has taught astrology, tarot, magic, Cabala, and Goddess lore in private homes and schools, public schools and facilities, bookstores, and summer camps. Her students have ranged in age from 4 to 94. She holds a vision of a new world arising like a phoenix from the ashes of the old.

Granny came of age in the 1960s, and has always believed that peace and love will transform the world. She is living proof that the spiritual path to higher consciousness can be exciting and lots of fun. She lives in the beautiful San Francisco Bay Area.

*Ageless Wisdom Welcomes You
to the Path of Return* ~

♥   *the Great Adventure into your True Self,*

♥   *most treasured of the Sages,*

♥   *where Angels are always on call.*

♥   *The goal is Freedom.*

♥   *Your Heart is the gateway.*

♥   *The Sun, Moon, and Stars light your way.*

TABLE OF CONTENTS

PLEASE NOTE:

Throughout this text, words in **bold** type
are defined by accompanying words in *italics*.
These words and definitions are also in the Glossary.

PART 1.

INTRODUCTION

This is a book about astrology
as an expression of Ageless Wisdom.
You stand before an infinite ocean of consciousness.
You may get your feet wet here,
or dive in anywhere.

LETTER TO READERS, FIRST EDITION

Dear Readers,

You do not have to be a high school student to read this book, and yet, I'm serious about this being a high school textbook. As I write, astrology is not being taught in high schools, but I feel that it could be, should be, and will be so taught. There will come a time when the ideas in this book will be commonly accepted and practiced.

You might be attracted to a course in astrology in the same way that you would be drawn to any other branch of study—chemistry, for instance. Psychology, mathematics, and philosophy are all incorporated into astrology. Astrology and astronomy are sister sciences.

This book sets forth the basic occult science of astrology. **Occult** simply means *hidden, concealed*. People may give it other connotations, but that is all it really means. Metaphysical disciplines such as astrology seek to understand what is happening <u>behind the surface appearances</u> of life. What magic lies <u>hidden</u> within humanity? What power is <u>concealed</u> in "empty" space? Occultists explore the mysteries of life. To their delight, this exploration is a never-ending quest.

Astrology is also an art, one of the ancient mystical arts that are becoming so publicized as we move into the Aquarian Age. There is a lot of talk about astrology these days, but we have barely scratched the surface of what it could contribute in terms of greater personal and world harmony. One purpose of this book is to help you interpret your own horoscope. Self-exploration is a most important use of astrology. I hope you find this pursuit very exciting and rewarding!   *(mostly) written 1978*

Dear   Friend

May light be extended upon you.
May you walk the Path of Peace.
In magic realms of wisdom
May your joy increase.
Trust your Self.
Love your Self.
Be your Self.

YES

Introduction

LETTER TO READERS, REVISED EDITION

Dear Readers,

It was a remarkable adventure to teach this course in a private high school in Berkeley, California, in 1978. My students were eager, smart, and talented. They grasped the torch of the Light of Ageless Wisdom and ran with it. Our experimental class proved that teenagers could be wise occultists. These young people showed a natural inclination to use their magical knowledge to make the world a better place.

Idealism soars high in youth. To help keep that precious flame of purpose and vision glowing brightly, I offer this manual again. Its many additions and changes have sprung from thirty more years traveling the Path of Return since *High School Astrology* was first published.

My beloved daughter was a high school senior the year I taught from this text. Now I am grandmother. All these years have not dimmed the fact that I still remember very clearly what it was like to be a child and a teenager. It wasn't easy. If I had known the Ageless Wisdom when I was young, it would have saved me a lot of grief. From an early age, I was looking for something but I didn't know what. Finally, at age twenty-nine I was introduced to the Cabala, High Magic, and spiritual occultism. Unbeknownst to me, this major event in my life occurred during an important astrological transit, my first Saturn Return. I didn't have a clue about Saturn at the time—but that was about to change!

Because I had heard that occultism was "bad," I had never considered having anything to do with it. Fate had to intervene. A friend gave me some tarot cards and a membership in an organization founded by Paul Foster Case, a mystical wizard of the greatest stature and magnitude. What a revelation it was to discover an ancient, yet timeless, philosophy that confirmed my own intuitions about the universe. Bit by bit, my misery transformed to joy.

So I offer these wisdom teachings to today's kids, in the spirit of love and compassion, so you can get good information early in life. More power to you. You are going to need it to straighten out this world. It is my heartfelt belief that positive metaphysical books should be widely used as high school textbooks. Courses could have names like: "The Meaning of Life," "How to Succeed as Your True Self," or "What Every Earthling Needs to Know About Where We Come From."

Blessings,

Granny Rainbow

Listening

PREFACE

From the ancient occult sciences "modern science" evolved. Magicians transformed themselves into "scientists."

Astronomers emerged from astrologers. **Webster's Dictionary** gives under the heading **astrology**, "1. [Obs.] astronomy." Obviously somehow astronomy escaped from its parent. In any case, for thousands of years, observations of the stars have been systematically recorded and interpreted. Our modern scientists are quite satisfied with mapping the heavens, charting the course of the stars and planets, and conjecturing about how it all started and when it will end. They scorn the idea that there is any inherent <u>meaning</u> in the sky patterns.

In contrast to this view the East believes, and has believed, that <u>all</u> the phenomena of life contain meaning. Astronomical data are still interpreted by astrology. The original impetus—the ancient search for meaning—enlivens the scene. In the Far East one expects guidance from the heavens.

Alchemists attempted to transmute base metals into gold, discover a universal cure for disease, and prolong human life indefinitely. Their early, crude experiments with Nature evolved into the scientific method. As they improved their skills, they gained respectability and became known as "scientists." The power drive that motivated them in the beginning continued to inspire them.

The exploitation of Nature for profit underlies most scientific research. The net result of these efforts is earth-shaking, as we all know. Mother Nature is stirring uneasily in her bed as she contemplates the scope of the experiments.

The actors on the ancient stage have returned in new costumes. Merlin, an accredited magician, is reborn Sigmund Smith, Ph.D., guiding light at Anti-Noxin Research Corporation where he is transforming oil into polyester. Paracelsus is back as head of Galactic Pharmaceutical Company. He has discovered that manufacturing <u>many</u> specifics is much better business than bottling one universal panacea. Mem-el-Habib, the master embalmer of the pharaohs, is in the operating room doing heart transplants. He firmly believes in the ancient dream that he can prolong life indefinitely.

In the cosmic time-scale, the startling change from occult science to modern science has occurred with magical swiftness. Undoubtedly, as we emerge from the present scientific age, we shall be forced to invent new descriptions for the masters of life and nature. "Scientist" is far too restrictive a title for the creators of the new age.

Written in 1978 by Jason Lotterhand
*Author of **The Spoken Cabala: Tarot***
Explorations of the One Self

To enter into the Kingdom of the Skies is to enter into the spirit of the cosmic order spread before us in the heavens.

Paul Foster Case

Hubble Photo of Spiral Galaxy M101

©NASA and STScI.

INTRODUCTION

Some of the ideas in this book may seem strange to you at first. Some of the language may appear difficult. When speaking of the Magical Arts, one is trying to talk about something that is really beyond words. The deeper wisdom in these studies is <u>felt by the soul</u>, not thought by the intellect. Many mysterious forces are at work behind the surface appearances of life. It is rewarding to search for the meaning that lies hidden inside. Astrological symbols, such as planets and signs, are keys that can open doors to the inner workings of the human psyche. Astrology is a powerful language, worthy of whatever time and energy commitment you are willing to make. This subject is not for the lazy.

The amount of astrology presented here is "the basics." The style is positive and life affirming. If everyone could get this information in the same way we get basic math and health education, then we would be better able to understand "what makes us tick." We could relax and enjoy one another without undue expectations or requirements that people be any different from who they are. We might actually discover more similarities than differences. After all, Earthlings all have the same ten planets and twelve signs (in infinitely varying combinations).

Parents and teachers who know basic astrology are able to nurture children according to their true natures. Inner and outer conflicts are healed, and relationships of all kinds flourish in the light of astrological acceptance. Individual self-awareness and sense of purpose deepen considerably through study of the natal horoscope, or birth chart.

This text contains all you need to know to be intelligent about astrology. Beyond this, there is a vast body of astrological knowledge spanning many cultures and millennia. You may or may not wish to continue these studies after working through this book. Just know that if you assimilate what is offered here, astrology will henceforth be a useful tool. Please test all theories. Do not "believe" without examination. Observe carefully, take your time, and gather experience. Be sure to get the facts straight; then you can be sure of the results!

The doctrines of the Universal Cabala, or Ancient Wisdom, are based on the philosophy that Life Itself is a unity. All genuine occult sciences aim at conscious awareness of this cosmic truth. Your own deep inner Self is your best guide and teacher in any effort to explore the mysteries of life.

Feel free to write your own discoveries and inspirations in this book. Color the pictures. Draw your own pictures. Please do the exercises. Try to <u>feel and live</u> what you are studying (not just think about it). The sages say that any effort we make along the Path of Return is never wasted. Our gradual enlightenment is built into our bodies and spread throughout our lives, so the rewards for our efforts become obvious. Then we know life is saying,

"Thank you for caring."

Revelation

Scholar penetrating the veil between the worlds

Swiss engraving, early 1500s

Introduction

PART 2.

AGELESS WISDOM

Astrology is one branch of an infinite vine
that twines throughout the universe.
This mystical vine of life, known as Ageless Wisdom,
grows from basic root principles,
grounded in the One Self.

THE TORCH OF TRUTH

YOU WILL KNOW THE TRUTH

AND THE TRUTH WILL MAKE YOU FREE.

Jesus

AGELESS WISDOM

A golden thread runs through the fabulous tapestry that is human experience on Planet Earth. Through all our wild ups and downs—our gatherings, separations, mistakes, revolutions, and triumphs, our work and worship, love and art, business and play, our inspirations, inventions, and investigations—through all the millennia, a shining light has guided our souls' journey. This unfailing light is the torch of Ageless Wisdom, burning brightest when events seem darkest. The One Light expresses itself differently in every culture, from the rainforest ceremonies of indigenous peoples, to the scriptures of organized religion, to the deepest stirrings of spirit in the hearts of today's youth.

There have always been children, women, and men of highest integrity and courage who embraced the truth, and through the power of that Reality, kept alive the vision of humanity's divine identity. These masters of life have always worked towards the time of our awakening. That time is upon us now. Humanity, and perhaps Earth herself, cannot long survive unless spiritual truth is widely known and applied on every level of society, from grammar schools to governments all over the world.

What is this truth, this light, this golden thread contained in the body of knowledge called Ageless Wisdom? What is the Secret Doctrine that has been taught in private, but now must be proclaimed around the world? It is this: God lives in you as your Self, your Christ, your Goddess, your Buddha-nature. The labels are not important. The simple fact is that the innermost Self of humanity is a divine being of limitless light and love who is One with All.

Believing we are mortal and limited, humans lost their way. Great teachers who were examples of Selfhood, such as Jesus, White Buffalo Woman, and Buddha, came to remind us of who we really are. Through the ages, sprinklings of ordinary people have awakened to Self-Realization. Now these are the days, foretold of old, when Ageless Wisdom is available to all. Human beings who want to remember and reclaim their Godhood are enabled to do so now. The world is ready. The choice is up to you.

It would be better to live one single day
knowing the Excellent Doctrine
than to live a hundred years
without knowing the Excellent Doctrine.

Buddha

GOD

GOD is a big topic. Eventually the world will agree on a definition of God. In the meantime, let us consider the viewpoint of Ageless Wisdom: God is all that ever was, is, or will be. Nothing exists outside of the ALL. This means that everything is part of God. Each person and creature, each rock, tree, and cloud, each and every atom of creation, is in no way separate from God. They <u>are</u> God. They are each unique, individual expressions of the One. They are all made of One Light. All share One Life and One Mind. They share One Body, too, which we call the universe. Put it all together and you have an inconceivably vast, indescribable, universal Being. Cabalists call this divine Being THE SELF.

Since there is nothing but God, it logically follows that <u>you are God</u>. You are not the whole big thing, but every part of God is equal to every other part of God, and that includes you. Consider the Biblical statement, "You are made in the image of God." Or as they say in the Yoga tradition of India, "God dwells within you as your Self." There is a deeper Self in you, a birthless, deathless, God-Self that infinitely outshines your mortal personality self. Spiritual occultists search beneath the outer appearance (the ego) for the "Pearl of Great Price," the innermost Self.

He [or she] who knows the Self...
sees it within his own soul, and sees all beings in it.

The Upanishads, ancient scripture from India

God, the One Self, is not male or female, but a unity with both masculine and feminine attributes. Sages through the ages have discovered that God-Realization is Self-Realization. God does not care <u>what</u> you call God, but does appreciate <u>when</u> you call God.

There are as many names of God as there are beings in the universe. Here are a few of Granny's favorites. What are yours?

All That Is	The Beloved (Sufi)	my Source and my Goal
Divine Mother	Great Spirit (Native American)	God/dess
Divine Father	Pachamama (Inca)	The Great Mystery
Divine Child	Nature (Earth Spirituality)	Light, Life, Love
Creator	Allah (Islam)	Heart of my heart

NOTE: For an up-to-date definition of **Creator**, see the Glossary, page 200.

To feel love is to experience God.

Ageless Wisdom

✳

Whichever way you turn, there is the face of God.

Muhammed

✳

Whatever you do to the least of these
brothers [and sisters] of mine,
you do it to me.

Jesus

✳

**The matrix of Buddhahood permeates all sentient beings.
All beings are therefore Buddhas in themselves.**

Buddha

✳

God is common to all.

Gandhi

✳

Kindness is my true religion.

Fourteenth Dalai Lama

A kindergarten teacher was observing her classroom of children while they drew. She would occasionally walk around to see each child's artwork. As she got to one little girl who was working diligently, she asked what the drawing was. The girl replied, "I'm drawing God." The teacher paused and said, "But no one knows what God looks like." Without missing a beat, or looking up from her drawing, the girl replied, "They will in a minute."

Circulating for years on the Internet

GOD IS LOVE

John, Disciple of Christ

"The question is whether you're ready to act as if you're loved by God. People think that God doesn't love them, and so they act as if that's true. That's why the world is the way it is right now. People say with their mouths that God is there and loves them like a mother or a father, but they don't believe it in their hearts. What would happen if they really did believe it? Then the love that's all around them would start to extend from them to touch other people, and then everyone would be healed. It's really very simple. So the question just has to do with whether people are willing to accept what is already true."

"To accept what is already true?"

"Yes, because that's how we feel it. The children are here to feel what is true, and to help others do that as well."

"Anna, if you could say anything to all the adults of the world, what would it be?"

"I would tell them to realize how strong they are, and that the more they love one another, the more that strength comes out. People are so afraid of their power because they think they will hurt one another. It only seems like there are a lot of us here. There really aren't. There is only one of us."

Anna, a 12-year-old Bulgarian girl,
speaking with James Twyman when he was
*doing research for his book, **Emissary of Love***

If you've opened your loving to God's love,
you are helping people you don't know
and have never seen.

Rumi

LIGHT

WE ARE LIGHT. In ancient temples this information was a closely guarded secret. Now science has made it available to all. In third grade this writer learned that everything is made of light. I was so moved with a sense of wonder by this astounding fact that it has captivated me all my life. Light is just as mysterious to me now as it was to that nine-year-old girl. As a child, I fell in love with light. Not knowing it at the time, I had set foot upon The Path.

Light is synonymous with atomic energy, except that from the viewpoint of Ageless Wisdom, light is <u>living and conscious</u>. Everything in the universe is made of atoms that come from starlight. Stars are suns. Our glorious Sun is a stupendous mass of ongoing nuclear explosions — the only nuclear reactor we need. The Sun gives us our life, our consciousness, and the atoms that make up our bodies, all transmitted as LIGHT. Sunlight is freely given to everyone without exception, with nothing asked in return. Light is manifested love, so Father Sun is a stellar example and teacher of unconditional love.

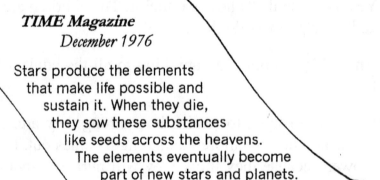

TIME Magazine
December 1976

Stars produce the elements
that make life possible and
sustain it. When they die,
they sow these substances
like seeds across the heavens.
The elements eventually become
part of new stars and planets.
Thus in death there is rebirth.

There are two truths, intimately known and reaching beyond all boundaries. The first of these is that joy does not come from outside, for whatever happens to us, it is within. The second truth is that light does not come to us from without. <u>Light is in us</u>, even if we have no eyes.

And There Was Light, *by Jacques Lusseyran,*
blind teenage hero of the French Resistance

NOTE: At 16, Jacques had formed and was heading 600 youth against the Nazi occupation. He wrote these words after surviving Buchenwald concentration camp. Nazis are stuck in dense darkness. <u>Only</u> light's higher vibrations can help them find their way back to love.

the True Self

WE ARE LIGHT.

the outer appearance

Most people object to the speed of light.
It arrives too early in the morning.

DARK

I form the light and create darkness.
I make peace and create evil.
I the Lord do all these things.

The Tanakh, Yeshayah (Isaiah) 45:7

Misunderstanding of the dark has caused untold havoc in the human mind, which in turn has created massive and needless suffering on this beautiful planet we all share. To correct this unhappy situation, we must stop calling the dark "bad," and realize that darkness is <u>necessary</u> in this dimension. The **Tai Chi symbol** *shows light and dark as partners.* This ancient Chinese diagram teaches us the nature of relationship.

Earthlings live in a world of **polarity**, *the interaction of opposites.* All polarities are held together by a **unity**, which is *love.* Love sees only pairs and equal partners, never enemies. A few examples of polar partners contained within a unity:

UNITY	YANG	YIN
magnetism	positive	negative
one Earth rotation	day	night
human beings	male	female
natural forces	fire (assertive)	water (receptive)
animals	dogs	cats
voting	yes	no
brain	left hemisphere	right hemisphere
understanding	obvious	mysterious
divinity	spirit	soul
human nature	God	animal
super conscious	self-conscious	subconscious

VERY IMPORTANT: <u>All people have both yang and yin, male and female qualities</u>. There is no real separation. We all have everything! In spite of this fact, humans have been resisting the yin half of life for thousands of years, forgetting that each half of a pair defines the other half. "Father" means nothing without "mother," "husband" is meaningless without "wife," night defines day, and NO can be a very liberating word.

The sad fact is that we humans have been denying our own dark side because we associate darkness with evil. What we resist, persists. A lot of seeming evil disappears when we start accepting the dark half of life. We need to make peace with what psychology calls our **shadow**, *the denied parts of our psyche*. Our Creator made us the way we are, dark side and all. Once we accept that there is nothing wrong with us, we can integrate the juicy energies of our animal nature (body), harmonizing them with our exalted divine nature (soul).

Making peace with the shadow does not mean throwing morality to the winds—quite the contrary. The highest moral stance is to <u>love at all times, no matter what</u>. Love transforms the difficult aspects of darkness, just as a lamp illuminates a room. Love lets us stop fighting, and relax.

Spiritually we live in a world of unity. Physically we live in a world of duality. *Not seeing the essential unity behind apparent opposites* is called **dualism**. Our right-brain feelings tend more towards spiritual unity, while our left-brain intellect tends more towards dualism and separation. Judgments such as "good" and "bad" are born from dualism.

Please ponder the Biblical statement, "I the Lord create evil." This means there are forces in this third-density world that are allowed to make things difficult, slow things down, cause fear and pain. These options exist for karmic balancing (page 141). What appears as evil is really the action of a loving universe that is offering us three great gifts. 1) CHOICE: a chance to use our precious free will, 2) GROWTH: a way to discover talents and strengths that lie dormant until we rise to meet a challenge, and 3) SELF-REALIZATION: to see our own light, we must go into the dark. Today we face enormous challenges on planet Earth. Will humanity bravely rise to meet them by choosing love? Each time <u>you</u> choose forgiveness over anger, you help everyone move beyond judgment.

> *As Light and Dark dance entwined throughout endless ages,*
> *their eternal embrace creates a great mystery,*
> *the RADIANT DARKNESS.*
>
> *Wisdom of the Cabala*

There is another aspect of darkness that has profound spiritual significance: The Great Unknowable Mystery of Life. In this case, darkness represents our ignorance. How can it be that anything exists? How does it all fit together in such awe-inspiring detail and complexity? These matters are <u>dark to our understanding</u>.

NATURE

In ordinary usage, the word "nature" is applied to plants, animals, mountains, the weather, etc. People often forget that humans are part of nature, too. A reminder is right there in the phrase "human nature." You are just as much part of nature in a big city as you are on a mountaintop.

When we capitalize the word **Nature**, it includes *all things in time and space, the entire universe.* This dictionary definition of Nature is very close to the Cabala's definition of God. We all come from Nature. We live and move and have our being within Nature.

Astrology is a direct expression and explanation of Nature's forces, cycles, and moods. Astrological signs change as the seasons change. For instance, there are signs of planting and signs of harvesting, which occur in the spring and fall. Nature is the macrocosm. Within the microcosm (you) similar natural forces, cycles, and moods are always unfolding. By correlating the macrocosm and the microcosm (page 34), astrology helps us to understand our natural selves.

At this point in our evolution, we humans tend to think of ourselves as separate from each other and the rest of life. Big mistake. Luckily, all the evidence points to the truth of unity. Consider the message of ecology: everything in Nature is interdependent, tied together. If you <u>look</u>, you will <u>see</u> that this is so.

All are caught in an inescapable network of mutuality,
tied in a single garment of destiny.
Whatever affects one directly, affects all indirectly.

Martin Luther King

It is of utmost importance for personal, family, and planetary health that we realize our inter-connectedness with all life everywhere. To remain ignorant of our unity with Nature is to insist on a lie, the lie of separation. Each individual is <u>distinct</u>, but not <u>separate</u>. We are ONE. As human beings realize their unity with All That Is, they join a global community of awakening souls who are transforming human consciousness. TOGETHER, we are God. Each being, human and otherwise, is no more and no less God than any other. All are equally loved and supported by our divine mother, Nature, and divine father, Spirit.

The earth is our Mother,
She gives us good food.
The sun is our Father,
He gives us warm light.
The stars are all our brothers and sisters,
And the moon guides us along

So don't you know how lucky you are,
To have so many friends.

The earth is loving you,
The sun is loving you,
The stars are loving you,
And the moon is loving you.

So don't you know how much you are
Loved.

Rami Vissell, at age 11
Rami's Book: The Inner Life of a Child

We are all Mother Nature's sons and daughters. Human babies are born with a natural love of Nature, and a feeling of unity with all life—especially with their mothers. Did you know that all human embryos begin as females? The Y chromosome that makes a male enters the embryo five to six days after conception.

EXERCISE: Observe yourself and other people with these questions in mind: What happens to our connection with the natural world as we grow up in this society? What can we do to strengthen, regain, or begin our relationship with Mother Nature? Do you personally believe it would be beneficial to do so? If so, what would be some benefits?

MAGIC

Magic is *the creation of something out of no-thing,*
or the transformation of one thing into another,
done by focusing one's will and feeling in the quantum Field of all possibility
(the Cosmic Mind).

Sensitive people have been appreciating the magic of life for a very long time. Consider these marvels: A large plant grows from a tiny seed. When you cut your finger, your body heals itself. When you really want something, the very thing you visualized may "just pop up out of nowhere." This book has no interest in so-called 'stage magic,' which is mere illusion. Rather, it is hoped that you will learn to observe, practice, and consciously use the real magic of life.

The astrological planet Mercury represents our intellect, which is our inner magician. We all have Mercury in our astrology charts, so we are all full-time magicians. Every human being is born with the power to create something out of what appears to be nothing. Ageless Wisdom explains that the cosmos exists within an invisible matrix called the Cosmic Mind, which holds all possibility. It is like a quiet field of fertile soil that awaits whatever seed the farmer chooses to sow. The matrix is not a thing; it is no-thing, yet all things come from it. Some ancient sages called this potentiality the Womb of God. Or they likened it to an infinite ocean. Today, quantum physics calls it the Field.

Through the power of focused desire, our intellect stimulates the Field, and what we have "asked for" (thought about) precipitates into our world of things. But let us not forget another of life's mysteries: things are actually made of atomic energy. The solidifying power known to astrologers as Saturn causes things to appear to exist in our three-dimensional world. A magical worldview looks at the physical world of things, bodies, and structures as being holographic, projected by the light of consciousness from the Cosmic Mind through the lens of our belief systems.

Magic happens within and around us constantly. The really important part, for us, is to realize we are creating our small-r reality with the power of our minds. There is an underlying big-R Reality that holds the whole cosmic magic show together. Our challenge is to recognize and appreciate our God-given powers of manifestation and transformation, and use them responsibly. Spiritual occultists realize that desire, the Will-to-Be, creates the world in partnership with the Cosmic Mind. In gratitude, they wisely do their best to bring about the highest good for all by focusing peaceful, heart-felt desire energy to create positive results. The most exciting challenge of all is the High Magic of spiritual self-transformation, wherein one's psychological "lead" is changed to spiritual "gold".

The Universe is mental, held in the mind of the ALL.   *The Kybalion*
Three Adepts

PART 3.

ESOTERIC SCIENCE

Astrology gives insight
into the inner meaning
hidden in certain patterns and relationships.
This insight is cultivated by
the study of esoteric science.

ESOTERIC SCIENCE

esoteric (adjective), from Greek, **eso**, *within*
1. mysterious or secret
2. said of knowledge understood only by the initiated

exoteric (adjective), from Greek, **exo**, *outside*
1. of the outside world, external
2. not intended for only a chosen few

These dictionary definitions need some explanation because they were written from an exoteric viewpoint. One cannot fully understand the inner world of mind and soul/psyche from the outside looking in. From that perspective, esoteric subjects certainly seem mysterious. Indeed, they do deal with life's mysteries. But they are not really a big secret that only a chosen few "initiated" people can know. It is just that esoteric things are <u>not obvious</u>, not yang, physical, or external. They are <u>internal</u>, yin, and subtle, only known through receptivity to feelings and sensations.

Our society has been emphasizing the intellect and mistrusting the feeling-emotional nature for a long time. This has led to a dangerous imbalance. The Cabala teaches that the intellect is designed to <u>serve and learn from</u> the feeling nature. <u>Feelings are a superior faculty</u>, able to sense the spiritual worlds. This is what makes babies holy; they have not developed their ego or intellect, so they are naturally at one with God and the universe.

Our feeling nature, connected to our right brain, does not go away when we grow up. It waits patiently for us to turn our attention **eso**, *within*. Anyone who wants to examine their own mind and soul is welcome to do so. Your innermost Self will initiate you. You become "chosen" for inner work when <u>you decide</u> to travel the Path of Return.

Historically, the leaders of organized religion have not wanted people to find God within themselves. That would have put the priests out of business! And government leaders did not want people to follow their inner feelings because they wanted to have all the control. As a result, humanity temporarily lost its God-connection and went crazy. The horrible insanities associated with human nature, such as greed, murder, war, destruction, etc., are only on the surface. The true human is a magnificent, divine, and peaceful being.

In the past, only the "few" had an opportunity to explore esoteric subjects. These matters <u>had to be kept secret</u>, to avoid persecution by the aforementioned power structure. Happily, in the current Aquarian atmosphere, opportunities to explore our true nature are becoming widely available. A tremendous spiritual revolution is occurring on Earth NOW! Dear reader, you can choose to be a part of the great awakening. Just say to God, "Put me in, Coach." God will say, "Okay, go for it!"

as in "Know Thyself"

science (noun), from Latin, **scire**, *to know*
1. systematized knowledge derived from observation, study and experimentation carried on in order to determine the nature or principles of of what is being studied
2. a branch of knowledge or study, especially one concerned with establishing and systemizing facts, principles, and methods by experiments and hypoteses, as in "the science of music"

physics, exoteric study of the physical world, the third dimension
metaphysics, esoteric study of spiritual worlds, fourth dimension and above
quantum physics, combines metaphysics and physics in non-dualism

Astrology is one of the esoteric sciences, also called occult, mystic, or spiritual sciences. The dictionary definitions of science given above apply to astrology. All science explores Nature. Esoteric science seeks direct knowledge of Nature, without the use of exterior instruments. Instruments of exoteric science, such as the telescope and microscope, are extensions of our outer senses. Esoteric science develops a corresponding inner sensorium. The famous "third eye" is our instrument of inner vision, which gives us the ability to <u>see into</u> things, behind their surface appearances. We also have inner hearing, taste, touch, and smell.

Inner knowledge and outer knowledge are both inherent in the universe, built into the way things are. The desire to know oneself is just as strong as the desire to know facts about one's environment. Natural law applies to mind and soul as well as to physics and chemistry. We need both kinds of science, since we apparently live in two worlds. The inner world is an experience of the right brain; the outer world is a left-brain experience. To develop a healthy balance of both sides is to have the whole brain experience. This fusion of opposites ☯ is more exciting than it sounds. Balancing of polarities leads to enlightenment. When there is no more separation, All is One! ☺

A person who embraces esoteric science is a seeker on the path that leads within. The goal of the quest is one's essential Self. Each aspirant makes this all-important discovery by himself or herself. Nothing outside of you can tell you who you really are. Take heart—God helps you, because God <u>is</u> you.

With God all things are possible.

Alchemical Principle

SISTER SCIENCES

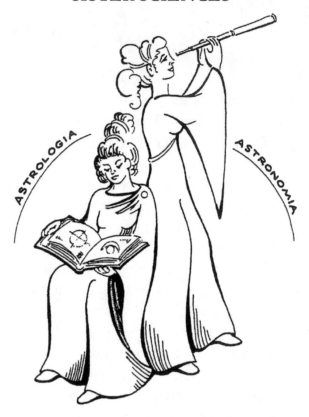

Astrology and astronomy are sister sciences.

In ancient times, "science" and "magic" were thought of as the same thing. Scientist-Magicians, who were students of Nature, practiced both astrology and astronomy as one branch of knowledge. Astrology probes inner space, just as astronomy explores outer space. Your inner universe is every bit as vast and exciting as the outer one.

In nineteenth century United States, astrology and astronomy were still taught together in public schools. Then people forgot the spirit of Ageless Wisdom, and came to think of astrology as a superstition or even a hoax. This change coincided with the mechanization of our world. Astronomy went its own way, disowning its "other half." In some ways, science has vastly improved the quality of our lives, but its separation from spirit has had drastic consequences. Modern people are just starting to realize that the twenty-first century does not have a monopoly on wisdom. We have much to learn from the wise ones who have gone before us on The Path. It is time to reunite those brilliant, beautiful Star Sisters, Astrologia and Astronomia.

> **The most beautiful and profound emotion we can experience is the sensation of the mystical. It is the sower of all true science.**
>
> *Albert Einstein*

26   Esoteric Science

ASTRONOMICAL BACKGROUND

All the planets are held in their orbits by the gravitational pull of the Sun. The Sun's influence is felt for at least 5.9 billion kilometers, which is the distance from the Sun to Pluto. Everything within that span is thought of as being contained in the *body of the Sun*, the **heliocosm** (HEE-lee-o-cosm). The planets orbit in *a force field that extends in space from the Sun's equator*, known as the **plane of the ecliptic**.

The apparent path of the Sun among the stars is called the **ecliptic**. The zodiac extends for approximately 8 degrees (8°) on either side of the imaginary line where the ecliptic touches the so-called "fixed" stars. From our Earthly viewpoint, the Sun, Moon, and planets all appear to move through the twelve constellations of stars that we see in this area of space. There are many constellations in the sky, but only these twelve form the zodiacal signs.

In old Greek, **planets** meant *wanderers*. The concept of planets has evolved to mean only those heavenly bodies that orbit suns (stars). The Moon orbits planet Earth, and obviously the Sun does not orbit itself. So in today's astronomy, the Moon and Sun are not called planets. Astrology still includes the Moon and Sun among the planets because they travel across our sky in the same path as the other wanderers. The stars are not really fixed in the sky, but they are called the **fixed stars** because they *appear as a stable background to the moving planets*.

Celestial bodies move at different rates of speed. The Sun takes one year to complete a cycle of the zodiac. The Moon takes about a month to complete the same cycle. Sometimes there are as many as six planets in one sign, and sometimes they are spread throughout the zodiac.

Approximate Spans of Time the Planets Spend in Each Constellation:

Sun ....1 month
Moon ....2½ days
Mercury ...... 2-4 weeks
Venus ....1 month
Mars .... 2 months
Jupiter ...... 1 year
Saturn ....2½ years
Uranus .... 7 years
Neptune ......14 years
Pluto .... 14-25 years

PRECESSION OF THE EQUINOXES

Due to the gravitational pull of the Moon, Earth's axis rotates like a slowly spinning top. It describes a gigantic circle in space, moving backward through the zodiac at the approximate rate of one degree every 70 years. *One backward cycle of about 26,000 years* is called a **Great Year**. Contained in the Great Year is another cycle called the **precession of the equinoxes**, which *pinpoints the zodiacal sign and degree with which the Earth's spinning axis is aligned at the moment of the spring equinox.* Every year this point moves backward .042 degrees.

An **equinox** *happens twice a year in the spring and fall, when Earth experiences equal amounts of day and night.* The vernal equinox marks the beginning of spring, when the Sun crosses the equator heading north. In the fall, at the autumnal equinox, the Sun crosses the equator heading south. In the northern hemisphere, the first day of spring is whatever day the Sun's northern crossing occurs, somewhere between April 19 to 22. This movement initiates the first day of autumn below the equator. Precession is measured from the spring equinox in the northern hemisphere.

An astronomical age is one twelfth of a Great Year, or about 2,160 years. In the Age of Taurus (the Bull), cattle represented wealth; gods and goddesses were symbolized by bulls and cows. The Age of Aries saw the rise of patriarchy. Jesus initiated the mystical, sacrificial Piscean Age. It is foretold that the Aquarian Age will bring peace on Earth. May it be so!

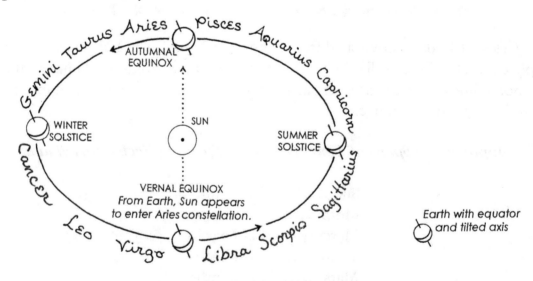

Earth-Sun Relationship at Equinoxes and Solstices
Spring begins when the Sun enters zero degrees Aries at the moment of equal night and day.
Each sign is thirty degrees, written 30°. The twelve signs make 360°, a full circle.

EXERCISE: Using this diagram, determine which signs the Sun enters at the summer solstice, fall equinox, and winter solstice, from the viewpoint of Earth..

TYPES OF ASTROLOGY

The precession of the equinoxes gives rise to two different types of astrology, **tropical** *western astrology* and **sidereal** (sy-DEER-ee-al) *eastern astrology*. Both are completely valid. This books deals only with the tropical system. Eventually, you may wish to study the sidereal or Vedic method, which arose in India long ago. Aries is the first sign of the zodiac. The zodiacal year begins with zero degrees Aries, 0°♈. The two different systems disagree on just what constitutes zero degrees Aries. This is not an either-or situation; both systems are correct.

Tropical astrology uses the yearly **spring equinox** as the starting point. *The exact moment of equal day and night* is called 0°♈. The whole year, until the next spring equinox, is divided up into a 360° circle, which is divided into 12 signs of 30° each. No matter where the precession of the equinoxes is pointing at the moment, tropical astrology sticks with this metaphysical definition of 0°♈.

Sidereal astrology is more physical. It sticks with the fact that, due to precession, each succeeding spring equinox (the vernal point of equal day and night) occurs in a slightly different place on the wheel of the Great Year. This means that astronomically, the vernal equinox occurs in 0° of the physical Aries constellation only once every 26,000 years—the time it takes for the Earth's axis to trace its grand circle around the zodiac. The rest of the time the vernal point happens in some other degree and/or sign. As this book is written, that degree is, and has been, in Pisces for centuries. It will enter Aquarius in about 400 years. Readers of this book only need to know that, from either viewpoint, the precession of the equinoxes is taking Earth into the Age of Aquarius, the Golden Age of Peace.

Most western astrologers agree that the long-prophesied Aquarian Age is beginning NOW. It is possible for many differing views to contribute to the whole picture. China has its own astrology, and the Maya of Central America have a kind of galactic astrology. Some of their calendars outline the evolution of consciousness, and predict the end of time <u>as we know it</u> on the Winter Solstice in 2012.

It takes all kinds to make **A WORLD.**

Old Saying

NOTE: If this precession discussion seems too complicated, forget it. You do not need to understand precession, or the differences between the types of astrology, to be a good astrologer. This information is an effort to explain the Aquarian Age in astronomical terms.

THE AGE OF AQUARIUS

Many prophecies in ancient cultures foretold an era of peace on Earth in the distant future. These prophecies are coming true in our time, as the precession of the equinoxes inexorably moves toward the constellation of Aquarius.

When man shall again conquer the ocean and fly in the air like a bird, when he has harnessed the lightning, then shall the time of warfare begin. Great shall be the battle between the forces of darkness and of light. Nation shall rise against nation, using dark forces to shatter the earth.

Then shall come forth the Sons and Daughters of the Morning, saying, "O man, cease from thy striving against thy brother. Only thus can ye come to the light." Then shall the Age of Light be unfolded, with all people seeking the light of God.

ancient Egyptian prophecy

♥ ♥

There will come a time when all the animals will be dying.
The Warriors of the Rainbow will come to save them.

old Navajo prophecy

♥ ♥

WE ARE THE ONES WE HAVE BEEN WAITING FOR.

recent statement by Hopi Elders

The Aztec sages tell us that we are entering the Sixth Sun, the Age of Flowers. The flowering of our planet occurs as we freely share and receive whatever we have to offer each other, creating our global village together, one person at a time. Similarly, whole cultures become fully appreciated by each other, until the entire world has achieved integration. We go inter-dimensional and inter-stellar, sharing our blossoming process to the max with all beings everywhere. Then the Sixth Sun will be fully risen, and Earth will be in much higher light. The Aquarian Age will be in full swing. The whole process is definitely gathering momentum now. Granny Rainbow fondly hopes that you, dear reader, will lead your life in such a way as to support and empower the dawning of the Golden Age of Miracles. What an amazing time to be alive!

Aquarius the Water-Bearer is beautifully depicted in Tarot Key 17, The Star. Mother Nature is pouring blessings into the inner world of mind and soul (the water) and onto the outer world of body and sensation (the land). She teaches us to balance inner and outer equally. The Great Goddess embodies the Life Force radiating from the stars. The right angle formed by her leg symbolizes truth.

The tree trunk in the background represents the human spine; its leafy crown symbolizes our brain. The ibis bird is humanity's intellect, which sees vibrations (wavy hair) from a distance, in a partial view. In order to truly see the Star Goddess, one must see with the heart. One must <u>love her</u>, for "No one has ever unveiled Isis." Isis-Nature unveils herself to her lover, her devotee. What does she reveal? All this and more: the mysteries of the universe, the Laws of Nature, and the truth in whatever form her devoted servant needs it at the moment. Here are some of the things Key 17 teaches us about the Aquarian Age:

✳ It is a time when Mother Nature is recognized and honored as a Divine Being. By following her laws, we restore our beautiful Earth to health and happiness.

✳ Humanity lives in the spiritual world as much as in the physical.

✳ We are aware of the Great Love that enfolds us, as we gratefully open our hearts to receive and share all Nature's gifts.

✳ Each person who appreciates Nature can have a loving personal relationship with her. She can be contacted in meditation (water) or through any aspect of the natural world (land).

✳ Humanity has a close connection to the stars.

✳ The Aquarian Age is a time of peace and beauty.

Tarot image from BOTA School of Holy Qabalah and Sacred Tarot 5105 N. Figueroa St., Los Angeles, CA 90042 323-255-7141 ✳ www.bota.org

The Shift of the Ages is the term applied to the process of Earth accelerating through a course of evolutionary change, with the human species linked by choice to the electromagnetic fields of Earth...The human aspect of The Shift may be consciously facilitated, even accelerated, through the use of choice, free will and emotion associated with the ancient wisdom of the human mind-body-spirit relationship. This is the purpose of The Shift, the ultimate balance and healing of the Earth and all the forms that are capable of sustaining the energy of that healing. This is the shift to a new way of expressing the human form, through the lens of higher frequency, a Christed energy. This is Awakening to Zero Point: The Collective Initiation.

Awakening to Zero Point
Gregg Braden

NATURAL LAW

The Sun, Moon, planets, and stars all follow exact patterns of movement. The timing, motions, positions, and interrelationships of the planets in our solar system may be measured precisely. By mathematical calculations, we may determine where Jupiter was in the zodiac on January 1st in the year 1 CE (Common Era). Or we can accurately predict where the Sun will be on the Summer Solstice in the year 2012. Exact positions of all the planets at the time of your birth can be pinpointed.

The celestial bodies operate according to Nature's perfectly designed machinery, Natural Law. Natural Law is completely dependable; it never breaks down. All individual parts of the universe cooperate with each other, working together in harmony. Some people see great beauty in the eternal dance of the sky-dwellers. They speak in glowing terms of the Order of the Heavens and the Music of the Spheres.

Astrology affirms that the same laws determining the order of heavenly bodies also operate in the lives of people, nations, and events. Natural Law underlies every happening, from the greatest to the least. The Law of Life determined a certain momentous event known as your birth. The sky-patterns that existed then will never be seen again. They are exclusive to that particular place and moment, which explains why <u>you are exceptional</u>.

But don't get puffed up about being special, because each and every person is special. The **ego**, *the sense of separate self*, might think if everybody is special, then "special" loses its meaning. However, from the perspective of your true Self, every person is an extraordinary miracle. (**Self**, *your divinity that is joined with all life*; **person**, *an individual personality and body chosen by the soul*.)

Natural Law has been working overtime to create all the people who live on planet Earth. We are so numerous that we can no longer escape from each other, so we <u>must</u> learn how to get along together. The Aquarian Age is the Age of Humanity. We will have peace on Earth when we can honor and respect each other, without wanting to change each other. Let's all become a human **rainbow**, *an harmonious collection of countless differently colored particles*.

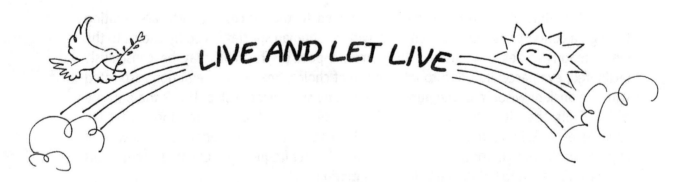

one of Granny Rainbow's all-time favorite sayings

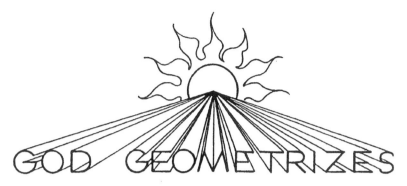

GOD GEOMETRIZES

Old Saying

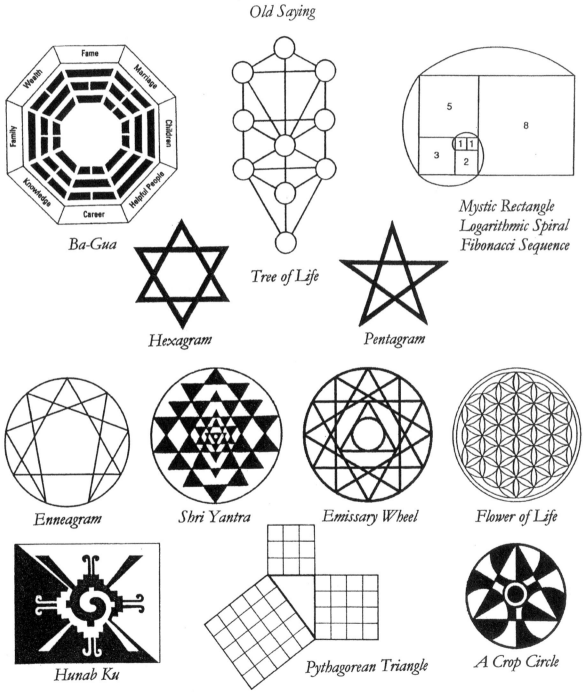

Ba-Gua

Tree of Life

Mystic Rectangle
Logarithmic Spiral
Fibonacci Sequence

Hexagram

Pentagram

Enneagram

Shri Yantra

Emissary Wheel

Flower of Life

Hunab Ku

Pythagorean Triangle

A Crop Circle

THE LAW OF CORRESPONDENCE

Astrology is based on the Law of Correspondence:

AS ABOVE   SO BELOW

MACROCOSM	MICROCOSM
Large World	*Small World*
HEAVEN	EARTH
GOD, NATURE	HUMANITY
THE UNIVERSE	AN INDIVIDUAL

The macrocosm is big; the microcosm is small, yet in essence they are the same. Each created being is a miniature universe, containing all the same qualities as the parent universe. Everything the larger cosmos can do, you can do too, and vice-versa. As below, so above.

Astrologers reason like this: You are not one thing and the universe a different thing. The universe is everything, the ALL. Since you are a part of the All, you must be like it. You must work the same way it works. The abilities of the universe are your abilities. Its desires are your desires. Its energies are your energies. And, very important for astrology, <u>everything that is going on in the heavens at the moment of your birth is going on in you</u>.

Life is infinitely creative. Every snowflake has a unique design. There are no two flowers or musical compositions or people or horoscopes exactly alike. Every "now moment" is different from every other. When you think about it, this is really amazing!

The universe is like a gigantic jigsaw puzzle. Each piece of the puzzle, each thing in creation, has a special shape. All pieces are needed to complete the whole picture. All pieces are equally important. Those who embrace this view are able to lovingly accept themselves and their fellow humans, and other creatures as well. We are all in this together.

EXERCISE: Think about this: In what way are you unique? What makes each of your friends special? Can you see that these traits are not "good" or "bad?" They just <u>are</u>.

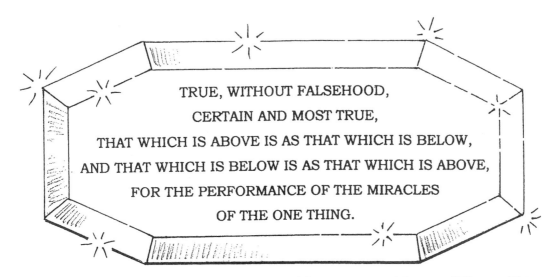

The Emerald Tablet of Hermes Trismegistus

TRUE, WITHOUT FALSEHOOD,

CERTAIN AND MOST TRUE,

THAT WHICH IS ABOVE IS AS THAT WHICH IS BELOW,

AND THAT WHICH IS BELOW IS AS THAT WHICH IS ABOVE,

FOR THE PERFORMANCE OF THE MIRACLES

OF THE ONE THING.

Astrology works because of the Law of Correspondence. Each moment in eternity has a distinctive vibration that extends through all levels of the universe, from the highest to the lowest (throughout the whole Tree of Life, page 145). Perception of up and down arises from separation thinking. In Reality, life is <u>all one thing</u>, so whatever is happening "up there" is also happening "down here."

An **astrological chart** *symbolizes a cross section through the universe at a particular instant, experienced at a particular spot on Earth.* The never-to-be-repeated energy of a specific moment is impressed upon a newborn infant for his or her lifetime. Each "slice of eternity" contains specific patterns and information arising from the interaction of cosmic forces, which are in constant flux. Since these living forces act according to Natural Law, we are able to make sense of them, and derive meaning from them.

Ageless Wisdom firmly asserts that every being gets the perfect chart for the most soul growth. No one is "dealt a bad hand." Heaven blesses all babies and their charts. Each of us is exactly who we are meant to be. No matter what worldly circumstances may occur, our essential Self remains innocent, pure and perfect.

> *Life is good and God is love,*
> *Grace is flowing from above.*
> *Stars their blessings do bestow*
> *On all creatures here below.*
>
> *corny song by Granny*

EXERCISE: Explore <u>As Above, So Below</u> by making a list of ten or more correspondences between yourself as a microcosm, and the universal macrocosm. For example, you might be an artist, and Nature paints sunsets. Or, you eat and assimilate food, and so do all living creatures. You have strong emotions; Nature has stormy weather.

LANGUAGE OF THE STARS

DERIVATION AND DEFINITION OF ASTROLOGY

aster, Indo-European, *star*
astron, Greek, *star* + **logos**, Greek, *word* = **astrology**, *language of the stars*
astrology *communicates what the stars have to say. It is a science of correspondences
between the macrocosm and the microcosm.*

In very ancient times, the first astrologers could converse with the planets and stars. Since everything is part of the One Life, it is natural for humans to receive messages from Nature. In today's mechanized world, it may seem outlandish to think of talking with the stars. However, even now, people who live close to Nature are often directly attuned to subtle (occult, hidden) forces. They can contact the **spirit**, *the intelligent life-essence within a person, place, or thing*, by communicating heart-to-heart, through feelings. We all have this ability. Spirit is in everything. There is a lot of communication going on in the universe that we can tune into if we open our hearts and minds to receive.

The stars seem far away in time and space, but in the Cosmic Mind there is no separation. You yourself may have personally experienced communication with animals, trees, stones, wind, water, clouds, the Sun, Moon, stars, or any number of natural forces. When we are in Oneness consciousness, we have no problem understanding a fellow creature, even if that creature happens to be a plant or a planet.

ALL HAIL THE ONE COSMIC MIND

message on the awning, Shambhala Booksellers, Berkeley, California

EXERCISE: Try an experiment in cosmic telepathy. Go where you can watch a sunset. When the Sun is <u>halfway under the horizon</u> it is okay to look at it. Do not look straight into the Sun at any other time. As our Day Star is setting, gaze into its glowing face, and send loving thoughts of thanks for the Sun's gift of life to you. Then sit quietly and pay attention to any feelings that arise within. You may feel the Sun loving you back.

It is possible to do a similar experiment with the Moon, except that you don't have to wait for a certain time. Anytime you can see the Moon is a fine time to commune. What would you talk to the Moon about? Or, you don't have to talk; you can just <u>feel</u> the natural connection between the two of you.

Esoteric Science

The Zodiac (extracted)　　　　　*Full Diagram with Zodiac and Other Constellations*

Ceiling in the Temple of Hathor, Dendera, Egypt
This was a huge birthing temple, where women came to have their babies.

Star beings who live in the heavens have a vast perspective compared to Earthlings. It is wise to pay attention to what they have to teach us. Modern astrologers use information bequeathed to us by the first astrologers. In other words, people did not just "make up" astrology. It was transmitted to humanity from the heavenly bodies themselves. We can tune into these same sources. They are all available, just waiting for us to pay attention. We can use the information to expand our consciousness, improve our self-awareness, understand each other, make plans, fulfill our destiny, and enrich our lives in countless ways.

The language of astrology is closely aligned with what science calls **psychology**, *study of the mind and soul.* Contrary to popular notions, most astrology is not about predicting the future. Astrology is best used for understanding the dynamics of the inner life of our mind and soul. The universe knows why we are the way we are, and communicates this wisdom via star messages. The wise astrologer uses these heavenly gifts to advise, heal, empower and enlighten—never to control others or create anxiety about the future.

As for the future, it only exists in our minds. What really matters is NOW. The future is not something already decided, just waiting to happen. Consciously or unconsciously, we create our own future in the present. When we are aware of divinity within, we naturally choose what will work out for the best. We sense the cosmic plan for us (our soul's chosen mission) and simply allow it to unfold, like a flower in the process of blooming. No forcing is necessary or advisable.

SONG OF THE STARS

Someone in the Algonquin tribe of Native Americans must have heard the stars singing this song one beautiful star-spangled night. Perhaps the song "just appeared" in their consciousness (inspiration). Or maybe the person heard the singing light with their inner, psychic ear (*extra-sensory perception*, or **ESP**, page 170). At any rate, that shaman taught the song to everyone so the whole tribe could appreciate the beauty, power, and mystery of the stars. A **shaman** (SHA-mon) is *an indigenous term for one who communicates with the spirit world.*

Judging by their song, the star spirits do seem to be joyous, friendly, and helpful, don't you agree? There is nothing to fear from them. So please don't scare yourself or others with astrology, the language of the stars. Remember the spiritual wisdom expressed in this song. Starlight is alive, aware, compassionate, and protective—and stars love to sing! Spirit is transmitted to us by starlight.

Important information from physics: Every particle of everything that exists on Earth is made of Sun-star-light (atoms). Metaphysics takes this information a further, far-reaching step, explaining that stars are the bodies of beings who are alive and conscious. Of course this aliveness includes our local star, the Sun. Ageless Wisdom teaches that <u>we get our consciousness from the Sun</u>. Listen with your inner ear. What song is the Sun singing? Does it sing in chorus with other stars?

EXERCISE: If possible, go out under the stars at night. Talk to the stars, attune to them, perhaps pretend you are a star. Then write an essay answering the following question: **What does it mean to sing with light?** You may illustrate your essay with a painting or drawing, or create a melody for the poem, ***Song of the Stars***, on page 39.

An **essay** is a *short literary composition on a single subject from a personal point of view.* So just grab a piece of paper and write how the stars make you feel. Like the Algonquin musician-poet, you might "take dictation" from the stars, or from a specific star. Some people may want to make a whole fancy page with calligraphy—whatever makes you happy.

While all the exercises in this book are meant to be enjoyable, there is a serious purpose behind these suggestions. One major aim of this book is to put you more in touch with your right brain, your intuitive awareness, so you know what you are <u>feeling</u>. You can stimulate a flow of wise, helpful information by doing **art**, which is *expressing what you are feeling.* Don't analyze your artistic expression. Just "go for it!"

SONG OF THE STARS

We are the stars that sing

We sing with our light

We are the birds of fire

We fly over the sky

Our light is a voice

We make a road

For spirit to cross over

Algonquin Song

MEDITATION

Meditation is *continued thought, holding a focus in the mind, serious contemplation, solemn reflection.* Through the practice of meditation, *the mind eventually becomes still.* Astrologically speaking, meditation (mental focus) is <u>fixed</u> <u>air</u>. There are two types of focus: 1) exoteric/outer and 2) esoteric/inner. By and by they blend.

In the first type, you may direct your conscious focus to something outside yourself in order to understand that thing more deeply. For example, look with sustained attention at Tarot Key 17, The Star (page 31), for insights into the meaning of Aquarius. Meditation may answer questions, such as, "What does Aquarius mean to me personally?" These kinds of practices stimulate feedback from your **intuition,** *your inner power of direct knowing.* The outer object or the question to which your focus is directed is technically called the "seed" of the meditation.

Meditative focus may also be directed inward, to get to know yourself more fully. In this case, the seed of the meditation is your desire to explore your vast inner world. Be prepared for amazing insights to arise from your subconscious. And be brave, because you may see some shocking aspects of your psyche. Our teachers, the masters of Ancient Wisdom, say the entire holographic universe exists in each of us. Do not criticize whatever you may discover within. Simply witness without judgment. Be honest with yourself, keep contemplating, and give yourself plenty of time. Behind every mask that looks like fear, anger, or hatred is the Face of Love. To get past surface appearances, dive as deep as you can into the infinite ocean of consciousness. And <u>listen</u> with your inner ear.

In all our dealings with occult science, it is wise to remember we are dealing with spiritual matters. If possible, you may want to create a simple altar, with sacred-to-you pictures and objects, where you can sit to meditate. Perhaps begin by lighting a candle and/or offering up a prayer. However, you can also meditate at your study desk, on the subway, walking in Nature, or listening to music—any place where you can sustain "solemn reflection" with spiritual intent.

Meditation is a primary tool in any metaphysical study. Since meditation activates the right brain, it can magically pull together separate bits of knowledge that were compartmentalized in the left brain. If you learn the facts and figures in this book, and then meditate on the information, big-picture patterns and significance will be revealed. Guidance for problem solving, connection with your feelings, a wealth of symbolic communication, healing of dis-ease, and unity with the center of your being—meditation offers all this and more.

Let the words of my mouth and the meditation of my heart
be acceptable in thy sight. O Lord.

Psalm 19:14

Note: "Lord" refers to the ruling power of the universe. This power lives in the human heart.

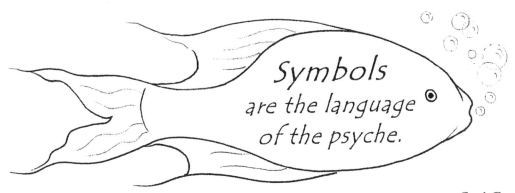

Symbols are the language of the psyche.

Carl Gustav Jung

A practicing astrologer is well versed in **symbolism**, which is *the language of the right brain/psyche/subconscious/intuition/soul.* Your soul may speak in sounds and sensations as well as symbolic images and colors. The **psyche** (SY-kee) is *the mind of the soul.* The **soul** is *an individualized spark of God.* Psyche and soul are contained in the **subconscious**, *a vast sea of awareness underlying the ordinary left brain/self-conscious/rational intellect.* Psyche, soul and subconscious are traditionally represented by water. Intellect is linked to the air element. In meditation, intellect is the "hook" that fishes symbolic communications up from subconsciousness to self-consciousness, from right brain intuition to left brain mentality.

Repeated meditation establishes an "open com link" between the two kinds of consciousness. Through practice, the deep information flows easily up to the self-conscious intellect. By this wondrous process, the intellect and the subconscious eventually merge. Super consciousness is the result of this happy union, known in Hermetic Science as the Alchemical Marriage (page 51).

Eastern philosophers tell us the universe is maintained by unceasing meditation in the Cosmic Mind. Therefore, you do not need to exert effort, but rather relax into the flow of what is already happening. You do not have to sit any funny way or do anything weird. It is perfectly natural to spend some time on the path that leads within. Simply be receptive to what Life and Nature and your Self want to show you. If you like to write, keep a journal of your meditational experiences. Dreams, and insights into dreams, may be included.

Learn from teachers and books but always remember, this is your research and your quest, so your own ideas, words, and methods are best. No person or thing outside yourself can complete or fulfill you. Deep meditation can reveal the most sacred desire of your heart, your innermost Self.

The Self is the dearest of all things, and only through the Self is anything else dear. The Self is the origin of all finite happiness, but it is itself pure bliss, transcending definition. It remains unaffected by deeds, good or bad. It is beyond feeling and beyond knowledge, but it is <u>not beyond the meditation of the sage</u>.

Brihadaranyaka Upanishad *(India, 800 BCE)*

GLYPHS

Glyphs are *symbolic writing.*

α	**alpha**	*area*	mathematics
𝄞	**treble clef**	*upper range*	music
♀	**ankh**	*life*	ancient Egyptian
♂	**Mars**	*energy*	astrology

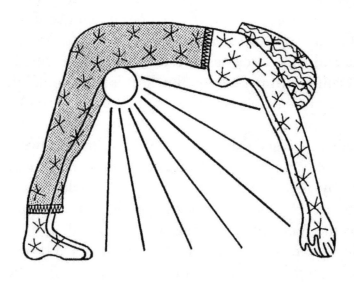

Hieroglyph of Nuit, the Egyptian Sky Goddess

Hieroglyphics (HI-row-GLIF-ics) Greek, *sacred picture writing,*
often with both exoteric (surface) and esoteric (hidden) meanings.

In ancient Egyptian thought, the heavens are one great over-arching body. Stars have different functions, yet they operate together as a whole, exactly like cells and organs in the human body. (As above, so below.) The conscious being whose body is the sky is called Nuit. She gives birth to Ra, the Sun, each morning. Daily rebirth of the Sun symbolizes the fact that each cycle—what we call a 24-hour day—is different, unlike any other. Planets are constantly changing positions in the sky, so Ra always rises on a new scene.

Thy priestesses go forth at dawn; they wash their hearts with laughter.

Egyptian sacred text

Esoteric Science

CIRCLE OF THE ZODIAC

WITH GLYPHS AND HIEROGLYPHS

Capricorn the SEA-GOAT

Aquarius the WATER- BEARER

Sagittarius the ARCHER

Pisces the FISHES

Scorpio the SCORPION

Aries the RAM

Libra the SCALES

Taurus the BULL

Virgo the MAIDEN

Gemini the TWINS

Leo the LION

Cancer the CRAB

THE FOUR ASTROLOGICAL SYMBOL GROUPS

A **horoscope** is *a zodiacal chart based on the time, date, and place of birth.* Astrologers work with four basic symbol groups in order to interpret a horoscope. The four categories are: planets, signs, houses, and aspects.

1. **PLANETS** are *natural forces and faculties that are living, conscious, and intelligent.*
   All humanity shares the same ten planets: ☉ ☽ ☿ ♀ ♂ ♃ ♄ ♅ ♆ ♇

   > **The Moon** ☽ is *our feeling, intuition, and emotional capability.*
   > **Saturn** ♄ *is our power of organization, definition, and self-mastery.*

2. **SIGNS** are *12 constellations of stars that influence the flow of planetary energies. Like the planets, the signs have life, consciousness, and intelligence.*

   We all share the same twelve signs: ♈ ♉ ♊ ♋ ♌ ♍ ♎ ♏ ♐ ♑ ♒ ♓

   > **Fire signs** ♈ ♌ ♐ *excite the planets to action.*
   > **Earth signs** ♉ ♍ ♑ *stabilize the planets.*

3. **HOUSES** are *areas, like fields, where the planets and signs operate.*
   Every chart has twelve houses, which are individualized in each horoscope. A chart's Ascendant begins the first house, which in turn determines all other house placements.

   > Example: **15° Leo ♌ on the Ascendant, ASC**
   > *Begins the 1ˢᵗ house and indicates a strong personality*
   > *who expresses much light and attracts attention.*

4. **ASPECTS** are *relationships between the planets.*
   Aspects are angular relationships determined by the number of degrees of arc between planets. Different angles have different effects. The possibilities for these interrelationships are infinite.

   > *A 90° angle* **square aspect** □ *Creates work and challenge.*
   > *A 120° angle* **trine aspect** △ *Creates harmony and talent.*

Planets = WHAT

    Signs = HOW

        Houses = WHERE

            Aspects = WHY

✪ ✪ ✪ The stars incline; they do not compel. ✪ ✪ ✪

Old Saying

The stars that comprise the circle of the zodiac never "make" us be a certain way, or do a certain thing. We are in charge of our life and our chart. Please avoid blaming heaven for the way things are. <u>The stars are mirrors</u> that we can look into and see ourselves—all of ourselves, including our highest and lowest energies. Heavenly forces are always helping us, whether or not we can understand their cosmic assistance. This is the teaching of Ageless Wisdom.

Sir Isaac Newton was a scientific genius who realized the laws of gravity when an apple fell on his head. To explain his discovery, he invented calculus. He was an astrologer and an alchemist, as well as an astronomer. To a man who derided his interest in astrology, Newton said, "Sir, I have studied the subject. You have not."

Newton proved mathematically that every thing in the universe attracts every other thing, proportional to mass and distance. Thus, all things affect each other. It follows that the planets must have some physical influence on us (and we on them). The Moon causes tides in the ocean, and we are just beginning to discover how much any activity of the Sun affects life on Earth.

However, astrology is not concerned with the physical influence of the celestial bodies. It focuses on the metaphysical relationship between humanity and the heavens. Astrology is a symbolic language that can be translated into ordinary speech. Astrological symbols are a code we can use to describe the functioning of energy and consciousness. Here are some examples of "code translation."

Sir Isaac Newton studied astrology and alchemy.

Venus ♀ is exalted in Pisces ♓ means *the love nature finds its most complete expression in a feeling of unity with all life.*

Gemini Rising, ♊ ASC represents *someone who is active in a diversified quest for knowledge, liking to speak and write about ideas.*

Pluto in the Ninth House, ♇ in the 9th indicates *the desire and power to destroy antiquated dogma, and create new expressions of spirituality.*

Sun trine Moon, ☉△☽ reflects *an integrated personality blessed with harmonious balance between will and emotion.*

NUMBERS

In the beginning,
God created the world
with numbers, letters, and symbols.

ancient Kabbalah Book of Formation

Numerical sequence underlies all manifestation. **Manifestation** is *the process by which the spirit of life creates forms in the physical world*. By the time a form – such as a body, an object, a thought, word, or action – has manifested here in the third dimension, it has gone through the whole process outlined below. If you want to change something that exists in the material world, go back to the top, to the Limitless Light, for a fresh start.

0 FREEDOM   As the Limitless Light, ZERO holds the infinite abundant potential of our boundless universe, from which anything can be created. In astrology, the circle of the zodiac forms a big ZERO.
Eternally existing before manifestation   SUPER CONSCIOUS

1 UNITY   The All-Power concentrates itself at a point of focus by an act of will, through a desire to create. ONE represents will, intention, beginning, initiation, originality, and the creative urge. It is yang and assertive. ONE is represented by a point (dot), TWO by an extended point (line). TWO is still part of ONE. (All the other numbers are also extensions of unity.) For all its divine power, in the manifestation process ONE needs TWO, which is the response to ONE's desire – the "yes" that is built into life. By extending itself into TWO, ONE begins its path to fulfillment. In astrology, the dot in the center of the Sun glyph ☉ stands for the power of ONE. And you are the ONE in the center of your horoscope.
Beginning of manifestation   SELF–CONSCIOUS

2 DUPLICATION   TWO brings polarity and duality, where choice enters the picture. Do you choose to see "the other" as an extension of yourself, or as an enemy? There is really only ONE, but the appearance of TWO makes diversity possible. TWO represents response, reflection, and duplication – a partner or teammate. Yin and receptive, TWO wants to help ONE manifest its desire. TWO rules sequence. In astrology, the signs flow in alternating sequence between yang and yin. Aries ♈ is yang, Taurus ♉ is yin, etc. The second planet, Moon ☽, symbolizes TWO's power of reflection.
Patterns and promise of manifestation   SUBCONSCIOUS

3 MULTIPLICATION Put a yang (male) rabbit together with a yin (female) rabbit, and what happens? Multiplication! This illustrates how the powers of ONE and TWO, combined as THREE, work in fruitful partnership to produce everything. THREE is Mother Nature's number of sexuality, fertility, reproduction, pregnancy, and fruitfulness. THREE is growth, development, expansion, and abundance. It rules imagination and instinct. In astrology, there are THREE qualities: cardinal, fixed, and mutable.
Creative process of manifestation   EROS

 4 ORDER The THREE phase of manifestation may appear chaotic, so FOUR follows with reason, logic, order, and control. FOUR defines, measures, and organizes. FOUR is the boss who lays down the law, creates systems, and writes constitutions. Dependable FOUR gives us a framework for stability and integration. It is associated with logos and language. In astrology, there are FOUR elements: fire, water, air, and earth.
Regulation of manifestation   LOGOS

 5 CHANGE FIVE has the unique distinction of being the middle number between ONE and NINE: 1 2 3 4 **5** 6 7 8 9. FIVE is the number of humanity because spiritually we exist in the middle between Heaven and Earth, and physically between an atom and a galaxy. The middle position is both a gift and a challenge, for it carries tremendous power. FIVE can change or adjust the direction of any manifestation process that has been set in motion. FIVE is exciting, resourceful, versatile, and spontaneous. A healthy FIVE shows strength and aspiration under pressure, and ability to alter things for the better. FIVE does best on the Middle Way between extremes. In astrology, a fifth is a quintile, the most adaptable aspect.
Manipulating and experimenting with manifestation   THE FIVE SENSES

 6 RELATIONSHIP As the number at the center of the Tree of Life, SIX stands for the heart, therefore love, sympathy, empathy, trust, and relationship. A SIX-pointed star combines a fire triangle and a water triangle in perfect equilibrium. This merger is an example of love between opposites, therefore peace, harmony, beauty, symmetry, and balance. SIX also offers acceptance, forgiveness, non-judgment, and cooperation. Now past the middle number, results are starting to manifest according to earlier choices. SIX's love and acceptance help the process to blossom fully. In astrology, a sixth is a productive sextile aspect.
Appreciation of manifestation   HEART OF HUMANITY

7 PROGRESS SEVEN can clearly see the goal represented by NINE. Here the manifestation process gains strength, purpose, and momentum. Progress inspires faith, certainty, safety, security, poise, art, and mastery. SEVEN puts purpose into action with intention, patience, perseverance and endurance; it says, "Keep your eye on the prize!" SEVEN knows life is a success process, and victory is a state of mind. The goal of spiritual life is enlightenment, which occurs when the SEVEN major chakras (page 157), go through an awakening process. In astrology, a seventh is a septile, the destiny aspect.

Advancement of manifestation   CHAKRAS

 8 RHYTHM EIGHT stands for **vibration**, *rhythmic movement back and forth*. Everything in creation vibrates, and EIGHT orchestrates all that flowing energy by the power of rhythm, oscillation, alternation, and variation. EIGHT is playfulness, the Dance of Life, and open-mindedness that encompasses all opposites in one. This next-to-last number possesses great skill. EIGHT is the number of **magic**, *the control of vibration*, therefore science, education, and culture. A sideways EIGHT symbolizes infinity. In astrology, the eighth sign, Scorpio ♏, rules magic and the occult.

Exploring and enjoying manifestation   MAGIC

 9 CONCLUSION NINE is the summation of all that went before, from the initial focus of ONE, through the entire process to the final goal. This is where "we reap what we have sown." If we have sown good seed on fertile ground then NINE bestows completion, harvest, fulfillment, satisfaction, and reward upon us. If our seed was faulty, NINE brings disintegration. There is no judgment either way, because mistakes are essential on the path to mastery. From all its experience, NINE has earned wisdom, maturity, and expertise. This is the number of adepts and sages, who through trial and error have learned <u>what works</u>. In astrology, these are the astrologers.

Final manifestation   WISDOM

 10 BEGINNING OF A NEW CYCLE The figure of TEN **10** shows that the power of ONE has extended itself through all the numbers, and having "come full circle," joins ZERO again. Through the wisdom gained in previous cycles, TEN carries the promise of expansion, new hope, and luck. Our loving universe always gives us another chance, since life cannot die. So TEN creates continuity, evolution, and revolution through ever-turning, ever-unfolding creativity. TEN represents the Alpha and Omega, the beginning and end. In astrology, there are TEN planets.

Renewal of manifestation   THE NEVER–ENDING STORY

THE NO-THING (ZERO)

> Everything an Indian does is in a circle, and that is because the power of the world always works in circles, and everything tries to be round...the sky is round, and I have heard that the Earth is round like a ball, and so are all the stars. The wind, in its greatest power, whirls. Birds make their nests in circles, for theirs is the same religion as ours...even the seasons form a great circle in their changing, and always come back again to where they were...and so it is in everything where power moves.
>
> ***Black Elk Speaks***
> *John G. Neihardt*

Sometimes called the No-Thing, zero is not any kind of thing at all, but rather the <u>potential</u> for things to exist. Zero represents the limitless freedom of all possibility. Things have shapes and characteristics; they can be defined. Even thoughts are things. Before things come into being, a mysterious undefined Source pre-exists beyond anything we can think, say, do, or have.

Ageless Wisdom audaciously asserts that this indescribable, before-the-beginning No-Thing is actually our own super conscious Being. In other words, we are not really things! We take on "thingness" when we incarnate into bodies, yet our divine soul remains eternally pure, free, and unattached. The essential Human transcends time and space.

This information may inspire you, confuse you, or both. So just "hold a space" for these teachings. How did the Masters of Wisdom find out about the No-Thing? Through direct experience. As you stroll, stride, or jog along the Path of Return, some fine day your own experience will prove it for <u>you</u>.

 Any circle is also a zero. A wedding ring is a popular circular object, said to symbolize eternal love. Astrological glyphs are made of circles, half-circles, and crosses. For example, the glyph for Venus places the circle of spirit over the cross of matter.

EXERCISE: Sing, draw, or write about one of these names of zero: the Beyond, the Cosmic Egg, Womb of God, Mystery of Mysteries, the Void. You may also create some new names for this cosmic non-number.

NOTE: About the quote at top by Nicholas Black Elk (1863-1950) He was an Oglala Sioux/Lakota holy man who, at the age of 9, had a tremendous heavenly vision that lasted 12 days. His relatives thought he was dying, but he lived to a ripe old age.

THE CENTER (ONE)

When you are **centered**, you are *in touch with your innermost Self.* You feel whole, "at one" with the truth of your being. Centeredness gives you strength, poise, and certainty. In astrological terms you are accessing the power of your Sun, the first planet, whose glyph ⊙ is a diagram of centeredness.

The Native American Sun Dance Ceremony celebrates and honors the star at the center of our solar system. By focusing on our Sun in the sky, the dancers connect with the spiritual Sun at the center of everything. As they encircle a central pole called the Tree of Life, they feel divine light in their own heart of hearts.

In esoteric science, CENTER means:
first point of consciousness
at the heart of things
place of balance
number one
focus
the Now
innermost essence
the super conscious Self
place of connection to Source
point from which a horoscope originates

Some people are under the impression that astrology is not valid because it was once practiced by people who believed in an Earth-centered universe. Here are three statements aimed at correcting that impression. 1) Not all the ancients were ignorant of the true nature of the solar system. There have always been adepts whose understanding far exceeds that of the ordinary person. 2) There is nothing wrong with working from an **apparent** center, *as it appears or seems,* as a basis of orientation. Astronomy frequently works from the apparent Earth-centered system. For example, we think to ourselves, "The Sun is rising and moving across the sky," when really the Sun is stationary (relative to Earth) and the Earth is rotating while orbiting the Sun. 3) The most important thing to remember in this discussion is that astrology speaks in symbols. Symbolically, each of us is at the center of our horoscope, just as we are at the center of our own life and environment—our microcosmic personal universe.

God is a circle whose center is everywhere and circumference nowhere.

Ageless Wisdom

EXERCISE: In meditation, feel into the mystic understanding, "God is centered everywhere." Perhaps dance the feeling with your Self or some friends.

Esoteric Science

THE HERMETIC ANDROGYNE (TWO)

For a discussion of duality, polarity, and otherness, please refer to pages 18-19. Accepting differences and opposites without judgment is an important practice on the Path of Realization. When we separate ourselves from each other for <u>any</u> reason, we create a split in our own psyche. Inner peace comes when we heal that split by embracing all of life <u>just as it is</u>, ourselves included. Wholeness within us is then reflected as unity in our world. To have a healthy psyche, we must forgive instead of blame. And we must see our own darkness in the light of compassion, so we can understand our brothers and sisters in the great family of humanity. Jesus asked us to "Love one another," not just because love feels good, but also because it is the only way to peace.

Beyond good and evil there is a Greater Good that has no opposite. This all-inclusive awareness is shown by the Tai Chi symbol's outer circle ☯. To indicate the same idea, medieval alchemists created a figure (example below) they called the **hermetic androgyne**, which *portrays the union of opposites in a person*. This **alchemical marriage** is greatly to be desired because it *occurs as the result of psychological harmony between a person's yang male and yin female energies* (page 18). Most outer bodies are either male or female, but our psyche has both genders. When we stop the wars between these parts of ourselves, war in the world will cease.

All words in **bold** come from Greek:

Hermes (HER-mees), *god of magic*
hermetic (her-MET-ic), *magical*
androgyne (AND-row-jyne), *dual-sexed being*
    from **andros** (AND-rowss), *man*
    and **gyne**, (GUY-nee), *woman*
Dual-sexed being is
also called **hermaphrodite** (her-MAFF-row-dyte)
    from **Hermes**, *Mercury*
    and **Aphrodite**, *Venus*

The Hermetic Androgyne: Yin and yang elements are equally balanced wtihin the unity of a human being. Doves represent the holy spirit of peace. The vessels symbolize human personality. The unadorned vessel is as nature made it; the other has been embellished by art.

right brain	+	left brain	=	whole brain
subconscious	+	self-conscious	=	super conscious
yin, female	+	yang, male	=	union, androgyny

THE ASTROLOGICAL MODES (THREE)

A **trinity** is *a set of three things that belong together and form one whole.* The astrological trinity is composed of three **modes**, *cardinal, fixed, and mutable.* The table below shows some of the trinities to be found in life.

astrological modes	**CARDINAL**	**FIXED**	**MUTABLE**
consciousness	self-conscious	subconscious	super conscious
atomic particles	proton (plus)	electron (minus)	neutron (neutral)
primary colors	red	blue	yellow
time	future	past	present
movement	fast	slow	vacillating
temperature	hot	cold	medium
alchemy	sulfur	salt	mercury
tarot	Magician	High Priestess	The Fool
Taoism	yang	yin	union
Hinduism	**rajas**, *life*	**tamas**, *substance*	**sattva**, *consciousness*
Tree of Life	**Chokmah**, *Wisdom*	**Binah**, *Understanding*	**Kether**, *Crown*

Astrological modes (also called qualities) are crucial to the formation of the signs. Each sign expresses one mode: cardinal, <u>or</u> fixed, <u>or</u> mutable. Since it is yang, cardinal takes the lead, so the first sign is cardinal. In response, the second is fixed. The third is mutable, a compromise between "irresistible force" and "immovable object." The permutations on page 88 show how the three modes and four elements combine in logical order to create the zodiac.

If most of your planets are in signs of one mode, that is a determining factor in your personality. The sample chart on page 134 portrays a cardinal personality, because half the planets plus the Ascendant are in cardinal signs.

CARDINAL people are active, yang, forward-looking, and full of new ideas. They envision what could happen in the future, so they love to begin new projects. The cardinal quality is INITIATING. Cardinal signs: ♈ ♋ ♎ ♑

FIXED people are stable and grounded, connected with tradition and the past. They form firm opinions and like to put down secure roots. They can sit and talk for hours. The fixed quality is STEADY. Fixed signs: ♉ ♌ ♏ ♒

MUTABLE people are oriented in the present. They have many interests, sometimes pursuing several at once. They are flexible, adaptable, and cannot be pinned down. The mutable quality is CHANGEABLE. Mutable signs: ♊ ♍ ♐ ♓

THE ASTROLOGICAL ELEMENTS (FOUR)

NOTE: The whole numerical process is contained in four: 1+2+3+4=10

Everything is made of combinations of the four elements: fire, water, air, and earth. (This is the order in the worlds of Cabala, page 145.) These ancient elements are different from those listed in chemistry's periodic table of elements. Occult fire is the Divine Father, the initiating spirit, will, and desire that activates the world of water, "impregnating" the Divine Mother. The water of life holds all possibilities in her infinite, oceanic "womb" of consciousness. Air represents the intellect, or Divine Son, who defines and chooses the exact form that will emerge from water. Air rules the "birth" process of seeming separation from the Mother. Finally, earth is the "baby," the result. The earth element contains the fire, water, and air elements. The original fiery impulse finds expression in the world of things. As the embodiment of spirit, the earth element is sacred. Earth is the beautiful, precious, beloved Divine Daughter.

All four elements are fully operational in everyone. Astrologically, it is possible to be **weighted**, *having strength and impact*, in one or two elements, or balanced between all of them. Here is an esoteric "table of elements."

Element	In a Being	Life Essentials	Process	In a Corporation	Cabala Worlds	Tarot Symbols
FIRE	spirit	light	desire	executive	archetypal	wand
WATER	soul	water	response	design dept.	creative	cup
AIR	intellect	breath	decision	machine shop	formative	sword
EARTH	body	food	result	final product	physical	pentacle

When contemplating these magical elements in connection with astrology (for example, a water sign such as ♋, or an air planet such as ☿), please refer to the following key words until you know them more or less by heart. As you continue your studies, add your own definitions.

FIRE   LIFE, spirit, consciousness, energy, action, power, will, initiative, drive, desire, passion, activation, inspiration, aspiration, excitement, zeal

WATER   FEELING, soul, sensitivity, intuition, emotion, psyche, receptivity, ESP, mystic awareness, psychic phenomena, dreams, right brain

AIR   INTELLECT, logic, thought, study, discussion, communication, breath, relationship, commerce, computers, media, logic, left brain

EARTH   BODY, health, values, practicality, endurance, animals, gardens, roots, wealth, manifestation, possessions, resources, temple of spirit

THE PENTAGRAM (FIVE)

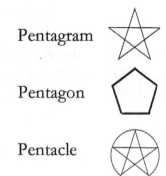

Pentagram

Pentagon

Pentacle

Diagram of the intimate connection between the pentagram and a human being, as exemplified by the Da Vinci Man

Five is the number of humanity (page 47). A five-pointed star, the pentagram, is our symbol. We enjoy five senses: sight, sound, taste, touch, and smell. We have five fingers and toes on each appendage, and we form a pentagram when we extend these appendages. As it says in the pop song by Earth, Wind, and Fire, "You're a shining star, no matter who you are."

The Fibonacci sequence (1-1-2-3-5-8-13-21-etc.) forms the golden spiral, which is a kind of logarithmic spiral. The pentagram embodies this most basic numerical formula by which life unfolds itself. Spiraling pentagrams and pentagons create the DNA of all organic life.

Fiboncci Series in the Pentagram

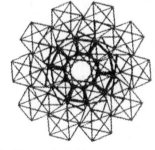

Cross section of DNA

 A pentagram within a circle is called a pentacle. In the tarot this symbol represents the earth element (page 108) and diagrams the alchemical teaching that God is to Man as Man is to Nature (Cosmic Man, page 152).

EXERCISE: Stand with your feet apart and your arms outstretched. Imagine you are a shining star. Feel golden white light coming from your inner God-self. Beam out blessings of peace, love, life, clarity, and joy to all beings throughout the cosmos. Know that your energy really does affect all life everywhere.

Esoteric Science

UNION OF FIRE AND WATER (SIX)

The fire is in the water.

Wisdom of the Cabala

"Fire and water can't be joined together," you might say. But the Cabala says they are never apart! The fire is actually <u>in</u> the water—a mystical statement meaning that spirit is always in the soul, life energy is in rainwater, passion is in emotion, and so on. In terms of the alchemical marriage (page 51), the Father is in the Mother. The cosmos is a never-ending love affair.

The interwoven six-pointed figure called the Star of David is known to Cabalists as the **Shield of Love**, made of *an upward-pointing fire triangle "married" or unified with a downward-pointing water triangle*. The Divine Father (fire) and Mother (water) give birth to the Divine Son (air) and Daughter (earth). Six is the number at the center of the Tree of Life, symbolizing heart, love, harmony, union, relationship, wholeness, and healing.

The alchemical glyphs for the elements are derived from the Shield of Love, following the elemental order given by Cabala. Father Fire flares upward; Mother Water seeks the lowest level. Son is a combination of Father and Mother, but yang, like Dad. Daughter is a combination of Father and Mother, but yin, like Mom.

FIRE	△	FATHER
WATER	▽	MOTHER
AIR	⩜	SON
EARTH	⩛	DAUGHTER

The Cabala order of elements occurs in the zodiac in the elemental rulership of cardinal signs. Cardinal signs initiate seasonal changes around the 21ˢᵗ of March, June, Sept. and Dec. Each season covers ¼ of a year, or 90° of the zodiac. Each season has three 30° signs; these follow the zodiacal fire, earth, air, and water order.

Spring Equinox	-	defines 0° ♈	-	the cardinal △ sign
Summer Solstice	-	defines 0° ♋	-	the cardinal ▽ sign
Autumnal Equinox	-	defines 0° ♎	-	the cardinal ⩜ sign
Winter Solstice	-	defines 0° ♑	-	the cardinal ⩛ sign

THE BEAUTY OF NUMBERS

Numbers are the pure essence of the highest **archetypes**, *the original ideas from which all creation flows*. One is the Most High that creates, contains, and rules all else. Numbers are the bedrock of creation. Behind all form lies sacred geometry. (page 33)

Any finite number can be reduced to a single-digit number from One to Nine. For instance, take Ten and reduce it by adding its digits: 1, beginning + 0, potential = 1. Therefore, Ten is a new beginning, just like One. Let's look at Twelve, the number of signs in the zodiac. 1, creative urge, God + 2, partnership, you = 3, productivity. Three also represents the Trinity of Consciousness/The Three Supernals, from which the three modes of astrology are derived. (See the Tree of Life diagram on page 142; it represents both God and a human being.)

To find your lifetime number, add and reduce the month, day and year of your birth. Example: June 18, 1991. 6+18+1991=2015. 2+0+1+5=8 (magic).

Pages 46-48 give the meanings of each number. Pages 50-55 show some aspects of life that derive from One through Six. Briefly, here are some contributions from Seven, Eight, and Nine.

SEVEN: Days of the week. Astrology's inner planets. The chakras (page 157).

Sunday	☉	Sun	
Monday	☽	Moon	
Tuesday	♂	Tiw	(Norse god)
Wednesday	☿	Woden	(Norse god)
Thursday	♃	Thor	(Norse god)
Friday	♀	Freyja	(Norse goddess)
Saturday	♄	Saturn	(Roman god)

EIGHT: Ancient Pagan Wheel of the Year.   Compass directions.

Winter Solstice	0° ♑	North
Candlemas/Groundhog Day	15° ♒	North-East
Spring Equinox	0° ♈	East
Beltane/May Day	15° ♉	South-East
Summer Solstice	0° ♋	South
Lammas/Midsummer	15° ♌	South-West
Fall Equinox	0° ♎	West
Samhain/Halloween	15° ♏	North-West

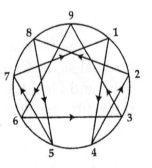

*The Enneagram
Arrows show energy flow.*

NINE: Nine has magical properties; ask any mathematician.

The **Enneagram** is *a system of human energy classification*. Each body expresses one of nine possible types of energy. These energies emanate from our souls and form a 9-pointed star.

VIBRATION

The ancient followers of Hermes realized from their direct experience that everything in the universe is moving, vibrating at different rates of speed. Modern science agrees. Even the most solid-seeming rock is composed of molecules, made of atoms, which in turn are made of sub-atomic particles. All are in rhythmic motion. Differences between manifestations of the One Light are due entirely to rates and styles of vibration. The faster the vibration of something, the higher is its frequency. Higher frequencies influence lower ones.

Vibration occurs on all planes of existence: spiritual, emotional, mental, and physical. Spirit is at the high end of the frequency continuum; dense matter is at the low, slow end. The Path of Return is always shown oscillating from side to side, as well as up and down. The Path gets higher and steeper because the aspirant's frequency is raised (spiritualized) as the soul gains more light.

There are vibratory correspondences between sound waves and color waves that are useful in occult science. Sound is a lower level of the same vibration that becomes light when it is raised several **octaves**, *repetitions of pattern in the spectrum of vibration*. This accounts for mystical tales of "hearing light" and "seeing sound." A color (light vibrating at a certain frequency) and its corresponding sound (same rate of vibration at a lower frequency) may be used to augment healing and awakening. All astrological planets and signs have Cabala sound and color attributions.

For humans, audible sound vibrates at about 20 to 20,000 cycles per second. Visible light vibrates at 450-780 billion cycles per second. As below, so above. Sound and color oscillations correspond as follows:

EXERCISE: With your voice or an instrument, play or compose a simple tune using some or all of these notes. With the corresponding colors, create a "visual" of the tune. You could create the picture first and the tune second. Perhaps base your work on your favorite colors, or create rainbows of sound and color, referring to the next page for the six or twelve colors of the rainbow.

COLOR ATTRIBUTIONS

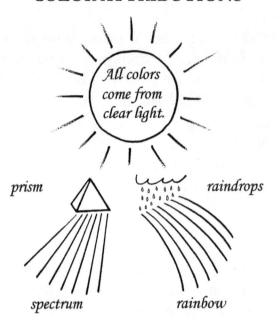

We live in an infinite ocean of light. Everything we see, hear, taste, touch, and smell is really light, or as a mystic might say, "God's holy light is All." The super-tremendous original source of light may be thought of as the Spiritual Sun, Great Central Sun, or **Lux Occulta**, *Hidden Light*. **Enlightenment** means *being able to see or sense the light (divinity) in everything.* The perception we call **color** *is caused by light vibrating at ascending frequencies through 12 distinct rates of oscillation.* Red is the slowest rate. Colors are associated with the signs and planets of astrology:

Red	♈	♂	♇
Red-Orange	♉		
Orange	♊	☉	
Yellow-Orange	♋		
Yellow	♌	☿	♅
Yellow-Green	♍		
Green	♎	♀	
Blue-Green	♏		
Blue	♐	☽	♆
Blue-Violet *	♑	♄	
Violet	♒	♃	
Red-Violet	♓		

*also called Indigo

COLOR WHEEL

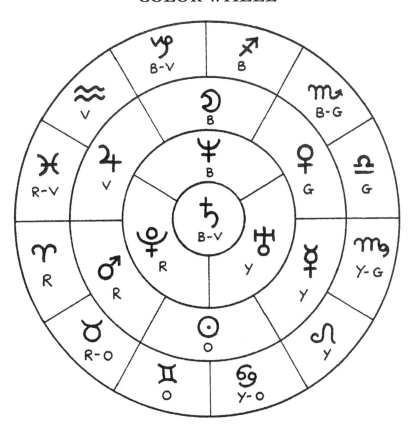

Clear (or "white") sunlight can be broken up into all the colors of the rainbow. There are 6 basic spectrum colors in the rainbow: Red, Orange, Yellow, Green, Blue, and Violet (Purple). Mixtures of these colors create 6 more, such as Red-Orange, Yellow-Orange, etc. Shown in the outer ring of the color wheel, the resulting 12 colors are allocated to the 12 signs of the zodiac, in rainbow order.

In the middle ring and central circle are colors for the 7 original planets. Each of these planets connects with one of the 7 major chakras, to which rainbow colors are often assigned (page 157). This chakra/planet connection is why it is sometimes said there are 7 colors of the rainbow: 3 primaries (Red, Yellow, Blue), 3 secondaries (Orange, Green, Violet), and 1 tertiary (Indigo, or Blue-Violet). The 3 primary colors of the inner ring are attributed to the trans-Saturnian planets (orbiting beyond Saturn).

PRIMARIES: Red, Yellow, Blue (not created by mixture)

SECONDARIES: R+Y=Orange, Y+B=Green, B+R=Violet (Purple)

TERTIARIES: Red-Orange, Yellow-Orange, Yellow-Green, Blue-Green, Blue-Violet, Red-Violet

EXERCISE: Color the wheel above, construct your own color wheel, or both.

THE PLAY OF NIGHT AND DAY

EXERCISE: Stare at this diagram for about a minute. Then close your eyes and see the polarities reverse.

PART 4.

THE PLANETS

Astrological planets symbolize various aspects
of human life, soul, mind, and body.
We are the planets;
the planets are us.
As above,
so below.

EPHEMERIS

A birth chart, or natal horoscope, shows the positions of the planets in the constellations at the time of your birth. These are calculated from figures found in an **ephemeris**, which *shows the planets' positions relative to the Prime Meridian*. The **Prime Meridian** is *the point of zero degrees of longitude*, located at the Astronomical Observatory in Greenwich, England. Here is part of a page from an ephemeris calculated for noon, Greenwich Mean Time.

At noon, at the Prime Meridian on Mother's Day, May 12, 2001, the Moon was in 19 degrees, 49 minutes, and 35 seconds of Capricorn. Written 19°49'35"♑, or 19♑50. There are 60 minutes in a degree, and 60 seconds in a minute. So in our example, 35 minutes is more than ½ of 60, therefore 49'35" was rounded off to 50'.

MAY 2001							Noon Greenwich Mean Time		
Day	☉	☽	☿	♀	♂	♃	♄	♅	♆	♇
1	11♉10 20	21♌32 25	20♉33	3♈46	28♐26	13♊36	1♊17	24♒31	8♒45	14R46
2	12 08 33	5♍45 47	22 38	4 10	28 33	13 49	1 25	24 32	8 46	14♐45
3	13 06 44	20 00 41	24 40	4 36	28 39	14 02	1 32	24 33	8 46	14 44
4	14 04 52	4♎13 48	26 40	5 03	28 44	14 14	1 40	24 35	8 46	14 42
5	15 02 59	18 20 58	28 38	5 32	28 49	14 27	1 47	24 36	8 46	14 41
6	16 01 04	2♏17 38	0♊34	6 03	28 53	14 40	1 55	24 37	8 47	14 40
⊕ 7	16 59 07	15 59 35	2 27	6 35	28 57	14 53	2 03	24 38	8 47	14 38
8	17 57 09	29 23 37	4 16	7 08	28 59	15 07	2 10	24 39	8 47	14 37
9	18 55 09	12♐27 58	6 03	7 42	29 01	15 20	2 18	24 40	8 47	14 35
10	19 53 08	25 12 30	7 47	8 18	29 02	15 33	2 25	24 41	8 47	14 34
11	20 51 05	7♑38 45	9 27	8 55	29 03	15 46	2 33	24 42	8R47	14 33
12	21 49 01	19 49 35	11 04	9 34	29R03	15 59	2 41	24 43	8 47	14 31
13	22 46 55	1♒48 54	12 37	10 13	29 02	16 13	2 48	24 44	8 47	14 30
14	23 44 49	13 41 18	14 06	10 53	29 00	16 26	2 56	24 45	8 47	14 28
● 15	24 42 41	25 31 50	15 32	11 35	28 57	16 39	3 04	24 45	8 47	14 27
16	25 40 31	7♓25 33	16 55	12 17	28 54	16 53	3 12	24 46	8 46	14 25
17	26 38 21	19 27 23	18 13	13 01	28 50	17 06	3 19	24 47	8 46	14 24
18	27 36 09	1♈41 40	19 28	13 45	28 45	17 20	3 27	24 47	8 46	14 22
19	28 33 56	14 12 00	20 39	14 31	28 40	17 33	3 35	24 48	8 46	14 21
20	29 31 43	27 00 49	21 46	15 17	28 33	17 47	3 43	24 48	8 45	14 19
21	0♊29 27	10♉09 09	22 49	16 04	28 26	18 00	3 50	24 49	8 45	14 18
22	1 27 11	23 36 35	23 48	16 51	28 18	18 14	3 58	24 49	8 45	14 16
● 23	2 24 54	7♊21 14	24 43	17 40	28 10	18 27	4 06	24 49	8 44	14 14
24	3 22 35	21 20 00	25 34	18 29	28 01	18 41	4 14	24 50	8 44	14 13
25	4 20 15	5♋29 08	26 20	19 19	27 50	18 55	4 21	24 50	8 44	14 11
26	5 17 53	19 44 38	27 02	20 10	27 40	19 08	4 29	24 50	8 43	14 10
27	6 15 30	4♌02 45	27 40	21 01	27 28	19 22	4 37	24 50	8 43	14 08
28	7 13 06	18 20 17	28 13	21 53	27 16	19 36	4 45	24 50	8 42	14 06
● 29	8 10 40	2♍34 34	28 42	22 45	27 03	19 49	4 53	24 50	8 41	14 05
30	9 08 13	16 43 27	29 06	23 38	26 50	20 03	5 00	24R50	8 41	14 03
31	10 05 44	0♎45 06	29 26	24 32	26 36	20 17	5 08	24 50	8 40	14 02

Celestial Guide 2001
©*Jim Maynard, Quicksilver Productions, www.CelestialCalendars.com*

EXERCISE: Answer the following questions with information found in this ephemeris. 1) Rounding off to the nearest whole number, how many degrees does the Sun move each day? 2) What day did the Full Moon occur? 3) On what day did Mercury move from Taurus to Gemini? 4) Which planet moved the fastest throughout the month? Which planets moved very slowly?

THE PLANETS

The **planets** *represent powers and faculties* bestowed by the universe upon its beloved children at birth. Shared by all people and creatures, these abilities can be used as a basis for understanding one another, so we can have an enjoyable ride together on Spaceship Earth. All living beings feel love. We all think, grow, and work. We all need to create, and fulfill our soul's purpose. Astrological planets symbolize the universal forces that make such activities possible.

Planets work within the zodiacal signs and houses. Like the signs and houses, planets have elemental strength. (Elements, page 53) Therefore, certain areas of the zodiac are stronger or weaker for each planet, depending on how the elements combine. **Ruling planets** *are very strong in the sign or house they rule*, and not so strong in the opposite sign or house. Originally, five planets ruled two signs each. That changed when the three modern planets received rulerships, but the original planets still influence the signs they used to rule (in parentheses below).

Each original planet has one sign and house where it is **exalted**, *raised to its highest expression*. The trans-Saturnian planets have not yet been assigned their exaltations; astrologers are still observing their cycles.

GLYPH	PLANET	POWERS & FACULTIES	RULES		EXALTED	
☉	Sun	life, consciousness, health, leadership, creativity, joy	Leo	♌	Aries	♈
☽	Moon	feeling, intuition, psyche, soul, responsiveness, ESP	Cancer	♋	Taurus	♉
☿	Mercury	thought, speech, writing, business, analysis, media	Gemini Virgo	♊ ♍	Virgo	♍
♀	Venus	love, beauty, art, wealth, nurturing, social graces	Taurus Libra	♉ ♎	Pisces	♓
♂	Mars	energy, physical power, work, bravery, passion	Aries (Scorpio)	♈ ♏	Capricorn	♑
♃	Jupiter	growth, expansion, luck, change, opportunity	Sagittarius (Pisces)	♐ ♓	Cancer	♋
♄	Saturn	wisdom, maturity, form, manifestation, mastery	Capricorn (Aquarius)	♑ ♒	Libra	♎
♅	Uranus	freedom, independence, science, friendship, play	Aquarius	♒		
♆	Neptune	mysticism, sensitivity, collective unconscious	Pisces	♓		
♇	Pluto	spiritual power, secrets, dark side, transformation	Scorpio	♏		

THE SUN

O living Aton, Beginning of Life,
you rise in beauty,
and fill every land with your perfection.
Great and glittering,
high above every land,
your rays encompass all that you have made.
Though you are far away,
your rays touch the Earth.
You embrace all in your love.

Egyptian hymn to the Sun

*Apollo, Grecian Sun God
who rides his chariot across
the sky every day*

The world is new to us each morning.
This is the Holy One's* gift,
and every person should believe
they are reborn each day.   *Baal Shem Tov*

* "The Holy One" refers to God, of course, but "The Sun,"
which is an embodiment of God, would fit perfectly here.

Hopi Sun Kachina

Love your enemies, do good to those who hate you, bless those
who curse you, and pray for those who mistreat you, so that you may
be children of your Father in heaven: for <u>he makes his sun to rise on
the evil and the good</u>, and sends rain to the just and the unjust.

Jesus
The Gospel of Thomas

64

THE SUN

Rules ♌ ★ Exalted in ♈ ★ Orange

The Sun is the source of all life in our solar system. It is the outer physical expression of "Our Father who art in heaven." When you think about the power and glory of the Sun, it is easy to see why it is the most important astrological planet. Because the Sun gives us life and consciousness, its position in the horoscope determines a person's sign and basic vibration. For example, if you were born early in August when the Sun ☉ is in Leo ♌, that means you are a Leo who is holding the basic vibration of fixed fire.

The word "sun" is synonymous with "star." All stars are living Solar Beings. Our Sun's body of light is created by super-colossal ongoing nuclear explosions; it is the only nuclear reactor we need. **Sunlight** *conveys life, consciousness, and love.* <u>Life</u> because we would not exist without the Sun. <u>Consciousness</u> as in "I see the light." (I am aware, conscious.) <u>Love</u> because the Sun gives us everything and freely supports all life on Earth, asking nothing in return. When we appreciate all these fabulous gifts, a grateful heart will help us use them well, and share them with others as Our Father shares them with us.

The glyph for the Sun ☉ emphasizes the importance of the center. The dot signifies a consolidation of cosmic power within the circle of potential. This solar awareness is sometimes called the I AM. It is the All-Power, or Primal Will-to-Good that expresses itself through every personality.

The astrological Sun rules the human heart. Just as the Sun is the center of our solar system, the heart is of central importance in the human body. In a broader, symbolic sense, the heart is the center of our lives. If "your heart isn't in it," you lose interest, because "home is where the heart is." Love may flow steadily from your heart just as sunlight shines constantly for everyone.

Ageless Wisdom tells us that God is Life and God is Love. An astrologer might add that God is the Spiritual Sun of the universe. In your chart, your ☉ is the God in you. All other planets are extensions and expressions of this One Source. All is light. You are light.

Health, vitality, regeneration, creativity, purpose, will, dignity, power, royalty, authority, leadership, charisma, flair, drama, courage, and heroism are all indicated by the ☉. You get your sense of individuality and Selfhood from God through our Day Star, who is known in our galaxy as Sol.

The Heart is King

Sufi Saying

THE HIGH PRIESTESS

☽ ○ ☾

**Most High Priestess
of the Inner Sanctuary,
I most humbly, reverently,
and devoutly bow before Thee.**

Masonic Vow

The Moon

Her bonnet is the firmament
The universe her shoe
The stars the trinkets at her belt
Her diminutives of blue

Emily Dickenson

Almighty Isis, Queen of the Universe, crowned with a throne

Who is the moon to us? She is the shining one, the magical one, she who shines on all equally. She is periodicity, the symbol of change that is consistent, the light of nighttime, birth-giver even before there was birth, dark and light mother.

Grandmother Moon
Z Budapest

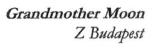

Diana, Roman Moon Goddess

The Moon part of us says we can measure a culture's evolution by whether that society protects, nurtures, and reveres its children, its elders, the environment, and all growing things.

Making the Gods Work for You
Caroline Casey

*Wolf and Owl from the **Medicine Cards**
Drawn by Angela C. Werneke*

THE MOON

Rules ♋ ★ Exalted in ♉ ★ Blue

The Moon is Our Mother who is in heaven. Father Sun is King of the Day, while Mother Moon is Queen of the Night. They are partners. ☉ stands for spirit (yang), and ☽ represents soul (yin). Just as the physical Moon reflects the Sun, so does your soul shine by the light of spirit. The more light your soul receives, the more inspiration and beauty it reflects into the world. The Moon is most radiant in her Full Moon phase when she is most completely illuminated, or "full" of sunlight. The ☉ goes around the zodiac once a year. The ☽ goes around the zodiac once every 28 days, creating 13 lunar months a year, and controlling the fertility cycle of women. The ever-changing Moon typifies humanity's feelings, which keep changing in response to the flow of life.

The Moon rules the psyche and the soul. When the psyche is calm, it acts like a clean mirror to reflect our divinity. But if it is disturbed, the psyche becomes like a dusty or cracked mirror, making it difficult for us to see our true Self. Obviously peace, not strife, is desirable in our mind and soul, our inner world. Fortunately, a damaged psyche can be healed. Inner peace may be cultivated by gentle acceptance of self and others. When daydreaming, meditating, creating, or otherwise experiencing the right brain, we are doing Moon work. Our psychic, feeling side is equally as valuable as our rational, thinking side. Feeling and thinking are designed by Nature to balance and assist each other.

Nurturing Moon governs the element of water—the vast feminine domain of tenderness, sensitivity, emotion, and intuition. The Moon and water also encompass memory, instinct, dreams, and the ability to respond to inspiration. Our feelings arise from oceanic inner depths and flow through us like water. Babies grow in a watery womb. Our bodies are mostly composed of water. Earth is predominantly a water planet. The Moon controls the tides and phases of our emotions as well as our oceans.

To understand your ☽, study all the ways water behaves in Nature, and find correspondences in yourself. Water can be hot, cold, steam, or ice. It evaporates from the ocean, forms into clouds and rainbows, then rains, hails, and snows on the mountains, finally descending as glaciers, streams, rivers, and waterfalls—only to rise from sea to sky again. Mysterious shape-shifter ☽ represents the universal matrix, subconscious mind, and Cosmic Womb. The Moon rules cycles, moods, prophecy, divination, the Third Eye, telepathy, and psychic phenomena. She is the artist's muse.

Go with the flow...

Mother Moon's Advice

PHASES OF THE MOON

The Moon's ever-changing phases are created by the different ways it reflects sunlight while orbiting Earth. To determine the Moon phase in a horoscope, see where it is in relation (aspect) to the Sun.

When the Moon is together with the Sun (conjunct), it is called the New or Dark Moon—"dark" because the Moon is in the daytime sky, which means no moonlight at night, very dark, a good time for stargazing. The Moon is not visible in this phase, as it is obscured by the Sun's blinding rays.

New Moon begins the waxing cycle, during which the light of the Moon increases every night. Throughout the next two weeks, it will pass through Crescent (sextile), First Quarter (square), and Gibbous (trine) phases, finally "peaking" at Full Moon (opposition). The precise moment of Full Moon occurs when the Moon and Sun are exactly opposite each other.

Full Moon initiates the waning cycle of Gibbous, Last Quarter, and Crescent, during which the Moon's light steadily decreases. The Moon comes up later and later, and only night-owl people are aware of it. Then it can be seen briefly in the early morning. Finally it merges with the Sun for another Dark Moon. A few days later, as the slender Waxing Crescent emerges from the Sun's embrace around sunset, the world begins to notice that the Night Queen is beginning her whirling dance again.

🌓 ○ ☾ ● 🌓 ○ ☾ ● 🌓 ○ ☾ ● 🌓 ○ ☾ ● 🌓 ○ ☾ ● 🌓 ○ ☾ ● 🌓 ○ ☾ ● 🌓 ○ ☾

It takes 28 days for the Moon to complete her 360° journey around the zodiac and return to the point from which she departed. This is why a lunar month contains 28 days. However, during this time the Sun has moved ahead approximately a degree a day, covering 30° in a solar month. So it takes the Moon 29½ days to catch up with the Sun and begin another cycle of phases. The New Moon is always in the same sign as the Sun, usually a different sign each month. It is possible to have 2 New Moons or 2 Full Moons in the same sign or Gregorian calendar month. To summarize: the Moon has two cycles. The 28-day zodiacal cycle goes once around the Earth to the same point in the zodiac from which it started. The 29½-day phase cycle is created by Sun-Moon interaction.

EXERCISE: 1) By looking at the Sun-Moon relationship in your chart, figure out your Moon phase. To determine if it is waxing or waning, see if the ☽ is moving toward or away from the point in the zodiac that is opposite the ☉. 2) Meditate on what your personal Moon phase means in your life.

NOTE: To get your natal chart, see bottom of page 132.

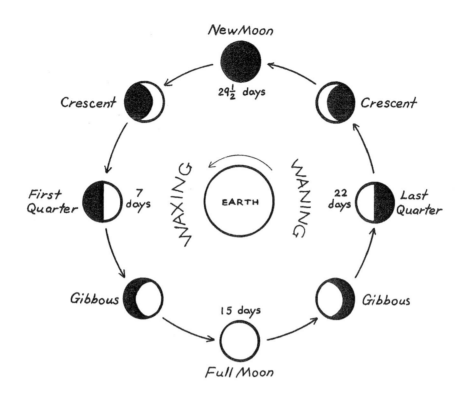

Dark Moon ☉☌☽ self-directed, imaginative, spontaneous, intuitive, subjective

Waxing Crescent ☉⚹☽ assertive, confident, adventurous, inventive, productive

First Quarter ☉□☽ strong-willed, active, creative, fearless, questioning

Waxing Gibbous ☉△☽ expressive, optimistic, gregarious, trusting, excited

Full Moon ☉☍☽ sharing, interacting, energetic, fulfilling, objective

Waning Gibbous ☉△☽ wise, thoughtful, compassionate, assimilating, sharing

Last Quarter ☉□☽ forceful, sensible, philosophical, transforming, mature

Waning Crescent ☉⚹☽ mystical, sensitive, sacrificial, prophetic, path of destiny

NOTE: In any horoscope, the ☽ will fall within one of these 8 phases
even if it does not have an aspect, or has a different aspect, to the ☉.
For more information about aspects, see pages 126-127.

EXERCISE: See the progression of phases for yourself by watching the Moon as much as possible for at least a month. To guide your observations, you may also refer to a calendar such as *Celestial Guide*, which indicates Moon phases.

THE MAGICIAN

*The most valuable force you can be
is an instrument of peace.*

Carlos Santana, who makes the words
"musician" and "magician" synonymous.

**His guide is Thoth,
who bestows upon him the gift of speech,
who makes the books,
and illumines those who are learned therein,
and the physicians who follow him, that they may work cures.**

Egyptian **Ebers Papyrus**

Because it orbits the ☉ so closely, ☿ can only go as far as 28° from the ☉. It can only be found in the same sign with, or in the signs behind and before the Sun. ☿'s position in relation to the ☉ gives rise to the following interpretations:

Closer to the ☉, within 14° – sane, focused
Farther from the ☉, more than 14° – versatile, flexible

Sign behind the ☉ – traditional, conservative
Sign ahead of the ☉ – inventive, radical

Rising before the ☉ (Morning Star) – experimental, takes direct action
Setting behind the ☉ (Evening Star) – theoretical, reasoning

Flying Mercury
Italian Renaissance Statue

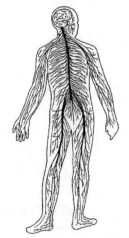

Diagram of Nerves in Human Body
Mercury rules the nervous system, which
delivers messages to and from the brain.

Whether you think you can, or think you can't, you're right. *Henry Ford*

MERCURY

Rules ♊ and ♍ ★ Exalted in ♍ ★ Yellow

Mercury represents the **intellect**, *our ability to perceive, think, reason, focus and analyze*. As the planet closest to the Sun, Mercury is intimately connected to the conscious living light that creates and sustains our solar system. Called Thoth in Egypt, Hermes in Greece, and Mercury in Rome, this planetary god was the messenger of the other gods, meaning that the intellect is a communicator.

Because we are children of the Most High, our intellect is an extremely powerful creative tool. Our focused concentration is like a magic wand with which we can "plug in" to the Source of Consciousness Itself. Consciousness is localized in each individual, but it is not personal. It comes straight from the Sun/Source/God. Whether or not we are aware of it, divine energy passes through our ☿, giving life to whatever the intellect is concentrating on, thinking about, aiming at—or worrying about. When we lift up our Mercury, our awareness, asking to be of service to the light, we become channels for grace to flow from above. Then we create strong, positive results in the world below. In a nutshell, we create our world with the power of our intellect because Life energizes what we think about. Magical Mercury is said to rule life and death. He brings things into being and makes things disappear, using a miraculous power freely given. ☿ makes us all magicians. What an awesome gift! And what an equally awesome responsibility!

Humans have the power to "play God" if we choose, but the wise have always found it better to "let God play you," much as a flute allows itself to be an instrument for the creation of music. In Tarot, the Magician card depicts the <u>enlightened</u> intellect, while the Devil card portrays the <u>un</u>enlightened intellect. Thinking he has cut himself off from God, the Devil is in bondage to egotism.

Mercury initiates the creative process by planting seeds of thought. Nature, as a multi-dimensional, conscious, creative matrix, receives your seed thoughts, gestates them, and develops them into forms. If you choose ideas that are as beautiful as flowers, Nature's response to your focus will be a lovely garden. Be careful what you choose to think about, because whether you are alert and disciplined with your mind, or unconscious and confused, the yin feminine principle will say "yes," and bring your thoughts into manifestation. What you think is so, is so for you.

In our daily lives, ☿ functions as our faculty of reason and logic, enjoying its ability to analyze, categorize, classify, and solve mental problems. ☿ is inventive, forever curious about what makes things work, interested in study or research, fascinated by technology and the media, and endlessly communicative. The "messenger" is witty, talkative, sociable, and well informed.

THINK ABOUT WHAT YOU WANT, NOT WHAT YOU DON'T WANT.

Buddha

THE EMPRESS

Nature is What Is.
We can accept or reject it;
we can even deny it,
but we cannot avoid it.

Jason Lotterhand

Venus is a bigger, brighter Morning and Evening Star than Mercury, because it is a larger planet that is closer to the Earth. It is a very special treat to see both ☿ and ♀ sparkling together at dawn or sunset. Mercury conjunct Venus, ☿ ☌ ♀, gives an idealistic, artistic mental outlook. For a viewer on Earth, and therefore in a horoscope, ♀ can only move as far as 47.5° from the ☉.

♀ as Morning Star – youthful, impetuous, innocent, emerging from the Sun
♀ as Evening Star – civilized, cultured, queenly, joining with the Sun

Demeter, Grecian Nature Goddess

Photo by Silma Smith

Drawing by Joey Ololodi
www.alocubano.com

Oshun, African Goddess
of Love and Abundance

She is the Great Mother
who cherishes all that is young and growing.
Her winged heart center is resplendent and glowing
with the greenray of healing.

Segment, **Hymn to Demeter**
Homer, 800 BCE

The Planets

VENUS

Rules ♀ and ♎ ★ Exalted in ♓ ★ Green

Venus is our beloved Earth Mother, who gives birth to everything we know and love. She takes universal conscious living light (atomic energy/spirit) and forms it into vehicles (bodies), so spirit can experience itself in form. Spirit is forever seeking to express itself in the physical world, so Venus is always pregnant with countless manifestations. The natural world is amazingly fertile and abundant. From one sheaf of wheat, a whole field of wheat can grow.

Mother Nature is the Great Artist and Creatress. Your creative process follows the way of Nature. Your psyche becomes "pregnant" when a desire (Mars) stimulates your creative imagination (Venus). The time period during which you are dreaming up what you want to be, do, and have, is a "gestation." Then you "labor" to bring your "baby" into the world. ♀ rules the whole procedure.

When you really look at any natural thing—a sunset, a ladybug, a tree—you can see the incredible artistry, intelligence, organization, and design that went into making it. That is why it is said that art imitates nature. Artists frequently call their work their "baby, " an acknowledgement of the power of Venus. Like ♀, an artist is open to inspiration, input from spirit. We are all artists, whether we are birthing a baby, a book, or a bright idea.

Having given birth, the Mother nurtures her children with tender loving care. Venus is the force within us that loves and nurtures other beings, just as Earth supplies us with a vast support system of everything we need for health and well-being. ♀ rules the plant kingdom, which sustains animals and people. By Nature's decree, all minerals, plants, animals, and people are interdependent. We were created to cohabit, collaborate, and cooperate with all other life forms in perfect harmony. To see examples of amicable coexistence, look at indigenous cultures.

The Moon is the Dark Mother, the mysterious lady of night and water who represents our subconscious world of feeling. Venus is the Bright Mother whom we see all around us in the beauty of Nature. The Venusian aspect of the Sacred Feminine gives us sensuality, pleasure, and enjoyment of the physical world.

Lady Venus loves to sing and dance in celebration of life. She delights in nice clothes and good company; she is the epitome of the gracious hostess. This goddess of art, love, and beauty rules partnership, romance, marriage, family, wealth, bodies, gardens, and ecology. She is attractive, harmonious, peaceful, kind, devoted, compassionate, and naturally wise. Venus teaches us to

HONOR AND RESPECT ALL OUR RELATIONS (all living beings).

Native American Wisdom

The Planets

73

THE TOWER

You never change things
by fighting the existing reality.
To change something,
build a new model that
makes the existing model obsolete.

Buckminster Fuller

ACE of SWORDS

*The Sword of Truth
and Justice*

**Be the change
you want to see
in the world.**

Gandhi

We look forward to the time
when the power of love will
replace the love of power. Then
will our world know the blessing of peace.

William Ewart Gladstone

Hymn to Ares (Mars)

*Hear me, helper of men, giver of dauntless youth!
Shed down a kindly ray from above upon my life,
that I may be able to drive away bitter cowardice from my head
and crush down the deceitful impulses of my soul.
Restrain also the keen fury of my heart,
which provokes me to tread the ways of blood-curdling strife.
Rather, O blessed one, give me boldness to abide
within the harmless laws of peace,
avoiding strife and hatred and the violent fiends of death.*

Homer, 800 BCE

A warrior's life is not about imagined perfection or victory; it is about love.
Love is the warrior's sword; wherever it cuts, it gives life, not death.

Way of the Peaceful Warrior
Dan Millman

In allowing all pathways to have equal validity, you will see the power and glory of the unified *family of humanity*. This is the gift of the Rainbow Warrior or Warrioress. The "I" has no place in this Whirling Rainbow that comes from the Great Mystery. It is replaced by the universal "we." All colors of the rainbow and all pathways are honored as one.

Medicine Cards, *Jamie Sams and David Carson*

MARS

Rules ♈ ★ Exalted in ♑ ★ Ancient Ruler of ♏ ★ Red

Mars is a valiant warrior whose basic instinct is protection. He has the courage to speak out for the downtrodden people of the Earth, chain himself to a 2000-year-old tree in an effort to save its life, and stand for truth when forces of falsehood threaten to engulf all that he believes in. Negative interpretations have misnamed Mars the god of war, but that is a perversion of his true nature. The human ego is the creator of war. In many ways it has enslaved Mars, forcing him to be violent, combative, competitive, and tyrannical. But the real Mars, the Divine Masculine Principle with which we are all born, is just as wise and loving as the other planets.

Like a bolt of lightning, God's weapon, Mars can blast away oppression! Mars seeks freedom and independence. His energy is always trying to jolt us out of complacency, and take us into new territory. ♂ is our life force, the animal power in our bodies, our strength and vitality, our blood and muscles. Mars is absolutely essential in every action we perform. We do need to tame and train the explosive power of this valuable gift because, like fire, pure ♂ energy can be used for destruction or construction. Mars may wisely destroy old forms in order to create anew. For instance, the metabolic process that keeps our bodies warm is constantly breaking down cells, recycling them, and building up new ones.

Our assertive and even aggressive nature has very good uses and purposes. We can put Mars to work in countless healthy ways. Dancing and sports are activities in which ♂ can shine. Any achievement requires help from Mars. Passion is a necessity, because you must really <u>want</u> something in order to create it—especially if you aspire to self-mastery. Mars rules desire, the hunger for life.

One astronomical term for Mars is "the red planet." Astrological Mars is also red, like fire and blood. The very descriptive glyph for this male planet shows an arrow going up and out. The yang nature of red Mars balances the yin nature of green Venus. ♂ is the life power in a seed; ♀ is the earthy environment that brings the seed to fruition. Together, these planets comprise a person's sexual energies. Mars is the fervent part of sex, and Venus is the cuddlesome part. Testosterone and estrogen are divine partners; theirs is a marriage made in the heavens.

Dynamic, outgoing Mars represents strength, power, courage, activity, speed, vigor, passion, excitement, exercise, and work. Mars stimulates appetite, initiates change, drives creativity, and undertakes countless adventures.

What is the highest and best use of my energy?

Mars' Quest

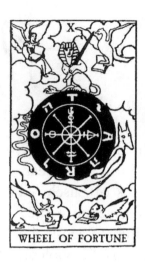

WHEEL OF FORTUNE

Everything will end in love
because everything was created in love.
Our work is simply to speed up
an outcome that is guaranteed.

Emissary of Light
James Twyman

In every deliberation,
we must consider the impact of our decisions
on the next seven generations.

Segment, **The Great Law of the Iroquois Confederacy**
Pre-colonized North Ameria

Jupiter
is
generosity.

The Logarithmic Spiral
May be observed throughout
Nature in such places as:
our Milky Way Galaxy,
the DNA molecule,
whorl of hair on a human head,
snails, sunflowers, pinecones,
and scorpion's tail.

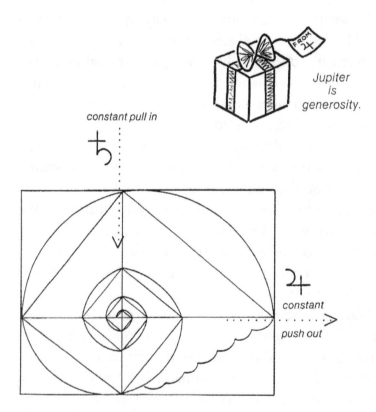

constant pull in

♄

♃

constant

push out

Write it on your heart that every day is the best day of the year.

Ralph Waldo Emerson

DO UNTO OTHERS AS YOU WOULD HAVE THEM DO UNTO YOU.

The Golden Rule

Treat others the way you want to be treated.

Golden Rule, modern version

JUPITER

Rules ♐ ★ Exalted in ♋ ★ Ancient Ruler of ♓ ★ Violet (Purple)

Jupiter holds a grand title in astrology: the Great Benefic. Its many helpful characteristics make it a popular planet, since everyone likes benefits from a benevolent benefactor. Jupiter represents the outpouring of God's mercy. In antiquity this planet was associated with the great sky god, father and ruler of the other gods, who wielded power with wisdom and justice. Lord of Life's exhaustless riches, ♃ the Giver of Gifts is very much like Santa Claus, except we don't need to wait until Christmas. Venus, also generous, is called the Lesser Benefic because she is smaller. Jupiter is so big that it could contain thousands of Earths.

Like the Big Bang that got everything spiraling at the beginning of time, ♃ keeps things in perpetual motion. Jovial Jupiter is always coming up with fresh opportunities for life, love, ideas, energy, resources, money, or whatever is needed to keep everything moving, growing, and circulating. Circulation is essential to our personal health and that of our whole planetary system. Jupiter's hand hurls the lightning-bolt (Mars), which is a life-giving double helix.

Jupiter and Saturn share responsibility for **karma**, *the cyclical law of cause and effect.* What we give out today, we get back tomorrow, when the energy returns on its spiraling path. ♃ expands the forces we put in motion, and ♄ makes sure they come back to us. The Golden Rule is a positive example of how karma works.

Everything is born, lives, and dies in cycles. Only Creator, the Cause of everything, is unchanging and eternal. If we welcome each new change as it comes along in the process of evolution, we can let go of what is finished. Many degrading energies have been clinging to human consciousness. Jupiter has the cure: OPEN UP to ever-greater awareness of our divinity! Old stuff will just fall away. Because the Principle of Expansion urges us to reach higher, ♃ rules aspiration, idealism, the big picture, and all spiritual paths. Philosophy, religion, higher education, and the upliftment of consciousness are Jupiterian concepts.

Big, breezy Jupiter rules the out-of-doors and inspires long distance runners. Whenever a record is broken in sports, ♃ has opened an evolutionary portal. Progress, far journeys, foreign lands, and pilgrimages are ruled by Jupiter, who teaches us that "travel broadens the mind." Increase, wealth, philanthropy, luck, and good fortune of all kinds are fostered by prosperous, generous ♃. Opportunity, optimism, enthusiasm, humor, good will, expansion, growth, rewards—the more gratitude we feel for these blessings, the more life we can embrace. Thank you, merciful Jupiter!

THE BEST IS YET TO COME ! ! !

Jupiter's Promise

XXI

THE WORLD

This above all, — to thine own self be true,
And it must follow, as the night the day,
Thou canst not then be false to any man.

Hamlet
William Shakespeare

They who dance not know not what is being done!
— Gnostic Mass

Saturn Cuts the Cookies
Life is like cookie dough. Use your ♄ to choose
the flavors and shapes that you like.

One who would master Nature must first obey her laws.

Hermetic Aphorism

Let your conscience be your guide.
Old Saying

conscience,

from Latin, **con,** *with*
and **science,** *knowledge*

the voice of truth in your mind
that guides you in support of
your soul's chosen mission

If you don't use it, you lose it.

The Power of the Center
The Magnetic Field of a Neutron Star (Pulsar)

SATURN

Rules ♑ ★ Exalted in ♎ ★ Ancient Ruler of ♒ ★ Blue-Violet (Indigo)

Saturn teaches **mastery**, *expert knowledge, eminent skill or power.* A master of any skill has dedicated long hours to study and practice, with devotion to excellence, usually for many years (or lifetimes). Great is the pleasure of being able to do something really well, but mastery is not a final state at which we arrive. A true master is always humbled by the infinite potential that lies ahead. This is especially true for one who desires **Self-mastery**, *expert knowledge of one's True Being, skillful directing of motives and behavior through graceful command of the ego.* Let's just say, mastery is a process. One who claims to be a master is not a master.

One must face and overcome serious challenges in order to earn mastery. Concerning self-mastery, the selfish, fearful ego provides plenty of challenge for most people. If you never give up, and just keep going toward your sacred heart's desire (what your soul loves), you automatically learn what works for you. Pay attention, and you can't miss seeing that what really works for you works for the higher good, as well. Voila! Love tames the ego! Saturn rules the aging process, which brings many rewards of **maturity**, *expertise and wisdom.*

Steady Saturn symbolizes the Principle of Contraction, which may be equated with the center of gravity. Its conservative pull to the center balances Jupiter's expansive outward thrust. Saturn is the yin to Jupiter's yang. When things are "spiraling out of control," call on ♄ to regain stability.

The logarithmic spiral is the universal pattern that energy follows in any growth process. In logarithmic cycles, the expanding **centrifugal force** of Jupiter *spirals outward*, while the contracting **centripetal force** of Saturn *spirals inward*. When these forces work in harmony, it is as if they are dancing together. Dance demands that we continually lose and regain our balance. Life gives us plenty of chances to test our inner mastery by throwing us off balance. The more we adhere to our center, the fewer pratfalls we have. ♄ rules gravity, a loving power that holds all our atoms and molecules together, so we don't go spinning off in space.

The last planet easily visible to the naked eye, Saturn used to be thought of as the outer limit of our solar system. Saturn represents the power of definition and limitation. It controls form, just as a cookie cutter defines shapes by separating them from the dough. You use ♄ whenever you make choices, create art, or build structures. ♄ is the teacher and authority <u>within</u>. It can act stern and decisive in order to uphold your purpose. Saturn will help you to be wise, firm, persevering, practical, organized, scientific, sober, productive, responsible, and self-disciplined.

There is no limit to what you can create with your power of limitation.

Saturn's Affirmation

THE FOOL

A good traveler has no fixed plans
and is not intent upon arriving.
A good artist lets his intuition
lead him wherever it wants.
A good scientist has freed himself of concepts
and keeps his mind open to what is.
Thus the Master is available to all people
and doesn't reject anyone.
He is ready to use all situations
and doesn't waste anything.
This is called embodying the light.

Lao Tzu

*W*e hold these truths to be self-evident, that all [people] are created equal, that they are endowed by their Creator with certain unalienable Rights, that among these are Life, Liberty, and the pursuit of happiness.

Declaration of Independence

Thomas Jefferson

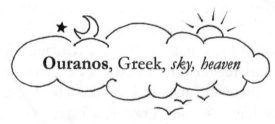

Ouranos, Greek, *sky, heaven*

THE ONLY WAY TO DISCOVER THE LIMITS OF THE POSSIBLE IS TO VENTURE PAST THEM INTO THE IMPOSSIBLE.

Arthur C. Clarke

Uranus
is
impulsiveness.

ZAP!

Believe nothing: entertain possibilities.

Caroline Casey

80

URANUS

Rules ♒ ★ Higher Octave of ☿ ★ Yellow

Uranus (yer-AHN-us) waves the Banner of Freedom. An irrepressible force within humanity is always looking for ways throw to off restriction, find independence, and give free rein to the spirit of life. Whereas the rings of Saturn symbolize the defining powers of limitation, the rings of Uranus are an example of wonderfully wild wackiness. Uranus rolls around on its side like a clown in a whirligig, at right angles to its orbit. And its direction of rotation is opposite that of the other planets. Playful, unpredictable, experimental, and sometimes totally outrageous, ♅ is a powerful stimulus to originality and invention.

When Uranus was accidentally discovered in 1781, it erased the old familiar idea that Saturn marked the far edge of our solar system. World consciousness suddenly and collectively expanded on a mass scale. Breaking through mental and physical boundaries, the human spirit flew out into space. Inspirational Uranus naturally rules space exploration and the unexpected. This liberated planet entered our perception just five years after the American Revolution and eight years before the French Revolution. Humanity has been uprising and rebelling against oppressive governments ever since.

Irrepressible ♅ always urges us to fully express what it means to be human. It is the patron planet of democracy, the Aquarian Age, and humanity in general. Of utmost importance to human beings is our individuality, our personal uniqueness and self-determination. The Uranian part of ourselves honors all beings as equals, and treasure's each one's distinctive qualities, especially when the distinction is very unusual or eccentric.

All three of the trans-Saturnian planets affect the masses. *Planets inside Saturn's orbit* are known as **personal planets**. *Planets beyond Saturn* are called **transpersonal** or **higher octave planets**. Untamed, untrammeled Uranus is the higher octave (faster vibration) of Mercury, the intellect. It represents our higher intellect, our super conscious ability to connect directly with Source, to see as God sees, and think creatively in the moment with no preconceptions.

Uranus rules technology, which is an ongoing series of breakthroughs and innovations. Using the higher intellect, our species is devising appropriate technologies that are in tune with Nature and therefore helpful to everyone. We can always count on emancipated ♅ to be spontaneous and uninhibited, eagerly jumping into life's limitless possibilities, all the while creating new ideas, methods, fashions, behaviors, and <u>whatever</u>! Uranus adapts in the Now with grace and ease.

FREEDOM IS OUR HUMAN BIRTHRIGHT

Banner of Uranus

THE HANGED MAN

The winds of grace are always blowing,
but you have to raise the sail.

Ramakrishna

One cannot help but be in awe when
contemplating the mysteries of
eternity, of life, of the marvelous
structure of reality.

Albert Einstein

The psyche is vast like the ocean, and full of possibilities, as the sea is full of fish.
Einstein (a Pisces, ruled by Neptune) said that he intuited the Theory of Relativity
before working it out mathematically. In other words, he fished it up from the
collective unconscious.

Chant

Folk Tradition

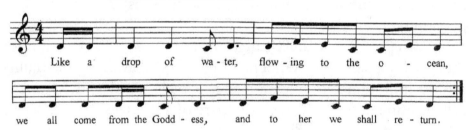

Like a drop of water, flowing to the ocean,
we all come from the Goddess, and to her we shall return.

Lord Neptune with his Trident

Within you lies the sea
of infinite knowledge
and inspiration.

Paramahansa Yogananda

ACE of CUPS.

The Holy Grail,
a Fountain of Life,
Love, Healing, Abundance,
and every conceivable Blessing

The Planets

NEPTUNE

Rules ♓ ★ Higher Octave of ☽ ★ Blue

Neptune is our portal to multi-dimensional and inter-time experiences. After Uranus frees us from restriction, Neptune offers endless opportunities for exploration. To travel through other dimensions, worlds, or epochs, we do not need to move in space. Everything exists in the Now. And wherever we happen to be, we are at the center of it all. This is the mystical awareness of Neptune.

The discovery of Neptune in 1846 was hailed as the greatest success of Newton's gravitational theory. Neptune was the second trans-Saturnian planet to impact all Earthlings simultaneously, bringing about a psychological awakening. Sigmund Freud told humanity something the sages have always known: we have a subconscious. This was big news. Then Carl Jung discovered the connection between psyche and soul. Investigation of the psyche has fascinated us ever since.

Soul, psyche, and subconscious work together. Water symbolizes this inner, hidden part of our nature. Named for the Roman god of the sea, Neptune's glyph ♆ is his trident. Whereas the Moon represents our personal "bay" into occult water, Neptune is a transpersonal "ocean" that fills and connects all the bays. It is the medium/matrix through which any activity in personal areas influences the whole. From the water and blue color correspondences, we see that ♆ is the higher frequency of the ☽. It rules what Jung called the **collective unconscious**, which is *the source and total of all human psyches put together, irrespective of time and space.*

This visionary planet contributes a cosmic perspective that transcends our third-density reality. Neptune's domain is a vastly bigger (big-R), Reality. At our current stage of evolution, the majority of Earthlings perceive physical things as totally separate from each other, and experience the individual mind as disconnected from other minds. This is a painful state. Fortunately, our inner Neptune enjoys ongoing unity with the One Being whose mind is a never-ending sea of consciousness and universal substance. Therefore, it does not play favorites, take sides, or engage in any polarity thinking whatsoever. As a Sufi master once said, "Swimming in an infinite ocean, who is nearer what shore?"

Compassionate Neptune's subtle influence invites us to feel the healing truth of wholeness deep within our soul. Mystic ♆ invites us to "pull up anchor" and float effortlessly in the sea of all awareness, where we may interact with numinous beings/selves amidst otherworldy scenes. Neptune may manifest in our life as an affinity for peace and harmony, talent for music or poetry, telepathy, attraction to meditation, communion with Nature—wherever sensitivity may lead.

Only Love is Real

Neptune's Meditation

There is a Secret One inside.
All the stars and all the galaxies
Flow through His hands like beads.

Kabir

Transform *can mean a change*
in outward shape or form, or in
character, nature, or function.
Metemorphose, transmute, convert.

Webster's Dictionary

Phoenix
(FEE-nix)
This fabled bird
dies in flames,
and is always reborn
from the ashes of
its previous existence.

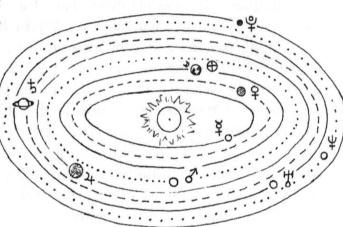

Solar System With Orbits
(not to scale)
Pluto takes almost 248 years to
complete one orbit around the Sun.
It can stay up to 25 years in one sign.

Caduceus
(ka-DOO-see-us)
   This symbol of healing illustrates the central channel of life force (the spine)
in a human body, around which opposing forces entwine. One serpent is
warm/solar; the other is cool/lunar. These currents cross at the chakra points.
The body is healthy when clear energy is flowing easily in all three channels.

Uranus, Neptune, and Pluto are Ambassadors of the Galaxy.
They are radically transformative, indeed subversive, forces at work.

Dane Rudhyar

The Planets

PLUTO

Rules ♏ ★ Higher Octave of ♂ ★ Red

Pluto holds the key to immortality, giving us the ability to unlock a mighty force within, a power known to some alchemists as the Risen Mars Force. When Mars/Pluto energy rises in frequency (as if going up a musical scale), it also moves up our physical spine. When the spirit fire reaches our brain, we "see the light." Ancient yogis, practitioners of **yoga**, *spiritual union*, were experts in enlightenment. They named the immortalizing power **kundalini**, *serpent fire*. Pluto power does not necessarily make the body live forever; it <u>awakens</u> us to the fact that we are <u>already</u> **enlightened masters** who *never die, and know simultaneous existence in infinite forms*.

Pluto knows that Life Itself cannot die. Whenever anything seems to die, it just means that the life energy in that form is ready to take on a new form/shape/body. Without the passing away of old forms, there could be no change, no creativity. As the third transpersonal planet, ♇ insists on grand, sweeping changes and completely new forms. This arousing planet rules **tranformation** and **transmutation**, *change from one state to another. Lead becomes gold; fear becomes love.* Along with these potent powers, Pluto also rules **regeneration**, *stimulation of new life, such as happens in healing*, and **reincarnation**, *rebirth in a different body*.

Life begins in fire, which is the will to Be. After awhile comes the will to Be something else…and then Be something else again and again. Pluto rules that magical place where LIFE GOES ON between apparent death of the old and miraculous birth of the new. The masters have always known about this awesome regenerative power, but since ♇ was discovered in 1930, billions of people have gotten the urge to regenerate our world, break with tradition, and instigate social, political, and religious upheaval on every level. Uranus opens our mind to fresh possibilities, Neptune dissolves old forms, and Pluto creates a completely new scene. Thus the outer planets shape whole generations. ♇ was recently demoted by astron-omers, who have, once again, re-defined the word "planet" (*wanderers* in Greek). Still, Pluto remains the most potent force for transformation known to astrologers.

Pluto the Awakener asks us to decide who we really are from a cosmic per-spective. ♇ is the spiritual revolutionary who brings resurrection of the world through the power of realization. If the renewing life force is held back, repressed, it festers within us as prudery, perversion, cruelty, tyranny, and a host of dark distortions. We must let Pluto's spiritual energy flow freely in order to overcome any ignorance born of fear. Let us remember our divinity, embrace a new destiny, and boldly go where humanity has never gone before—into a world of health, peace, and freedom for all!

FEAR NOT! LOVE CONQUERS ALL — EVEN DEATH.

Clarion Call of Pluto

ST. PATRICK'S BREASTPLATE

Now that you have studied the planets, you might start finding evidence of their influence everywhere. You can look at what is happening around you and see the planets at work. When you are thinking, Mercury is active. When you are feeling intuition or emotion, your Moon is in charge. When you go jogging, your Mars energy and Venus body are having a good time. Ask yourself what planets rule different school subjects, and so forth. Just for fun, let's assign a planetary correspondence to each of the ten lines of St. Patrick's famous invocation.

I arise today . . . . ♇
through the Strength of Heaven . . . ♅
Light of Sun . . . . ☉
Radiance of Moon . . . . ☽
Splendor of Fire . . . . ♂
Speed of Lightning . . . . ♃
Swiftness of Wind . . . . ☿
Depth of Sea . . . . ♆
Stability of Soil . . . . ♀
Firmness of Rock . . . . ♄

St. Patrick obviously had a great relationship with Nature. He appreciated and acknowledged the Source of his life, and experienced conscious unity with universal forces. Judging by this statement, there was no separation between God and Nature in his philosophy. A breastplate is a piece of armor worn for protection and display, but St. Patrick's "breastplate" was actually a shield of words, a charm or kind of prayer used by Patrick and his followers to invoke divine safeguards in the wilderness. An astrologer might have called upon the planets for protection.

Nurture Nature, and Nature will nurture you.

Granny Rainbow

EXERCISE: Try saying St. Patrick's affirmation when you wake up in the morning. See if it makes you feel healthy and strong. You may even feel loved by Nature. Consider your relationship to Heaven and Earth. These ancient words are still true no matter where you happen to be "arising."

PART 5.

THE ZODIAC

As Mother Earth spins in her dance with the stars,
her extended equator traces a circular path
through twelve constellations
known as the signs of the zodiac.
Each sign offers its unique support to Earthlings.

THE PERMUTATIONS

Astrological permutations *combine the modes and elements in a given order, creating a coherent set of signs.* Permutations cause the characteristics of the signs. Once you know the order of the permutations, it is easy to remember the order of the signs.

Order of 3 modes: cardinal, fixed, mutable (page 52)
Order of 4 elements: fire, earth, air, water (page 53)

Which astrological mode is found in the spelling of the word "permutations?"

PERMUTATIONS of 3 Modes x 4 Elements = 12 Signs

1. cardinal	fire	Aries	♈
2. fixed	earth	Taurus	♉
3. mutable	air	Gemini	♊
4. cardinal	water	Cancer	♋
5. fixed	fire	Leo	♌
6. mutable	earth	Virgo	♍
7. cardinal	air	Libra	♎
8. fixed	water	Scorpio	♏
9. mutable	fire	Sagittarius	♐
10. cardinal	earth	Capricorn	♑
11. fixed	air	Aquarius	♒
12. mutable	water	Pisces	♓

TRIPLICITIES

signs that belong in sets of three, sorted by element

FIRE	Aries	♈	Leo	♌	Sagittarius ♐
EARTH	Taurus	♉	Virgo	♍	Capricorn ♑
AIR	Gemini	♊	Libra	♎	Aquarius ♒
WATER	Cancer	♋	Scorpio	♏	Pisces ♓

QUADRUPLICITIES

signs that belong in sets of four, sorted by mode

CARDINAL	Aries	♈	Cancer	♋	Libra	♎	Capricorn	♑
FIXED	Taurus	♉	Leo	♌	Scorpio	♏	Aquarius	♒
MUTABLE	Gemini	♊	Virgo	♍	Sagittarius	♐	Pisces	♓

THE SIGNS OF THE ZODIAC

The zodiac is an abstraction and a symbol, like a Wall that separates all inhabitants of the Earth's surface from the universe. Symbolically, this Wall has twelve gates, twelve signs of the zodiac, twelve channels through which universal energies flow.

Dane Rudhyar, ***Astrology of the Personality***

GLYPH	SIGN	AREAS OF FOCUS	RULER	EXALTS
♈	Aries	self awareness & development, youth, vision, will, desire, assertion, speed	Mars	Sun
♉	Taurus	physicality, purpose, practicality, money, fertility, patience, pleasure, possessions	Venus	Moon
♊	Gemini	relationship, duality, information, networking, language, writing, adaptation	Mercury	
♋	Cancer	birthplace, family, maternal instinct, safety, food, receptivity, emotion, depth	Moon	Jupiter
♌	Leo	creativity, courage, heroism, charisma, spiritual light, power, theater, fashion	Sun	
♍	Virgo	analysis, discernment, refinement, healing, integration, helping others	Mercury	Mercury
♎	Libra	social consciousness, appreciation, harmony, peace, partnership, balance	Venus	Saturn
♏	Scorpio	hidden forces, sexuality, reproduction, mortality, magic, transformation	Pluto (Mars)	
♐	Sagittarius	travel, sports, the circus, enthusiasm, optimism, idealism, religion, guidance	Jupiter	
♑	Capricorn	status, influence, authority, ambition, paternity, responsibility, maturity, age	Saturn	Mars
♒	Aquarius	truth, independence, invention, friends, humanitarianism, brother-sisterhood	Uranus (Saturn)	
♓	Pisces	ocean, openness, psychism, devotion, empathy, mercy, mystery, past lives	Neptune (Jupiter)	Venus

Planets in parentheses ruled these signs in antiquity, and still have an underlying influence, although the trans-Saturnian planetary rulers have more **weight**, *influence*.

Each zodiacal sign has specific characteristics that influence the behavior, and empower the expression, of planets located in that sign. Start your interpretations with the idea that everything in a chart is exactly and perfectly where it should be, for the greatest growth and fulfillment of the individual, as chosen by the soul of that distinct individual.

THE EMPEROR

A heart that loves
Is always young.

Greek Proverb

YOU MUST BE AS LITTLE CHILDREN
TO ENTER THE KINGDOM OF HEAVEN.

Jesus

*Where the spirit does not work with the hand,
there is no art.*

Leonardo da Vinci – an Aries

Life is a pure flame, and we live by an invisible sun within us.

Thomas Browne

There is one thing stronger
than all the armies in the world,
and that is an idea
whose time has come.

Victor Hugo

ACE of WANDS

The Magic Wand
of Will and Desire

RULE OR BE RULED

Old Saying

The Zodiac

ARIES

The Ram ★ Cardinal Fire ★ Ruler ♂ ★ Exalts ☉ ★ Red
(late March - late April)

Aries begins the zodiacal year. When the Sun enters zero degree Aries, 0° ♈, at the Vernal Equinox, Nature says, "Rise and shine!" as she gives us springtime. Cardinal fire brings the joy and excitement of new life bursting forth from the composted old year. An enlivening influence on everyone, the headstrong Ram bounds ahead with a built-in desire to be first. Pioneering Aries just naturally likes to be out in front, lead the way, and get to the top. Ruled by fiery Mars, the Ram's disposition is vigorous, eager, and daring.

Enthusiastic Aries is associated with childhood, the first stage of life. Its red color is the favorite of most young children. Red is the first color in the rainbow spectrum, having the most basic vibrational frequency of all the colors. Natives of this primal sign retain a youthful, innocent quality throughout their lives. All children have incredible wisdom and power. Their positive, clear I AM awareness is unmistakable. They are simple, direct, and honest. In youth is renewal of the species. With the courage of Mars, youth stands ready to change the world for the better. And so, as the poet Wordsworth wrote, "The Child is father of the Man." And of course, the Child is also mother of the Woman.

In our bodies, ♈ rules the head and the power of sight. This inventive sign has potent visionary capabilities. Symbolically, everything begins in fire, with the will and desire to BE. Fiery Aries gets the manifestation process started by thinking up possibilities of what could be created, as well as envisioning variations and inventing strategies. The brain of imaginative ♈ is always popping with ideas. Cardinal fire needs fertile ground for its ideas to grow. Luckily, the fruitful fields of Taurus lie right next door in the zodiac. Venus, ruler of Taurus, the fixed earth, is ever ready to nurture the seeds that Mars generates.

Cardinal fire is the ultimate ruling power, the Life Force within each living being. When this power is resurrected in the spring, rites of renewal such as Passover and Easter are celebrated. Yang Aries is a sign of eruption, emergence, and exuberance—qualities that are suggested by the ♈ glyph. Ruling Mars can be energetic and forceful, but ♂ can also be playful and lots of fun. The high energy of youth is truly marvelous to experience when one is young, or behold when older. Like a spring flower, young Aries deserves encouragement for free expression.

Our Divine Father Sun is exalted in the sign of beginnings, because a grand influx of living spirit is needed to initiate and sustain the whole zodiacal cycle that is to come. Mars plus Sun equals so much power that Aries has a responsibility to consider the good of the whole in order to keep its fire under control. When focused on helping life to blossom, passionate Aries can empower others without overwhelming them. Aries easily maintains its own originality and independence.

THE HIEROPHANT

In the Garden of the Senses

lies a pathway to the Spirit.

Tantric Scripture

*Every blade of grass has its angel
that bends over it
whispering. "Grow, grow."*

The Talmud

This very earth is the Lotus Land of Purity,
And this body is the Body of Buddha.

Hakuin, Zen poet

A seed's a star, a star's a seed.

*Stevie Wonder – a Taurus
from soundtrack of the movie*
The Secret Life of Plants

There is a universe of knowledge and understanding that we are meant to receive from and through our bodies. This knowledge and understanding is not about science or the mechanical workings of our organs. [It] will not be found …through poking, prodding, testing, injecting, cutting, radiating, or altering in any way. This is higher knowledge. It can only be directly experienced and observed when you…trust your inner truth. Your body has a lot to show you about who you are. By allowing the body to function as nature intended, it will demonstrate to you that you truly are interconnected to everything in creation.

Soul Speak
Solomae Sananda
(previously Cheryl Stoycoff)

**If you don't love it,
then it ain't worth it.**

George Lucas – a Taurus

Ferdinand the Bull, a powerful yet gentle image of Taurus

TAURUS

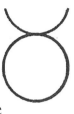

The Bull ★ Fixed Earth ★ Ruler ♀ ★ Exalts ☽ ★ Red-Orange

(late April - late May)

Taurus is astrology's second sign, the partner who helps Aries manifest its desires. Fixed Earth is the substance that the Aries/Mars life force uses to "flesh out" its visions. This substance has a potential phase and an actual phase, which are represented by the two planets most closely connected to ♉, Moon and Venus. Moon is the Divine Mother's dark, mysterious womb that receives the spark of life and nurtures the fiery desire to Be. Venus is the bright, observable Mother Nature who creates an outward form/body to express the divine creative spark. ☽ = possibilities before insemination, ♀ = pregnancy and birth. Taurus exalts the Moon in recognition that astrology's Moon is the First Feminine Elder, the primal Source of form. If she did not receive the seed desires, nothing physical would exist. If your mother had not received your father's seed, you would not exist in a body. You would be formless.

Everything starts in spirit, goes through a continuum process, and ends in form. There is no essential difference between spirit and its embodiment. Spirit is in every atom, and every atom has some kind of form. (What we call "empty space" is a reservoir of formless, pre-atomic spirit.) From the fast frequencies of spirit to the slow frequencies of physicality, all things are expressions of divinity. This is why Ageless Wisdom is very clear that the earth element is holy.

Taurus is our Sacred Mother Earth. Beautiful ♉ occurs in May, when springtime is in full glory, inviting us to joyful worship of Life in fragrant fields of wildflowers and hallowed groves of trees. Queen Venus, the planet of art, love, and beauty, is at the height of her splendor when ruling in this sign.

Your body, governed by ♉, is a very lively piece of planetary substance. Sages of every tradition have called the human body a Temple of Spirit. If you always keep a non-judgmental part of your attention on what your body is feeling and doing, you will come to experience the wisdom and presence of God Within. The divine voice of **intuition**, your *inner tutor or teacher*, is built into your body.

Taurus rules the throat, our center of self-expression. Natives of this sign enjoy singing, conversation, and the arts. Due to Venusian influence, Taurus is affectionate, gentle, and patient. Pleasure-loving Taurus likes comfort and luxury, but is not afraid of hard work. It can be firm, determined, and persevering—even obstinate. Like the buffalo in Native American lore, the Taurean Bull embodies great strength, endurance, fertility, abundance and prosperity. Poetic references to horns of the crescent Moon evoke the sign and glyph of the Bull. Steady, sensible ♉ is oriented towards practical and physical matters such as diet, fitness, basic values, finances, gardens, real estate, and personal resources. It is natural for fixed earth to be unmoving, but if an overly stubborn or "set in stone" condition arises, Taureans can remember this example: Earth herself is always moving in space.

THE LOVERS

The ornaments of a house
are the friends who frequent it.

Ralph Waldo Emerson – a Gemini

Vive la difference!
(Long life to maleness and femaleness)
(Hurray for sexuality)

French Saying

English Saying

The universe constantly and obediently answers to our conceptions.

Henry David Thoreau

Find your home in the heart of every living creature; make yourself higher than all heights and lower than all depths; bring all opposites inside yourself and reconcile them; understand that you are everywhere, on the land, in the sea, in the sky; that you are still in the womb, that you are young, that you are old, that you are dead, that you are in the world beyond the grave; hold all this in your mind, all times and places, all substances and qualities and magnitudes; then you can perceive God.

Hermetic Writings, *3rd Century*

The world is so full
Of a number of things,
I'm sure we should all be
As happy as kings.

A Child's Garden of Verses
Robert Louis Stevenson

Photo by Ira Fabricant

*Ira & Shana Fabricant with their twins,
Sima & Eli*

Love of an idea is the love of God.

*Epitaph on the grave of
Frank Lloyd Wright – a Gemini*

GEMINI

The Twins ★ Mutable Air ★ Ruler ☿ ★ Orange
(late May - late June)

Gemini is the third sign of the zodiac. Mars in Aries "married" Venus in Taurus, and then they had children—twins!—very alert, active, curious twins. Three, the number of fertility, reproduction, and development, is joined with mutable air, the intellect. This combination creates maximum mental activity in ♊.

The Twins represent the dualities in life. Natives of this sign are gifted with avid interest in exploring polarity. When looking deeply, they discover a unifying factor that connects the opposites. This magical cohesive link is the Self, the observer, the conscious witness. It is represented by Gemini's ruling planet, Mercury, the "messenger" who connects heaven/above and earth/below. When ☿ bridges a pair of opposites, a relationship arises that is really a third entity, having a life of its own. Ageless Wisdom tells us that polarity exists to make relationship and communication possible. People do not have to be "opposites" to be in relationship. Each person or creature we meet gives us an opportunity to establish relationship. Infinite possibilities for interaction keep Gemini busy networking everywhere. An excellent communicator, charming ♊. takes a light, airy approach to society. Gemini rules commerce and business, which are all about communication.

In the psychological makeup of an individual, the polarities exist as self-conscious and subconscious. In alchemy and Jungian psychology, these *inner polarities* are called **animus** and **anima**. A symbiotic, mutually beneficial relationship between these inner twins gives rise to the unifying third factor of super conscious awareness. This is why our teachers ask us to accept both light and dark in ourselves. Self-love, acceptance between animus and anima, creates psychological harmony. Venus naturally <u>feels</u> the relationship between opposites, but humans also use intellectual Mercury to <u>logically</u> <u>understand</u> the inherent connection and ultimate oneness of opposites. An egoic belief in separation does not allow much inner or outer peace. When ☿ comprehends the truth of unity, peace enters the mind

In our body, ♊ rules these pairs of opposites: right and left lobes of the brain, two lungs, two shoulders, arms and hands. The essence of mutable air is breath. Throughout our time on Earth, we experience our life-giving in-breath and out-breath working together with perfect agreement inside our lungs.

Observant Gemini is an information specialist who likes to know what makes things tick, the versatile jack-of-all-trades. Interested in people, talkative, adaptable, always "on the go"— Gemini is often called **mercurial**, *swift of mind and fleet of foot, ever-changing*. Communication through writing and all forms of media is a strong talent for ♊. This clever sign can dazzle with sparkling wit or word play, and excel at juggling or prestidigitation (sleight-of-hand).

THE CHARIOT

Hᴇᴀᴠᴇɴ ɪs ᴜɴᴅᴇʀ ᴏᴜʀ ꜰᴇᴇᴛ

ᴀs ᴡᴇʟʟ ᴀs ᴏᴠᴇʀ ᴏᴜʀ ʜᴇᴀᴅs,

Henry David Thoreau – a Cancer

The women in the Golden Dawn were inspired
to discover the light within the dark,
the inner within the outer, the God-Self within the shadow self.
Bringing the shadow into the light, both were seen to be One.

Women of the Golden Dawn
Mary K. Greer

Love and compassion are necessities, not luxuries.
Without them, humanity cannot survive.

14th Dalai Lama – a Cancer

There are no mistakes,
no coincidences.
All events
are blessings
given to us
to learn from.

Elizabeth Kubler-Ross –
a Cancer

Security is the soul
knowing itself, its
direction, its course
of learning.

Illuminations for a New Era
Matthew

My home is my castle.

Gazing at the Moon and Cherishing Thoughts of a Distant Friend

Above the sea the bright moon is born
From the horizon it lights up the whole length of heaven
Passionately I mourn your absence throughout the night
All night long my loving thoughts arise
I put out my candle in compassion for the light of the moon
I put on my cloak because the dew is heavy
Sorry I cannot fill my hands with moonlight and give it to you
I go back to bed and dream of meeting you again

Chang Chu Ling

The Zodiac

CANCER

The Crab ★ Cardinal Water ★ Ruler ☽ ★ Exalts ♃ ★ Yellow-Orange
(late June - late July)

Cancer is the fourth astrological sign, combining 4, the attribute of stability, with the yin principle symbolized by water. Zero degrees Cancer 0° ♋ is the **nadir**, *the lowest, deepest, darkest point on the wheel of the zodiac.* It is the foundation, a place of privacy, safety, and security. Therefore, Cancer is called the Root of Being.

A root holds a plant in position, draws up nourishment, and stores food. Humanity's root extends down into water, not earth, because occult water represents the hidden mental substance that comes before physical embodiment. The alchemists called this substance their **Prima Materia**, or *First Matter.* In Latin, **mater** means *mother.* The first, most basic and subtle matter that supports all life may be called the Great Mother, or Cosmic Mind. Our <u>feelings</u> are the roots through which we connect to her nourishing matrix. The Crab who lives in the dark and teeming depths of cardinal water moves by feeling its way.

The Moon naturally rules Cancer, since it represents the subconscious mind, a vast realm of feeling. A person born in ♋ is a Moonchild who feels at home in the receptive, ever-flowing water world. The Crab is given a hard outer shell to protect its inner sensitivity. All three water signs deal with sensitivity; Cancer is particularly tuned-in and responsive to emotions. The Moon's ever-shifting phases create a full emotional experience of life for moody Cancer. The privacy of home is a needed refuge. Cancer rules the home, and natives of this sign may be quite domestic. Natives of either gender like to "mother" others, and provide security. They can be fabulous cooks. Physically, ♋ rules the breasts and stomach.

Jupiter, the planet of expansion, is exalted in Cancer's endless ocean, where everything is telepathically connected. ♃ in ♋ is like a great friendly whale who inhabits the sanctuary of our inner world. Moonchild's glyph is an embrace, a hug.

The Sun leaves Gemini and enters 0° Cancer at the Summer Solstice. ☉ at the nadir is like a consummation for the Gemini Twins. The brightest light in the sky and the darkest depths of the ocean become One. Then—happy summer days.

When ♋ gets overly dramatic or emotionally out of balance, it has some excellent options. One is to express the feelings artistically. Another is to accept and <u>fully</u> <u>experience</u> every emotion without repression or censure, no matter how intense. By experiencing extremes, one may learn to recognize the central place of balance, the Middle Way. Then ♋ can come home to itself at the Root of Being, having won great inner strength. Victorious over the sway of the opposites, and filled with compassionate understanding for the emotional life of others, sympathetic Cancer encourages everyone to "go deep sea diving." At the deepest point of the Inner Ocean lies the Pearl of Great Price, one's true Self.

VIII

STRENGTH

Be praised my Lord
for all your creatures
and first for brother sun
who makes the day bright and luminous.
He is beautiful and radiant
with great splendor
He is the image of you
Most High.

Segment, **Canticle of the Sun**

St. Francis of Assisi

𝔗𝔯𝔲𝔱𝔥 𝔦𝔰 𝔩𝔦𝔨𝔢 𝔞 𝔩𝔦𝔬𝔫;

𝔧𝔲𝔰𝔱 𝔩𝔢𝔱 𝔦𝔱 𝔬𝔲𝔱 𝔬𝔣 𝔦𝔱𝔰 𝔠𝔞𝔤𝔢.

C.S.Lewis

Alchemical Emblem of Solar Power

Nequaquam Vacuum, Latin, *Nowhere a Vacuum*
The living fire of the Spiritual Sun radiates throughout every force and atom,
every level and dimension of all formed and formless universes.

The heavens declare God's glory
    and the magnificence of what made them.
Each dawn is a new miracle;
    each new sky fills with beauty.
Their testimony speaks to the whole world
    and reaches to the ends of the earth.
In them is a path for the sun,
    who steps forth handsome as a bridegroom
    and rejoices like an athlete as he runs.
He starts at one end of the heavens
    and circles to the other end,
    and nothing can hide from his heat.   *Psalm 19*

Astrology represents
the summation of
all the psychological
knowledge of
antiquity.

Carl G. Jung – a Leo

God is my strength.   *A simple statement of fact*

The Zodiac

LEO

The Lion ★ Fixed Fire ★ Ruler ☉ ★ Yellow
(late July – late August)

Leo is the fifth sign of the zodiac. It combines 5, the number of humanity, with the immense authority of fixed fire. Golden Leo has always been a sign of glory, providing natives with both an advantage and a challenge. Leo can easily exhibit either the greatness of a human being, or an ego blown out of proportion. The key to happiness for Leo is remembering there is a small self and a great Self that are not separate, but One. The One holds both greatness and smallness, or humility, equally. It never pretends to be exclusively great. Leo's natural grandeur can be a reminder of the One God-Self that we all share.

Fixed fire refers to the Sun, which is permanently fixed at the center of our solar system. The ☉ is literally the divine Source of Life for all its planets. It is easy to see why the Sun is used as a symbol of God in every culture. Ageless Wisdom holds the deeper awareness that the Sun is an actual expression and extension of God/Source. All light extends itself in continuity. When we feel warm sunlight across 93 million miles of space, we are actually being touched by the ☉. Suns (stars) shine for billions of years, giving all their power in service to life. The physical bodies of stars do eventually burn out, but God's spiritual Light extends itself in infinite creative expressions forever, in humble and loving service to life.

Leo rules the heart and spine. Our teachers tell us the heart is an inner sun, smaller in size, but in essence exactly like the Sun, which is exactly like the Source. (As below, so above.) When our heart is blazing with love, others are warmed by our presence. The sages also say the spine is the route up which Kundalini (page 202) spirit-fire rises as we gradually awaken into ever more light , truth, and wisdom.

The Lion is a regal "king of beasts," and ♌ has long been "the sign of kings." Now that Earth is moving into the Aquarian Age, humanity no longer wants outer rulers. ♒ is opposite ♌. Now we each claim the ruling power within, and become king or queen of our own lives. Lion-hearted Leo has a proud, commanding presence. Leo is brave, exciting, resourceful, joyous, gracious, and genial. Just as lions live in "prides" (groups), Leo loves company. The ♌ glyph is a lion's tail; it also symbolizes a wave of energy. Waves are classified as yin, and straight lines as yang. The Sun emanates both waves of heat and beams of light. We call the Sun "father" for the sake of left brain classification. Really, everything has both yin and yang, especially things directly connected to Source.

Leo occurs at the height of the summer season, giving people born under this sign a "summery" nature. Charismatic Leo has a dramatic flair, often taking center stage in the same way the Sun naturally stands at the center of our planetary family. Above all, ♌ is a sign of creativity and self-expression.

THE HERMIT

LIFE is CHANGE.

Old Saying

CHANT FOR EARTHLINGS

A chant is a flowing song, meant to be repeated many times. Try singing this one to a drumbeat.

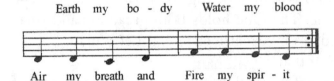

Earth my bo - dy   Water my blood

Air my breath and   Fire my spir - it

We have it within our power to begin the world again.

Thomas Paine, American Revolutionary

(and again, and again, and again, and again.........)   *Granny*

Life's most urgent question is: what are you doing for others?

Martin Luther King

Photo: www.webshots.com

Be kind and merciful.
Let no one ever come to you
Without leaving better and happier.
Be a loving expression of God's
kindness...to children, to the poor,
to all who suffer and are lonely,
give always a happy smile.
Give them not only your care,
but your heart.

Mother Teresa – a Virgo

Our core purpose is to practice and promote the principle that every life is precious.

Society for the Prevention of Cruelty to Animals

When you work with love, you bind yourself to yourself, and to one another, and to God.

The Prophet
Khalil Gibran

VIRGO

The Maiden ★ Mutable Earth ★ Ruler ☿ ★ Exalts ☿ ★ Yellow-Green
(late August-late September)

Virgo is the sixth astrological sign, in which we experience the healing, harmonious nature of mutable earth. The planets teach us about mutability, because they are always moving and changing in perfect order. By watching the heavens above, we come to realize that the same systematic progressions are reflected here below, moment by moment. Virgo is sensitive to the magical mutations constantly occurring all around us. Precise, methodical Virgo knows how to pay attention, appreciate details, and treat each precious instant with care. ♍ is the nurse/caretaker in the zodiac, and the "patron saint" of animals.

In Leo, we learn that all is light extending itself in countless directions, expressing itself in mind-boggling diversity as this physical universe. The conscious living light does not just create stuff and then leave the scene. Rather, it keeps on creating, using Jupiter to keep everything moving, while Saturn gives an appearance of stability. Virgo, the flowing earth, is the result of all this divine artistry. As a summation of the entire ever-shifting blend, Virgo is the sign of integration, wholeness, and health. ♍ rules the intestines, where assimilation takes place.

The Maiden or Virgin is a symbol of the unsullied Universal Mind (partner of the light), in which all things arise and recede without changing the nature of Mind in any way. The Maiden also represents the purity and perfection of the natural world. She is traditionally shown bearing a sheaf of wheat, an emblem of Nature's abundance. Bountiful ♍ brings the beginning of harvest, and completes the first half of the zodiac, the phase of individual development. The "fruit" of individual development is Self-awareness. At the end of the sixth sign, we have the significant opportunity to fully integrate all the different parts of our self into a *unique wholeness*— a process called **individuation** by Jung. This "alchemy of the Self" prepares each unified being to confidently and lovingly enter Libra, there to begin the phase of social expression in the second half of the zodiac.

Mercury rules and is exalted in Virgo, the only planet to be exalted in a sign that it rules. ☿ observes the gradual flow of mutable earth, which it directs by those precious intellectual tools, focus and choice. In Gemini, ruling Mercury concentrates on communication with others. In Virgo, Mercury emphasizes communication with the Self, and intimacy with life as a whole. ♍ rules true purpose, work, and service, which are natural expressions of the integrated personality. Virgo's great powers of concentration can sustain long periods of practice and discipline, making sure to cover all the steps in a process. Virgo is famous for its ability to examine, analyze, organize, classify, and keep records of all the delightful varieties of mutable earth. When it gets lost in details, ♍ needs a vacation from work!

If you can conceive it,
you can believe it.
If you can believe it,
you can create it.

Dennis Kucinich – a Libra

LOVE

is omni-inclusive,
progressively exquisite,
understanding and tender,
and compassionately attuned to other than self.

Buckminster Fuller – a Libra

In all things great and small, I see the Beauty of the Divine Expression.

Paul Foster Case
– a Libra

Learning to love one other person completely, teaches you how to love all people. Learning to love all that is unlovable in your partner, learning how to rise above the pettiness, disagreements, and judgments, establishes in you a love for all humanity.

The Shared Heart
Barry and Joyce Vissell

Blessed are the peacemakers,
for they shall be called the Children of God.

Jesus

Let the beauty that you love be what you do.

Rumi

The Beauty Way

Beauty before me, beauty behind me.
Beauty above me, beauty below me.
Beauty all around me.
All is finished in beauty.

Native American Poem

EQUILIBRIUM IS THE BASIS OF THE GREAT WORK.

Alchemical Saying

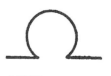

LIBRA

The Scales ★ Cardinal Air ★ Ruler ♀ ★ Exalts ♄ ★ Green

(late September - late October)

Libra is astrology's seventh sign, where the poise and purpose of 7 merge with cardinal air. Libra's mission is to balance relationships—not by any rigid rules, but by dynamic, in-the-moment interweaving of energies. This Venusian sign uses diplomacy to create peace and beauty from whatever energies are occurring between people. Thus noble Libra helps humanity to learn the art of living.

Known as the peacemaker of the zodiac, Libra is a sensitive and skillful communicator. The first air sign, Gemini, is about communication with your birth family, extended family, neighbors, and business associates. The second air sign, Libra, is about choosing the people with whom you want to be close friends or lovers, and establishing a mutual basis for familiarity. Your creativity in personal relationships can take many forms, from a single life partner to a cooperative community or tribe of kindred spirits. In its highest expression, ♎ thinks of each person it meets as a friend.

Libra highlights partnerships. The song of Libra, "We Are," initiates social expression. Opposite Libra, Aries declares, "I Am," emphasizing individual development. Whereas ♈ brings the spring equinox, ♎ ushers in the fall season at the autumnal equinox. Red Mars rules Aries, and green Venus rules Libra, switching the colors associated with their seasons (spring green, autumn red) like the "seed of the opposite" in ☯. This archetypal couple holds hands across the zodiac, along the horizon. To the left, ♈ represents symbolic sunrise on the Ascendant, while to the right, the ♎ glyph pictures sunset on the Descendant.

Exalted Saturn is the fulcrum point of equilibrium in Libra's Scales. The Scales are balanced when partners have equal "weight," or worth. ♄ determines what is real, what is false, and what must be eliminated in art or relationship. When the ego pulls us off balance, Saturn can draw us back to the Self at our center. One of the most important lessons we can learn is how to maintain peaceful, respectful relationships. Physically, Libra rules the kidneys, which maintain peace in the body.

Venus knows the true basis of relationship: we are all family, born from the same Source. In the Balance of Nature all lives are designed to fit together **symbiotically**, in *beneficial inter-dependence*. Love always knows how to keep the peace. Due to Venusian endowments, tasteful Libra governs the arts. Art is a major force for the advancement of culture. The arts are concerned with placing diverse parts in cooperative proportion/relationship to each other. Natives of this sign are refined, graceful, polite, diplomatic, cultured, and artistically talented, with a deep desire for harmony. Easy-going Libra enjoys comfort and companionship. Because ♎ sees both sides of any issue, it can sometimes have difficulty making a decision. When Libra aims at what it loves and finds beautiful, the decision will make itself.

I DIE DAILY.

St. Paul

St. Paul is describing a spiritual exercise in which one surrenders one's whole being to God every night, and rejoices in resurrection every morning.

I have loved the stars too much to be fearful of the night.

Epitaph on the gravestone of an anonymous astronomer

God Works in Mysterious Ways.   *Old Saying*

To let go of the last moment and open to the next
is to die consciously moment to moment.

Stephen Levine

Try to paint your world as though you are the first person looking at it.

*Georgia O'Keeffe
– a Scorpio*

Scorpio Rising
from a painting by Arisa Victor

Here is a quote from a booklet by a priest of the *indigenous African divination system* known as **Ifa**. His words are well worth your study. **Awo**, the *secret and invisible forces* of which the diviner speaks, can also be called *occult powers*.

Within the discipline if *Ifa*, there is a body of wisdom called 'awo,' which attempts to preserve the rituals that create direct communication with Forces of Nature. *Awo* is a Yoruba word that is usually translated to mean "secret." ... *Awo* refers to the hidden principles that explain the Mystery of Creation and Evolution. *Awo* is the esoteric understanding of the dynamics and form within Nature ... These invisible forces are not considered secret because they are devious; they are secret because they remain elusive, awesome in their power to transform, and not readily apparent. As such they can only be grasped through direct interaction and participation. Anything which can be known by the intellect alone ceases to be *awo*.

OBATALA: Ifa and the Spirit of the Chief of the White Cloth *by Awo Falokun Fatunmbi*

SCORPIO

The Scorpion ★ Fixed Water ★ Ruler ♇ ★ Blue-Green
(late October - late November)

Scorpio is the eighth sign of the zodiac. The magical control of vibration is held in fixed water. Water symbolizes the matrix of life that Ageless Wisdom calls Universal Mind (page 153). Our intellect (air) is derived from mind (water). We live and move and have our being within the infinite ocean of consciousness. Everything in the ocean abides by the laws of the ocean. Just as humans have "certain inalienable rights," so does God/Nature have certain unalienable laws, which are forever true and "right." These laws are <u>fixed</u>, that is, unchanging.

Esoteric and exoteric science both seek to discover and apply the laws of Nature. Aquarius rules science, while the authority/ability <u>behind</u> the science is ruled by Scorpio. Extremely potent forces operate beneath the surface appearances of life to enforce the laws of Nature. These divine Powers carry out cosmic will in unseen ways. ♏ rules this underworld of hidden influences. There is absolutely nothing to fear from these energies. Ageless Wisdom always reminds us that love is the strongest power there is. On an outer level, Scorpio energies can be potentially dangerous, like tools in the hands of children. But an alert child with a good teacher won't have any trouble. And a sincere student of occultism who wants the truth can benefit greatly from working with what Paul Foster Case liked to call "Nature's Finer Forces."

A few of these mysterious forces are gravity, kundalini, karma, death, rebirth, sexuality, and the love that conquers all. We cannot really grasp or understand these things. What we can do is apply the scientific method: observe and learn, then use whatever knowledge we have gained as wisely as we can. The results of our experiments show us whether or not we are attuned to the magic of life. Occult powers are extremely enticing to the ego, so this is where The Path can get steep and rocky. Keep asking for divine assistance to know the truth. And remember! These powers do not belong to anyone personally. As Children of Light, we are given everything for our mutual benefit, as Libra teaches us.

Traditionally, Scorpio is the sign of transformation. Ruling Pluto asks us to change in order to grow, to be willing to "die" and be "reborn" spiritually and psychologically many times throughout our life. **Transformation** is *a major shift of life energy from one form to another.* An acorn dies in order to transform into an oak tree. Life <u>never</u> gives up, <u>especially</u> in Scorpio, making it a sign of great intensity and determination. ♏ rules the sex organs. It has strong feelings and intuitions. Working in the underworld, ♏ is secretive and self-protective. But when transformation time arrives, ♇ is released from darkness to light through the three phases of the Risen Scorpio Force—from a scorpion with stinging tail as shown in the ♏ glyph, to kundalini energy snaking upward, to a great eagle or phoenix who flies in heaven.

XIV

TEMPERANCE

You will show me the path to life,
fullness of joy in your presence,
and happiness at your right hand forever.

Psalm 16:11

Far better things lie ahead
Than any we leave behind.

C.S. Lewis – a Sagittarius

The goal of the Cabala is to lead a guided life.

Jason Lotterhand

Student: I have been seeking for the Buddha, but don't know where to look.
Master: It is very much like looking for an ox while you are riding on one.

paraphrased from **The Spirit of Zen**
Alan Watts

philos, loving

sophos, wise

philosopher, lover of wisdom

The future belongs to those who
believe in the beauty of their dreams.

Eleanor Roosevelt

Come, let us go up
To the mountain of the Lord,
That we may walk the paths
of the Most High.

Jewish Peace Prayer

How beautiful
on the mountains
are the feet of one
who brings good news!
Who hearalds peace
brings happiness,
proclaims salvation!

Isaiah, Hebrew Prophet

The Zodiac

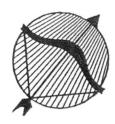

SAGITTARIUS

The Archer ★ Mutable Fire ★ Ruler ♃ ★ Blue
(late November - late December)

Sagittarius is ninth in the cycle of zodiacal signs. Attainment and fulfillment join with mutable fire to bring the light of inspiration to seekers on The Path of Return. <u>We are all seekers</u>, whether we know it or not. At least, that is the inclusive viewpoint of Sagittarius. In this energetic sign, the Path ascends to the very top of the zodiac, the highest point of consciousness. There we understand the big picture of how everything fits together in a way that makes total sense.

If you want to see the world from this expansive perspective, put on your spiritual hiking boots! It's quite a climb from the ego's imaginary stories of so-called "reality" to the eternal Reality. Fortunately, we have the help of Scorpio's unseen forces, powers that far exceed the ego's grasp. Something called "ego-death" happens when the intellect surrenders to truth, realizing that all power comes from <u>the</u> All Power. But the ego does not really die, because it never really existed apart from the One. It is our consciousness that transforms from a dark little scorpion into a great eagle, as it overcomes illusion and soars through ♐. Mutable fire helps us adapt to the rarified atmosphere on the high peaks of awareness. As we climb, we must continually modify our self-definition, thoughts, and behavior, becoming ever more pliable to the Primal Will. This is the tempering process by which Sagittarius turns us into philosophers, lovers of wisdom.

Recognition of the need for divine guidance replaces the "I can do it myself!" attitude. As we let go of what we thought was so, we are shown as much Reality as we can handle. Ageless Wisdom affirms that our essential Self helps us from beginning to end along the Path. Our goal is the Crown of Enlightenment at the end of the trail. Of course, once we get there, we come back down the other side and begin a new cycle. Jupiter, planet of journeys, cycles, and great blessings, naturally rules ♐.

All this Sagittarian path symbolism is completely psychological. In Reality we are already enlightened masters. Our God-Selves purposely forgot this fact, for the thrill of the Return. Humans have gone as far as possible into the hellish ego-mind experiment, and still have a body to live in on this planet. It is the greatest relief imaginable to remember that true heavenly Reality is already here right now.

The Archer is our spirit that aims for the stars. Sagittarius is idealistic, keen-witted, optimistic, and enthusiastic. The Archer is usually depicted as a centaur (part horse, part human), suggesting that we may aspire to the highest wisdom even while we live in an animal body. ♐ rules the thighs, the most horse-like parts of the body. Freedom-loving Sagittarius governs long distance travel, higher education, speculation, exploration, and the evolution of consciousness. Athletic ♐ loves sports and the out-of-doors. If feeling ungrounded and over-zealous (too "fired up"), Sagittarian natives can seek out water and earth experiences.

THE DEVIL

Cowardice asks the question – is it safe?
Expediency asks the question – is it politic?
Vanity asks the question – is it popular?
But conscience asks the question – is it right?
There comes a time when one must take a position
That is neither safe, nor politic, nor popular,
But one must take it <u>because it is right</u>.
The time is always right to do what is right.

Dr. Martin Luther King – a Capricorn

Teach only love, for that is what you are.

A Course In Miracles

An Investment in Knowledge Always Gives the Best Return.

Benjamin Franklin – a Capricorn

*God does not look at your forms and possessions:
He looks at your hearts and your deeds.*

Muhammad

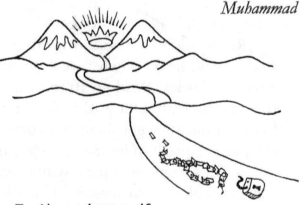

Oh God,
Lead us from the unreal to the Real;
Lead us from darkness to Light;
Lead us from death to Immortality.
OM Shanti, Shanti, Shanti

Upanishads, *Ancient Scripture of India*

ACE of PENTACLES

*Health, Wealth,
and Success*

The Earth and myself
are of one mind.
The measure of the land
and the measure of our bodies
are the same.

Chief Joseph

Apparent "evil" is an evolutionary stimulus.

The Hathors
Tom Kenyon

The Zodiac

CAPRICORN

Sea-Goat ★ Cardinal Earth ★ Ruler ♄ ★ Exalts ♂ ★ Blue-Violet

(late December - late January)

Capricorn is the tenth sign. The number of new beginnings starts a new sun cycle. Zero degrees Capricorn, 0°♑, is the **zenith**, *the highest or mid-heaven point of the zodiac.* It marks the sacred moment of the Winter Solstice. This is when the northern hemisphere celebrates the Sun's birthday, because daylight hours begin to increase at this time. In cardinal earth the yang, assertive aspect of Mother Nature is at work. Outwardly her powers appear withdrawn for a hibernation period. But in the dark winter cave of the bear, new cubs are born.

The most fulfilling gift of Sagittarius, the ninth sign, is Self-realization. Now in the tenth sign we get to express as much of our truth as we are able. This is where we stand firm for what we believe in, put our ideas into cardinal action, and resolutely manifest our spirit in earthly form. The masters of wisdom explain that we can't help but "teach what we are." So Capricorn is the sign of the teacher or coach, who teaches integrity by example.

Capricorn holds a position of prominence, authority, and influence. People "look up to" the highest point of consciousness. Cancer takes us into oceanic depths and Sagittarius takes us to the heights, while Capricorn encompasses both. The Sea-Goat glyph ♑ = horn + fishtail, or mountaintop + wave. Having journeyed to the zenith, we now begin our descent down the other side of the mountain through the zodiac's last 90°, consisting of Capricorn, Aquarius, and Pisces. This get-back-to-work aspect of Capricorn is why, for all its exalted position, it can be humble and dutiful. In the body, Capricorn governs the knees, on which we kneel to get closer to the Earth.

Masterful Saturn's rulership guides Capricorn to apply the wisdom of experience to practical matters. ♑ understands that every idea, person, place, or thing has a useful purpose, and it is up to us to discover the purpose so that we may use things well. Once we become Lords of the Secret of Saturn, we know this is a magical universe in which we may do anything we want—and all we want to do is serve the rest of life. We accept that we live in an outwardly limited body and environment. The difference is that now we consciously choose our own limits. Life becomes a game. How can unlimited divine beings have a positive experience of limitation? The sages say, when you realize the truth, you burst out laughing!

Mars enjoys exaltation in Capricorn, where the life force is dedicated to career and accomplishment of goals. ♂ in ♑ is an efficiency expert (speed + order). Hard-working Capricorn is the governor, director, and organizer of the zodiac. It is said that young Capricorns tend to be quite serious and responsible; sometimes they are expected to act like adults. Resilient ♑ mellows with age and experience, develops great capacity to enjoy the good things of Earth, and embodies the secret of health, wealth, and success.

THE STAR

Their faces looked like this: Each of the four had the face of a man, and on the right side each had the face of a lion, and on the left the face of an ox; each also had the face of an eagle...Wherever the spirit would go, they would go.

Ezekiel, Chapter 1

Astrology in the Bible: In his tremendous biblical vision, the prophet saw the symbolic "living creatures" associated with the <u>four fixed signs of the zodiac</u>. He tried to describe how they are everywhere at once, and what awesome power they have. Words are inadequate to convey this kind of inner multi-dimensional experience. Notice that Man (Aquarius) is one of the creatures.

All parts of God are equal.

Ageless Wisdom

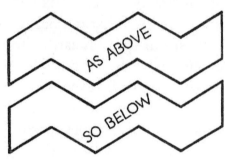

AS ABOVE

SO BELOW

Government of the People, by the People, and for the People shall not perish from the earth.

Abraham Lincoln — an Aquarius

Lasting peace will never come to a world that thinks it has a choice between peace and war. The only choice you ever really make is between truth and illusion. When you choose truth you discover that peace is always present ... When you choose illusion it is like closing your eyes to what is right in front of you. This is what it means to wake up from the dream of separation. It's like opening your eyes. Reality was never compromised by your dream. It remained whole and unchanged while you made up your own world where hatred and fear seemed to have meaning.

Emissary of Light
James Twyman

The gravitational force between any two objects is proportional to the product of the two masses, over the distance squared.

Sir Isaac Newton

AQUARIUS

The Water-Bearer ★ Fixed Air ★ Ruled by ♅ ★ Violet (Purple)
(late January - late February)

Aquarius is the eleventh sign. The number 11 is a partnership of two individual ones. Sideways, eleven is an equal sign =. The glyph for Aquarius ♒ is also a kind of equal sign, meaning as above, so below. Combine these ideas with the air element, and equality of relationship is the result. Then add the fixed characteristic to make the equation into a stable, unchanging law.

The four fixed signs hold the zodiac squarely in place. Taurus holds the solid earth; Leo controls creative fire; Scorpio knows the ways of water; Aquarius constitutes the laws of air. The hieroglyphs of the fixed signs—Bull, Lion, Eagle, and Human—are featured in Ezekiel's biblical vision (page 110). He saw the spirits of four "living creatures" turning great wheels in the sky. In other words, he was given a mystical experience of Cosmic Law. Ezekiel's use of astrological symbols is evidence that "the language of the stars" was part of ancient Hebrew culture.

The Water Bearer is humanity. Our bodies are composed of a very high percentage of water, just like our Mother Earth, so we "bear" water everywhere we go. We also carry and share the mind/psyche/soul that is occult water. But remember that Aquarius is an air sign, not a water sign, because occult air deals with relationships. This third air sign rules one's relationship to society. There are billions of us Water-Bearers inhabiting this planet. Our major lesson here is to learn how to relate to one another in a way that works for everyone. Therefore, Aquarius is known as the sign of humanity and brother-sisterhood. Natives of ♒ are friendly, accepting, and curious about any and all sorts of people. Ruling planet Uranus freely enjoys all.

Newton discovered a formula to express the physical law that everything in creation affects every other thing. Pisces feels this law as mystic truth, while Aquarius sees it as scientific fact. Both are correct. As an air sign, ♒ has a strong intellectual bent. Observant, analytical ♒ loves mental stimulation. Ruled by eccentric Uranus, the higher octave of Mercury, Aquarius is innovative, open-minded, inventive, and free. Aquarius governs computers and the world wide web, which is like a global brain. The internet puts us all in mental contact with each other, and frees us to explore countless viewpoints. If ♒ gets too mentally "wound up," it is time for a walk outside. This sign rules the calves and ankles, which steadily hold us erect.

In our current era of Earth history, the precession of the equinoxes makes Aquarius the "new frontier." The now-dawning New Age of Peace brings all people together in mutual respect. Tolerant, accepting Aquarius celebrates each unique individual, and welcomes the amazing diversity we create together as a big family. Aquarius is the sign of truth and clarity. As humanity enters the long-awaited Aquarian Age, let us open to the revelation that all parts of God are created equal.

XVIII

THE MOON

There are two ways to live your life.
One is as though nothing is a miracle.
The other is as though everything is a miracle.

Albert Einstein – a Pisces

*Cease trying to work everything out with your minds.
It will get you nowhere. Live by intuition and inspiration
and let your whole life be Revelation.*

Eileen Caddy

The New Millennium is all about compassion and getting along with one another.

Jason Lotterhand

Your union ought to be considered as a main prop of your liberty, and
the love of the one ought to endear to you the preservation of the other.

Farewell Address
George Washington – a Pisces

Photo (c) 1992 Stephen Frink

"Gravitational attraction"
is a scientific term
for LOVE.

Ms. Mystic

Everything else can wait. The search for God cannot wait.

A favorite saying of George Harrison – a Pisces

Nothing real can be threatened.
Nothing unreal exists.
Herein lies the peace of God.

The Course In Miracles

PISCES

The Fishes ★ Mutable Water ★ Ruled by ♆ ★ Red-Violet

(late February - late March)

Pisces is the twelfth and final sign. It demonstrates the teaching of Ageless Wisdom that every ending is a new beginning. During this completion of the zodiacal year, potential is gathering for the rebirth that will come in Aries. Add the digits in 12, 1+2=3, to see that Pisces is a sign of infinite promise and possibility. Also, 12 is the product of the 3 modes multiplied by the 4 elements, fertility times stability, a dynamic interaction of eros and logos that includes all zodiacal signs. Pisces is the synthesis or "wrap-up" at the end of the cycle.

Just as all rivers run into the sea, so do all experiences of our journey through the zodiac merge at last into the great ocean of Pisces. There, the Fishes of individualized consciousness enjoy a blissful feeling of being One with All. Sometimes spiritual aspirants imagine that upon enlightenment they will lose their sense of self, but this is not the case. They only lose their hallucination of separation from the whole, while their true Self peacefully encompasses the universe.

Shape-shifter Neptune, god of the sea, is the rightful ruler of Pisces. Some interpreters call it the planet of illusion, but often the actual facts are the other way around: Neptune recognizes the deeper Reality behind outer illusion. To a mind still identified with the ego, ♆ may seem otherworldly and mysterious. However, we all have Neptune and Pisces in our charts, so we all have a mystical side to our nature.

Like fish in the ocean, Piscean consciousness is very sensitive to subtle shifts and moods in the environment. This receptive, intuitive sign is innately psychic, able to <u>feel</u> information that would go unnoticed by less perceptive awareness. Because of its depth of feeling, ♓ is empathic and compassionate. Great loving-kindness flows forth from Venus in this sign of her exaltation. Pisces is especially tender towards those who are vulnerable, such as children and small animals. Knowing deep inside that all beings are One Being, mutable water easily merges with others. If ♓ gets lost in others, deep breathing helps restore awareness of the body; body awareness reminds us of our individuality. Also helpful is the fact that beneficial effects of our spiritual work are built into our bodies by subconsciousness.

Pisces rules the feet, which carry us on the Path of Return. The Path leads <u>within</u> (yes, we do have inner feet). Natives of this sign have an active inner life "behind the scenes." To Pisces, imagination is a divine creative faculty. Introspective ♓ is fond of daydreaming and/or night dreaming—states in which dimensions are bridged and other "mansions in God's kingdom" may be visited. The Pisces in us needs privacy, that we may at times retire from the outer world, connect with our deep core of inner peace, and merge in mystical union with all life in the boundless cosmic Ocean of Being, Consciousness, and Bliss.

KEY WORDS

The planets, signs, houses, and aspects are all concepts. Astrological key words are basic meanings associated with these concepts. It is good to have a few key words on the tip of your tongue when thinking or talking about astrological ideas. These are commonly accepted meanings that come in handy as starting points for discussion and interpretation. Examples:

"Your Sun is in Aquarius, the sign of humanity, truth, and freedom."
"You and I are born in the sign of Libra, so we are both interested in art, love and beauty."
"Gemini, the sign of short journeys, is opposite Sagittarius, the sign of long journeys."

EXERCISE 1: On page 117, three key words are given for each <u>sign</u>. Memorize all 36 words. You will be glad you did, because these keys will open many doors.

EXERCISE 2: Using a separate page for each sign, create lists of other meanings, descriptions, and characteristics for all the signs. Begin by writing down the three key words from #1 above, then add other words from this text. Leave space at the end for your own words later. Example from Cancer, pages 89 and 97:

Cancer is the sign of home, mother, security, birthplace, family, maternal instinct, safety, food,
emotion, depth, receptivity, stability, yin, cardinal water, nadir, lowest, deepest, darkest,
foundation, privacy, Root of Being, nourishment, First Matter, mind-stuff ...etc.

EXERCISE 3: Repeat #2 above, creating another set of meanings, this time for the <u>planets</u>. Start with page 63. Example from Mars, pages 63 and 75:

Some meanings for Mars are: energy, physical power, work, bravery, passion, valiant,
warrior, protection, courage, stand for truth, lightning, freedom, independence, life-force,
animal power, strength, vitality, blood, muscles, action, explosive, fire ...etc.

EXERCISE 4: From your work in #3 above, create a list of three key words for each planet, for a total of 30 key words. If you are studying on your own, make your own choices. If you are working with a group of friends, or with students in a class, compile this list of planetary key words together. Group consensus will ensure that you are all on the same track. Memorize the 30 words.

EXERCISE 5: From time to time, expand your information in the various lists you created in #2 and #3 above. Read other books, talk to astrologers, and jot down ideas that come to you. You might also want to make notes on astrological characteristics you are observing in family, friends, or famous people.

EXERCISE 6: See key words for <u>houses</u> (pages 120-121) and <u>aspects</u> (page 127). Please learn them, and add to them over time. Thank you for doing these exercises.

PART 6.

THE HOROSCOPE

The horoscope is a practical application
of Ageless Wisdom, esoteric science,
and the astrological meanings of planets and signs.
Horoscopes offer endless opportunities
for self-discovery.

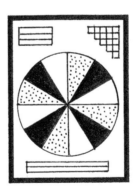

Home Sweet Home

Photo © NASA 1972

THE BIG CHART OF HIGH SCHOOL ASTROLOGY

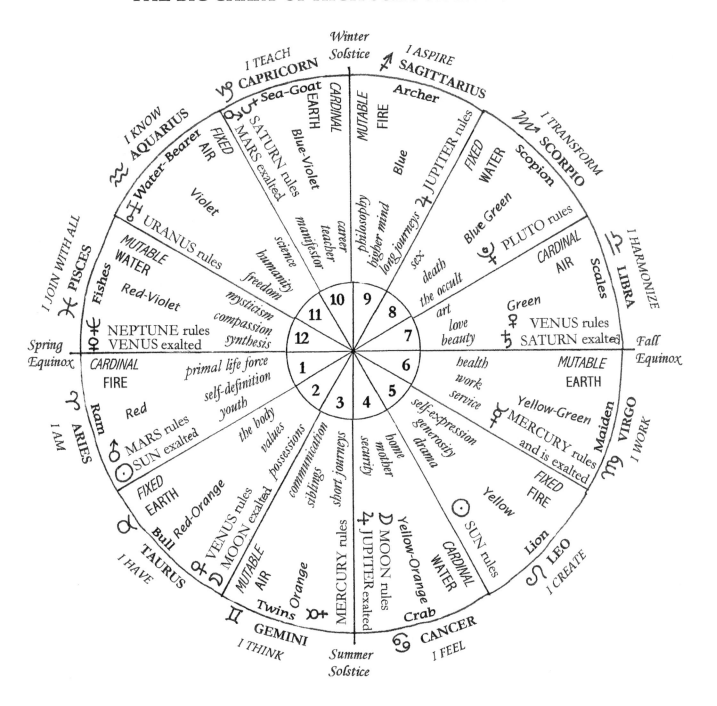

Just for fun, you could think of this diagram as Earth's horoscope.
Please use this information to become ever wiser and more loving.

Peace,

Granny Rainbow

HOUSES

Planets are <u>what</u>. Signs are <u>how</u>. Houses are <u>where</u>. Signs empower the planetary energies, while houses provide different territories where these energies live and express themselves in this world. Houses represent the conditions and circumstances that shape the planets' daily activities.

A person who becomes an actor may have one or more planets in the fifth house
(or a powerful Leo emphasis).
A soul who incarnates for the purpose of teaching may have a prominent tenth house
(or strong Capricorn planets).

In these examples, notice that the fifth house and the fifth sign are given equal weight; the same is true for the tenth house and sign. This direct correlation between houses and signs is due to the way in which houses are determined. Here is a "recipe" for understanding and remembering what the houses mean:

Houses 1 through 12 have the same basic meanings as signs 1 through 12. Houses deal with daily affairs, while signs influence fundamental character. Houses always stay in one place, while signs can be anywhere in a chart (depending on what sign and degree are on the Ascendant). Houses are created from the **natural zodiac** that *begins with zero degrees Aries,* 0°♈. When learning and using the houses, always picture the natural zodiac in your mind's eye.

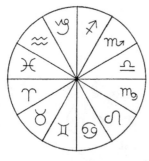

natural zodiac

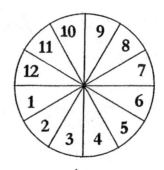

houses

The first house will always have Aries characteristics, no matter where the sign of Aries happens to be in an individual chart. The second house will always have Taurean traits, no matter where Taurus actually occurs. The third house will reflect Gemini qualities, and so forth through all the houses. Often, a chart will exhibit house <u>and</u> corresponding sign emphases.

In the chart on page 134 the native has 3 planets, including the ☉ (identity)
in the 7th house (peace), while ♎ (the 7th sign, peace) is rising and ruling
in the 1st house (identity). This person identifies as a peacemaker.

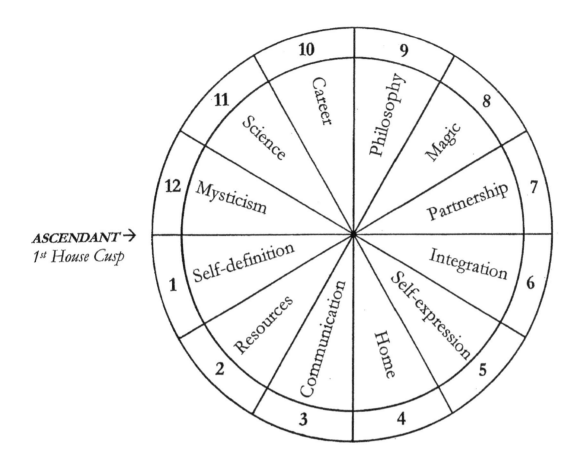

Key Words for Houses

Houses are cardinal, fixed, and mutable, just like the signs.
They are sometimes classified as angular, succedent, and cadent.

Cardinal houses	1, 4, 7, 10	dynamic, creative, activating
Fixed houses	2, 5, 8, 11	reliable, steady, consolidating
Mutable houses	3, 6, 9, 12	diverse, adaptable, changing

EXERCISE: 1) In the sample horoscope on page 134, how many planets are in cardinal houses? Fixed houses? Mutable houses? 2) Make the same analysis in your own chart. How do your findings relate to your personal experience?

NOTE: If you don't have your chart yet, see instructions at the bottom of page 132.

HOUSE DESCRIPTIONS

1st house: *self-definition*

emergence from formlessness, conditions of birth, early childhood, ego development, personal identity, self-awareness, zest for life, potential, instinct, basic energy, will power, drive, assertiveness, creative visions, independence, pioneering, leadership, subjective springtime

2nd house: *resources*

embodiment of spirit, substance, solidity, stability, all bodies and forms, temples, values, talents, finances, worth, wealth, banking, ownership, attachments, possessions, objects, practical matters, abundance, comfort, luxury, sculpture, gardens, roots, eco-systems, Nature, Earth

3rd house: *communications*

family relationships, siblings, neighbors, childhood education, language, writing, conversation, debate, commerce, business, intellectual activity, knowledge of environment, short travels, maps, calendars, media, information, diversity, curiosity, wit

4th house: *home*

family activities, the chosen environment, interior decorating, protection, safety, security, privacy, sensitivity, emotion, moods, psyche, sanctuary, deep inner knowing, First Matter, mothering, nurturing, cooking, food, "where the heart is," subjective summer

5th house: *self-expression*

creativity, flair, theater, drama, costumes, spectacle, display, heroics, bravery, risk, speculation, prizes, excitement, center of attention, fame, glory, admiration, romance, love affairs, offspring, generosity, self-esteem, honor, pride, royalty, majesty

6th house: *integration*

patience, practicality, focus, study, details, examination, scrutiny, competence, work, co-workers, craftsmanship, perseverance, skill, loyalty, reliability, care of animals, nursing, all levels of health, self-analysis, self-improvement, individuation, service to others

7th house: *partnership*

love, marriage, intimate relationships, close friendships, participation, teamwork, co-operation, sociability, diplomacy, contracts, courts of law, justice, fair play, balance, equality, peace, serenity, harmony, artistry, aesthetics, beauty, sweetness, grace, subjective autumn

8th house: *magic*

The Powers That Be, secrets, mysteries, shamanism, initiation, the occult, concealment, the underworld, death/transition, transformation, regeneration, healing ability, kundalini, sex, intensity, determination, investigation, research, legacy, inheritance

9th house: *philosophy*

mind expansion, exploration, circulation, opportunity, fortune, long journeys, spiritual quest, spiritual guidance, aspiration, zeal, optimism, sports, fun, gifts, circus, the out-of-doors, vistas, visas, higher education, goals, religion, higher law, karma, wisdom, the big overview

10th house: *career*

profession, recognition, public influence, government, responsibility, teaching, authority, fathering, rules, structure, organization, self-control, discipline, accomplishment, success, self-mastery, principles, scruples, ethics, conscience, reality, manifestation, subjective winter

11th house: *science*

pursuit of knowledge, experimentation, invention, social awareness, global awareness, the Aquarian Age, friends, tribes, brother-sisterhood, individuality, uniqueness, eccentricity, independence, freedom, truth, reform, causes, revolution, visions and hopes for the future

12th house: *mysticism*

ocean, oneness, universality, infinity, eternity, return to Source, unconditional love, mercy, compassion, merging, the masses, collective unconscious, cosmic citizenship, idealism, imagination, going with the flow, past lives, inter-dimensional experiences, telepathy, ESP

CUSPS

An astrological **cusp** is *the point where one cycle ends and another begins, always a sensitive and powerful area that holds great potential.* Cusps occur at the beginning of signs, houses, and ages. The completion of one cycle blends into the beginning of another in a kind of death and rebirth that brings change and opportunity.

> *The world is on the cusp of the Aquarian Age.*

Sign cusps occur regularly every thirty degrees. In the ancient, classical Equal House system used in this book, house cusps also occur every 30°. (There are other house systems in which house cusp degrees and house sizes vary.) An Age lasts 2,160 years; the cusp of an Age covers an undetermined number of years.

> *At present, Earth consciousness is partly in the Piscean Age and partly in the Aquarian Age, giving humanity a great opportunity to leave behind outworn ideas of collective subjugation, and reinvent itself with more freedom and social awareness.*

The sign in which a house begins is said to rule that house, no matter what degree of the sign is on the cusp. In exploring charts, you can combine the vibrations of any house with the energies of its ruling sign. The various combinations will disclose the native's* natural tendencies as they operate in daily circumstances.

> *If the 11th house cusp falls in Pisces, then Pisces rules the 11th house.*
> *The native will feel compassion (♓) for all humanity (♒ energy in the 11th house).*

Sometimes planets are located on sign and/or house cusps. Cusp planets have a broad field of operation. They may function on either side of the cusp. In its yang expression, a cusp planet will work in the sign or house ahead; its yin expression will be in the sign or house behind.

> *A person born on October 23, 1961 has Sun on the Libra/Scorpio cusp, six hours before the ☉ went into ♏. In action, she is determined and powerful; in receptivity, she is peaceful and loving. When centered within herself, she is both ways at once.*

The **cardinal points** are *the cusps of the cardinal houses: 1st, 4th, 7th, and 10th or Ascendant, Nadir, Descendant, and Midheaven* (page 124). They are particularly potent demarcations. Planets or aspects that touch these points have a strong effect on the native, and receive extra emphasis in chart interpretation.

> *Saturn on the cusp of the 10th house gives an ability to master the world of form.*

*****native**, from Latin **natus**, *born. One for whom a natal chart, or birth horoscope, is made.*

ASCENDANT

The **Ascendant** *defines the 1ˢᵗ house cusp, the most important cusp in any horoscope.*

The Ascendant is the primal beginning point from which the whole chart is developed. It is the sign and degree that were rising over the physical horizon at a person's time and place of birth. It is a doorway through which you enter this world, and also through which you can then step out to experience the world.

For natal horoscopes, the sign and degree of the Ascendant are mathematically calculated according to the native's time and place of birth. For horoscopes of events, the Ascendant is calculated according to time and place of the event. Correct times are essential to correct horoscopes.

Once the Ascendant has been located in a specific degree of a specific sign, that location becomes the first house cusp. In the Equal House system of 30° per sign, the Ascendant degree reoccurs on successive house cusps.

> *A chart Ascendant is calculated to be in 15°♏. Therefore, the 1ˢᵗ house cusp is 15°♏,*
> *the 2ⁿᵈ house cusp is 15°♎, the 3ʳᵈ house is 15°♏, and so on.*

A **rising planet** *is situated on the Ascendant or in the beginning of the first house.* A **risen planet** *is just above the Ascendant in the twelfth house.* If you are born at dawn (sunrise), the Sun is on the Ascendant in your chart, and you are a **double** whatever-the-sign-is, because *Sun and Ascendant are in the same sign.* If *Sun and Moon are in the same sign,* that is also called double. When *Sun, Moon, and ASC are all in the same sign,* that combination is a **triple** whatever.

> *☉ and ASC in ♓ = double Pisces*
> *☉ and ☽ in ♊ = double Gemini*
> *☉, ☽, and ASC in ♌ = triple Leo*

Your Ascendant degree marks the door through which you enter into life and self-awareness on this planet. It is your astrological "address." The most important determinants in a natal horoscope are the Sun, Moon, and Ascendant. The Sun is your basic yang; the Moon is your basic yin; your Ascendant connects and works to balance those two Lights. *The sign of your Ascendant* is called your **Rising Sign**. It contributes greatly to your physical appearance, the first impression you make on others, and your personal expressive mannerisms. What kind of relationship do you have between the qualities and elements of your three major determinants?

> *☉ in ♉ = fixed earth. ☽ in ♏ = fixed water. ASC in ♋ = cardinal water.*
> *A basically earthy nature (Taurus) with willpower (fixed),*
> *sensitivity (water), and originality (cardinal).*

CARDINAL CUSPS

The **cardinal house cusps**
*form an equal-armed cross within a
circle, which is a very ancient symbol
for the balance of universal forces.*

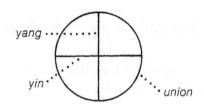

When constructing the horoscope, one first draws a circle. This circle, or zero, symbolizes the cosmos and all potential. Insofar as it is a boundary, the circle also stands for a specific field of potential within the All. The circle of the zodiac is an astrological boundary defining a field of activity for us Earthlings.

The rising degree is placed on the left, or eastern portion, of the circle, establishing the Ascendant and the beginning of the 1st house. Then the **horizon line** is *drawn from the Ascendant degree to the Descendant degree* in the western portion, exactly halfway, *180° across the circle.* Next, the **meridian line** is placed *at right angles to the horizon, 90° from the ASC and DSC.*

The cross that is formed by this construction marks the center of a horoscope. Imagine yourself at this essential point when viewing your chart. From this position of power, all the various chart components may be balanced and coordinated. You are surrounded by the three hundred sixty degrees of the zodiac. All 360° are there for your use, as your support. From the center, you connect to the wheel of the zodiac at four main points: above, below, to your left, and to your right. These *four key points of entry to the zodiac* are the **cardinal points**, *where one contact the cardinal house cusps to access four different types of consciousness.*

ASCENDANT ★ *awareness of being* ★ *consciousness of self*
East, left side of chart, 1st house cusp.
Your sign of emergence, <u>symbolic sunrise</u>

MID-HEAVEN ★ *rational awareness* ★ *outer consciousness*
South, top of chart, 10th house cusp.
Your public sign, <u>symbolic high noon</u>

DESCENDANT ★ *awareness of relationship* ★ *consciousness of others*
West, right side of chart, 7th house cusp.
Your partnership sign, <u>symbolic sunset</u>

NADIR ★ *intuitional awareness* ★ *inner consciousness*
North, bottom of chart, 4th house cusp.
Your home sign, <u>symbolic midnight</u>

CENTER OF THE ZODIAC ★ *you* ★ *super consciousness*

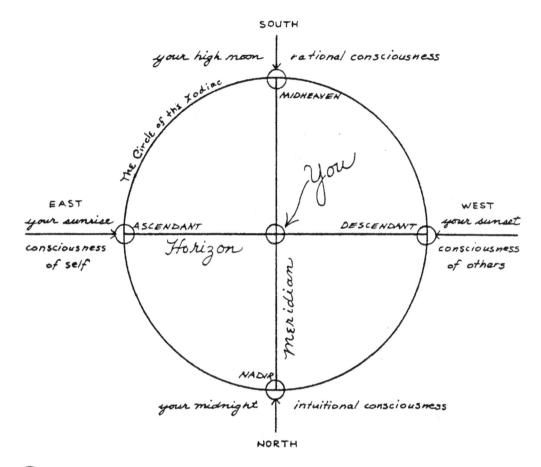

The figure of a circle containing an equal-armed cross is the astronomical symbol for Planet Earth. In astrology this symbol is embodied in the cardinal cusps, and is also used to represent *an important point of integration* called the **Part of Fortune**. The same pattern is used by Native Americans to construct their sacred Medicine Wheel. In Hawaiian indigenous art, this design is considered to be the most powerful tattoo. Why such big magic in these few lines? To answer, let's start with geometry and end with Ageless Wisdom.

In occult geometry, any circle corresponds to the number 22, because circumference equals Pi times the diameter, C= π D. The closest approximation of Pi in simple numbers is $3\frac{1}{7}$. Thus the smallest whole number that can represent a diameter is 7, corresponding to a circumference of 22. In astrology there are 22 basic components: 10 planets + 12 signs = 22. There are 22 letters in the Hebrew alphabet and 22 Major Arcana in the tarot (page 162).

An equal-armed cross represents number four. So a circle (22) plus a cross (4) is 22+4=26. This makes 26 the number of the figure under discussion. In the Cabala, 26 is the number of the Name of God, because the **Tetragrammaton**, the *Name of Four Letters*, totals 26 (page 146). The "Letters" represent living, intelligent, creative powers of the universe, embodied in the four elements and directions. Four is the number of system and stability. Therefore, the circle/cross combination, in its most profound interpretation, symbolizes both God and Earth simultaneously. All is One Big Magic.

ASPECTS

Aspects are *relationships between planets, or between planets and other chart components (such as the Ascendant), defined in terms of angular degrees.* Planets are always moving, so the aspects between them keep shifting. This mutability makes one moment in time different from another, even on the same day. A natal horoscope maps the aspects as they existed at the moment of birth.

If Saturn is in ten degrees Gemini, ♄10♊°, and Neptune is in ten degrees Aquarius, ♆10°♒, there is a 120° angle between them, an exact trine aspect, ♄ △ ♆. The two planets have a harmonious relationship. There is talent for giving form to mystical awareness, perhaps through music or film. Wisdom and compassion empower the native to help society.

The example above uses the exact number of degrees in a trine aspect, but in real charts, the numbers are rarely exact, so there is an **orb allowance** of *a few degrees on either side of the point where an aspect would be exact.* Planets still have an aspect if they fall within the orb allowance.

If Saturn is in 9°♊ and Neptune is in 12°♒, there is 117° between them. Or if Saturn is in 12°♊ and Neptune is in 9°♒, they are 123° apart. Either way, with a 3° orb, the native still has a trine aspect, with the same talents and empowerments.

Astrologers do not agree on the size of orb allowances. Every chart is different, which is why exact orb allowances are not offered here. In general the Lights, the Sun and Moon, are allowed larger orbs, up to 10° between each other, and 8° in relation to other planets. Major aspects have larger orbs than minor aspects, which have 3° or less. It depends on the dynamics of the chart. With practice and experience, you will get the feel of it. In the end, it all comes down to the astrologer's intuition. What feels right? As you study your chart, looking deeper and deeper into yourself, answers will arise from your subconscious storehouse of wisdom. Then you will <u>know</u>.

Some computer calculations show whether planets are **applying**, *moving toward the exact aspect degree,* or **separating**, *have contacted the exact aspect degree, now are moving away from exact aspect.* Applying aspects are lessons to be learned. Applying aspects with close orbs indicate important life lessons. Separating aspects denote grasp of the lesson, and perhaps ability to teach it to others.

There are many astrology books that describe the meanings of the aspects in detail. For a balanced view, you may want to check into several of them. If you do, you will notice that sometimes certain aspects are considered "bad" and others "good." There is also a non-judgmental way of looking at aspects. Like everything in life, they exist for a purpose. Our job is to discover their purpose, then put them to use.

There are major and minor aspects. It would be perfectly fine if you just want to focus on the major aspects. Some curious people always want the whole story, so minor aspects are included in the chart on the bottom. For the sake of clarity, the diagram of angles and degrees shows only major aspects. You can make your own diagram of minor aspects, if you so desire.

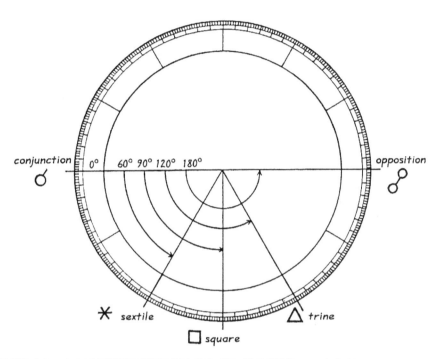

DEGREES	ASPECTS	GLYPHS	FRAC-TION OF 360°	COMPUTER APP. SEP.	KEY WORDS
0	**conjunction**	☌		**CON con**	**cooperation, emphasis**
30	semisextile	⚺	1/12	SSX ssx	fast, intimate, subtle
36	semiquintile	Q/2	1/10	SQT sqt	clever, artistic, immediate
40	novile, nonagen	N	1/9	NON non	initiation, endurance
45	semisquare	∠	1/8	SSQ ssq	slow, ponderous, intense
51:26	septile	S	1/7	SPT spt	destiny, fate, the occult
60	**sextile**	**✶**	1/6	**SXT sxt**	**productive, skillful, able**
72	quintile	Q	1/5	QTL qtl	expressive, spontaneous
90	**square**	**□**	¼	**SQR sqr**	**work, effort, determination**
102:50	biseptile	2S	2/7	BSP bsp	destiny with another
120	**trine**	**△**	⅓	**TRI tri**	**harmony, talent, ease**
135	sesquiquadrate	⚼	3/8	SQQ sqq	pressure to express
144	biquintile	2Q	2/5	BQT bqt	teamwork, social activism
150	quinquncx	⚻	5/12	QCX qcx	need for compromise
154:15	triseptile	3S	3/7	TSP tsp	destiny with a group
180	**opposition**	☍	½	**OPP opp**	**balance, awareness, others**

PLANETARY PATTERNS

Completed horoscopes in which all the planets, signs, houses, and aspects are drawn frequently reveal certain patterns. It is always good to make an over-all scan for patterns. View the chart as a whole. If you don't see any of the major patterns in this list, perhaps you will notice kite shapes, star shapes, or whatever. Ask your intuition what they might mean.

BUNDLE: *All planets contained within 120°. Conjunctions, perhaps a stellium, are likely.*
Powers of concentration and focus. Hermitage.

BOWL: *All planets contained within 180°. Opposition defines chart. May have T-Square.*
Receptive, desiring to be filled. Or if tipped, may be pouring out.

BASKET: *A bowl with one exterior planet (a **singleton**) not within the opposition.*
The singleton is a power planet that "carries" the basket.

SEE-SAW: *Planets grouped on either side of the circle. Oppositions are featured.*
Two major areas of expression balance and challenge one another.

OPEN ANGLE: *All planets within 240° leave an empty trine. May contain a Grand Trine.*
Open-minded, freedom-loving, adventurous.

SPLASH: *Planets spread around circle. Few or no conjunctions. May have a Grand Square.*
Widespread interests and activities. Multi-talented.

Planetary formations, *aspect-defined groupings of some planets in a chart*, may occur within whole-chart patterns. Orb allowances apply, so they don't have to be "perfect." It is possible for a planet to be in more than one formation at once. The four most common formations are as follows.

STELLIUM: *Group of three or more planets with multiple conjunctions in the same sign or house.*
This cluster gathers much energy in one place, controlling the chart.

T-SQUARE: *Three or more planets are located at three specific points: Two points are in opposition to each other, and square the third point. Aspect lines drawn to the three points create a pyramid shape with a right angle (T-square) at the apex.*
The planet(s) at the peak of the pyramid works to resolve any imbalance occurring in the opposition.

GRAND TRINE: *Three or more planets are located at three points 120° apart, all in the same element, either fire, water, air, or earth.*
Skill in working with the element that holds the formation.

GRAND SQUARE: *Four or more planets are located at four points 90° apart, all in the same quality, either cardinal, fixed, or mutable. A perfect Grand Square contains four T-Squares.*
Lots of work can accomplish great things.

RETROGRADES

Retrograde (verb, noun, adjective) *a term used in astronomy and astrology;*
real or apparent motion in a direction contrary to the signs of the zodiac

A Great Year (pages 28-29) is the result of Earth's axis retrograding through the zodiac in <u>real</u> backward motion. That is why we are moving from the Piscean Age to the Aquarian Age. On the other hand, sometimes planets <u>appear</u> to be moving backward in the sky, although planets never actually reverse their orbit. Their apparent contrary direction is due to differing positions and orbital speeds in relationship to Earth.

When a planet appears to be in *reverse motion*, it said to be **retrograde**, "R." When it is *moving forward relative to Earth*, it is said to be **direct**, "D." When *changing direction*, it is called **stationary**, "S". It may be either SR or SD, depending on which way it is headed. For examples of R see ♂, ♅, ♆ and ♇ on page 62. For R and SD see sample chart, page 134. Sun and Moon are included among the astrological "planets" (cosmic, intelligent life-forms) for convenience, but astronomically they are not planets and do not retrograde.

When a planet is retrograde, its expression is yin, inward, and subjective. It may be slow to express itself. The native is likely to ponder and "sit with" the power of that planet, so its eventual expression is thoughtful, considered, and philosophical. Direct planets are yang, outward, and objective in expression. Stationary planets are sensitized, with potential for focus and determination amidst change.

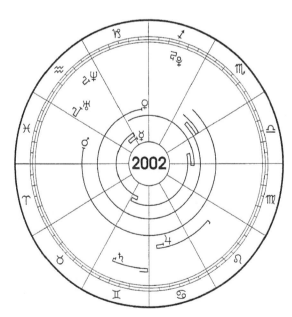

Diagram of Planetary Motions in 2002
Mercury went retrograde three times that year, Venus once,
and Mars not at all. The outer planets hardly moved forward.

The Horoscope

HIGHER OCTAVES

The three outer planets, Uranus, Neptune, and Pluto, are often called the spiritual planets. Of course all the planets are spiritual, because they are ensouled expressions of divine order and embodiments of divine light. But the trans-Saturnian planets are special, because their discovery has coincided with the onset of humanity's awakening from a low-density/third-dimensional belief in separation to the higher fourth-density frequency of unity consciousness.

Uranus made its appearance just five years after the American Revolution, as if it were announcing an important step forward in humanity's spiritual evolution: "Hear ye! Hear ye! Be it known that all people are free and equal!" Neptune has been helping to stimulate humanity's compassion and sense of oneness. Pluto is busy transforming outworn ideas and methods through revolutions in consciousness.

These higher-octave planets have always been operating in our solar system, but now we are <u>more aware</u> of their influence. Because they move slowly, they link together the consciousness of whole generations of people. In your chart, whatever sign an outer planet is in shows how you share it collectively with everyone in your generation. The house it is in shows where it has personal meaning for you.

Pluto in Virgo, ♇ in ♍, indicates revolutions in medicine, industry, and employment.
Pluto in the 6ᵗʰ house stimulates personal transformations in the native's
health and work; self-awareness develops through service to others.

Each planet has a certain energy signature, or pattern of vibration. The astrological **higher octaves** are *faster speeds of the energy signatures of Mercury, Moon, and Mars, expressed as Uranus, Neptune, and Pluto.* Higher frequencies are created by more light—in everything—planets and people included. Look at the octave diagramed on page 57. Middle C on the left corresponds to Mars, while higher C on the right corresponds to Pluto. Pluto in full swing in a horoscope could reach oscillations of three octaves on the piano, or even go right off the keyboard!

In this table, earth is the synthesis, container, and result of the other three elements, just as your body contains intellect, feelings, and life-force. To review planetary color correlations, refer to pages 58-59.

OUTER PLANET	INNER PLANET	ELEMENT	PRIMARY COLOR
Uranus ♅	Mercury ☿	Air	Yellow
Neptune ♆	Moon ☽	Water	Blue
Pluto ♇	Mars ♂	Fire	Red

HOUSE RULERS

The planet that rules a sign always rules the corresponding house, even if it is not actually in that house, and no matter what planets are actually in that house.

Jupiter ♃ rules Sagittarius ♐. The 9th house corresponds to ♐. ♃ rules the 9th house.

Likewise, a planet that is exalted in a sign is **dignified**, *exalted by house*, in the corresponding house. *☽ is exalted in ♉, therefore ☽ is dignified in the 2nd house.*

A planet gains weight when it is placed in the house that corresponds to the sign of its rulership or exaltation. *♂ is very strong in the 1st and 10th houses.*

Outer circle — house numbers
Middle circle — house rulers
Inner circle — dignities

A diagram of sign rulers and exaltations would duplicate all planets' positions.

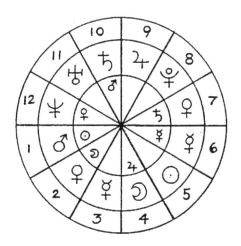

PART OF FORTUNE AND NODES OF THE MOON

Three symbols, ⊕, ☊, ☋ are added to most horoscopes. They are not planets, and have very small orbs when aspected by planets. They do add understanding to chart interpretation, so are included here.

Part of Fortune, *where the Moon would be if the Sun were rising; a combination of Sun, Moon, and Ascendant energies.* A point of integration and natural ease that offers the least resistance to who you are. Its sign indicates the type of activity that is fulfilling. The house shows where the action happens.

Nodes of the Moon, *points where the Moon goes north/above or south/below the ecliptic. Always exactly opposite each other in any chart.*

☊ **North Node**: "Dragon's Head"— *where to take in and assimilate freely*

☋ **South Node**: "Dragon's Tail"— *where to let go, release, and eliminate*

CHART INTERPRETATION

You can know a lot about astrology without seeing a lot of horoscopes. Eventually you may want to research the charts of everyone you know, as well as charts of famous people and events. In the beginning, it is essential to study just one horoscope—your own. In order to experience the impact of what you are studying, you must apply it to yourself. All astrologers learn their subject by working with their own charts. Your horoscope is a blueprint for this incarnation. Don't expect to understand it overnight, since YOU are not so easily explained!

Through direct experiment and experience, you discover what works, what is true, and what to avoid (for example, negative interpretation can cause fear and upset). In this process of self-examination through applied astrological science, you gather **empirical evidence**, *results that are directly experienced by you.*

For mathematical calculations, a computer can perfectly print your planets' positions. Computers have limited capacity for chart interpretation, however, since they do not possess intuitive sensibility. A comprehensive chart interpretation by an experienced professional takes many factors into account simultaneously. As the reader focuses his or her knowledge and intuition on a chart, a tapestry of information emerges, woven of many different threads.

Astrologers have different styles of chart erection, so if you gather copies of your horoscope from different sources, they will vary in appearance a bit. They should all agree on essentials. Similarly, each astrologer will give a somewhat different reading of your chart, because each person sees and speaks through the lens of a personal world view. Still, they will agree with each other overall. A comparison of chart readings is one way to "prove" astrology. Discussion can be informative and fun, but if you want privacy, you do not need to discuss your chart with others. This book will help you to understand it for yourself.

To get your chart, be sure you have an accurate birth time. If you were born in a hospital in the USA, your birth time should be on record in the Department of Birth Records in the capital city of the state in which you were born. If you were born elsewhere, hopefully someone made note of the time you drew your first breath. If you have a birth certificate, it should show your birth time. There is a process called **rectification**, *calculation of birth time by extrapolation from events in a person's life*, but you would have to hire an expert.

HOW TO OBTAIN YOUR HOROSCOPE: When you know your date, time, and place of birth, you can order your chart from a metaphysical bookstore or computer service, or use an astrological home computer program. We would be happy to serve you at www.GrannyRainbow.com. Ask for your natal chart and calculations in the Equal House system. Once you have your chart in hand, "get down" with this book and get to know yourself through Ageless Wisdom.

EXERCISES IN INTERPRETATION

What does it <u>mean</u>? This is the big question in astrology. The "ancient search for meaning" referred to in the Preface of this book has led humanity to discover the Ageless Wisdom. Ageless Wisdom is built into the universe; it is "the way things are," insofar as these things can be expressed in ideas and words. Beyond thoughts, the real truth awaits. When we connect with Ageless Wisdom, a deep knowing in us says, "Yes! In the core of my being, this feels right." Meaning cannot be found in a rulebook of dogma that you are expected to believe. It is the divine understanding <u>in you</u>, in your authentic Self.

Reading a chart is a time-honored sacred art. As with any skill, the more you do it, the better you get at it. The more you look into a chart, the deeper you will see. Astrological interpretation is a never-ending, always rewarding process. Since you can only start on a journey from where you are, it makes sense to begin learning to read charts by exploring your own horoscope. You become the native, the person whose natal chart is under discussion/interpretation.

EXERCISE 1: Write a paragraph that begins, "My Sun in (your Sun <u>sign</u>)…" Describe how you experience your Sun sign. Example: *My Sun is exalted in Aries. This means I have a lot of fiery energy. My basic life force always wants to explore new things. I love to climb to the top of trees and mountains. I am independent, a tomboy with a warrior spirit. I think of myself as a self-sufficient winner.* Then write paragraphs about each of your other nine planets, and how they behave in their signs.

EXERCISE 2: Write a paragraph that begins, "My Sun in (the <u>house</u> of your Sun)…" Describe your Sun's experience of that house. Example: *My Sun in the 7th house enjoys partnerships and activities with other people. I am an artist. Beauty is very important to me, and I love to share the wonders of life. I work for peace within myself and in the world.* Continue writing about the other planets and their houses.

EXERCISE 3: Combine #1 and #2 above. Notice if the sign and house of each planet are in agreement, or if adjustment is needed. Using above examples: *My Aries Sun makes me independent, while its location in the 7th house means I want to be with people. For the sake of relationship, I create win-win situations. To fulfill my primal life force, I seek to tame my aggression, and be a peaceful warrior.*

Now that you know the sign and house of each of your planets, and have some grasp of how they operate in your life, you have basic astrological self-knowledge. Be sure to remember your Ascendant, as well. If you want more in your "tool kit" of self-awareness, add the aspects. Then on to planetary patterns and formations, nodes, etc. There is <u>a lot more</u> in other books, as well.

SAMPLE CHART

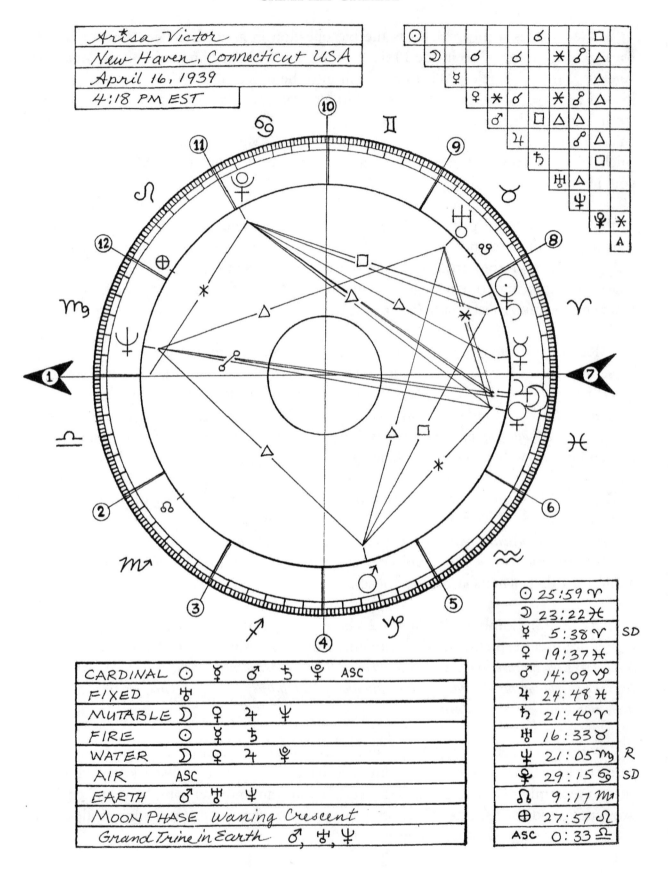

Arisa Victor
New Haven, Connecticut USA
April 16, 1939
4:18 PM EST

CARDINAL	⊙	☿	♂	♄	♇	ASC
FIXED	♅					
MUTABLE	☽	♀	♃	♆		
FIRE	⊙	☿	♄			
WATER	☽	♀	♃	♇		
AIR	ASC					
EARTH	♂	♅	♆			
MOON PHASE	Waning Crescent					
Grand Trine in Earth	♂, ♅, ♆					

⊙ 25:59 ♈		
☽ 23:22 ♓		
☿ 5:38 ♈	SD
♀ 19:37 ♓	
♂ 14:09 ♑	
♃ 24:48 ♓	
♄ 21:40 ♈	
♅ 16:33 ♉	
♆ 21:05 ♍	R
♇ 29:15 ♋	SD
☊ 9:17 ♍	
⊕ 27:57 ♌	
ASC 0:33 ♎	

SAMPLE CHART CHECKLIST

Planetary ruler of Sun sign, *no matter what sign the planet is in* ♂ rules ♈

Ruling planet(s), *located in signs they rule* —

Planet(s) ruling in house ♇

Planet(s) in detriment, *in sign opposite rulership* ♇

Exalted planet(s), *exalted in sign* ☉, ♀, ♂

Fallen planet(s), *in sign opposite exaltation* ♄

Dignified planet(s), *exalted in house* ♄

Overall pattern of planets and aspects   *open angle*

Planetary formation(s): stellium   ☽, ♀, ♃ *in* ♓, *6th house*

t-square —

grand trine   ♂, ⛢, ♇ *in earth*

grand square —

Close applying aspect(s)   ☽☌♃ *1°*, ♂△⛢ *2°*

Close separating aspect(s)   ☉□☿ *3°*, ☽☍♇ *2°*, ♀☍♇ *1.5°*

Angular planet(s), *conjunct cardinal cusps (usual orb allowances)* —

Retrograde or stationary planet(s)   ☿ *SD*, ♇ *R*, ☿ *SD*

Singleton planet, *stands out from the others* —

Elevated planet, *closest to midheaven. All charts have one of these.* ♀

Planet(s) above the horizon   ☉, ☿, ♄, ⛢, ♇, ♀

Planet(s) below the horizon   ☽, ♀, ♂, ♃

Planet(s) in the "self" hemisphere   ♇, ♀

Planet(s) in the "others" hemisphere   ☉, ☽, ☿, ♀, ♂, ♃, ♄, ⛢

Preponderance, *a lot more of one kind of mode, element, or aspect*   *7 trines*

Absence, *none of one kind of mode, element, or major aspect*   *Not an absence, but*

notable: 0:33° ♎ ASC is the only air component in the chart.

EXERCISE: Refer to your computer chart calculations and the sample chart to create your own horoscope in the blank form on page 137. If you plan to do more charts, you might find it handy to have several blank forms available, in which case you may make copies of both sides of the form before filling it in. After you have drawn your chart, fill in the checklist on the back. Suggestion: Use pencil (not ink) at first. Colored pencils are fun for planets and aspects.

Study your chart by filling in all checklist categories that apply. As time goes by, discover what these things mean and how they work for you. Use your own insights, as well as details you pick up from other sources. Keep feeling into the meaning behind the symbolism, and see how different pieces of your chart fit together in the unique combination of components that is you. Every piece has a <u>positive purpose</u> in your overall existence. After you complete these two forms for yourself, you may want to try the same process on a friend's chart.

SAMPLE INTERPRETATION OF SATURN

Saturn in Aries, ♄ in ♈

>makes rapid decisions
>energetic organizer
>likes working with young people
>interested in the practical use of energy; clean, efficient
>young at heart, yet appreciates the wisdom of age

Saturn dignified in the 7th house, ♄ in the 7th

>needs to work in various art forms
>likes stability in relationships
>drawn to partnerships with elders
>seeks balance through relationships
>envisions new social structures
>>*Envisions* and *new* come from Aries, and *social* comes from the 7th house. *Structures* are Saturnian, as are *work, stability, elders,* and *balance.* Balance is also a Libran trait, which in one reason why Saturn is exalted in Libra and dignified in the 7th house.

Saturn in a 4° separating conjunct aspect with Sun, ☉ ☌ ♄

>lover of truth, justice, and wisdom
>vitality for building the new and cleaning up the old
>self-identifies as a teacher
>chooses to be positive, constructive, and responsible
>establishes roots in the Self

This Saturn is tested by its location in Aries (in fall in the sign opposite its Libra exaltation), while it gains strength from conjunction with the exalted Sun, dignity in the 7th house, and Libra Rising. It has no other major aspects, except wide-orb (7½ degrees each) applying squares to Mars and Pluto. These contribute some setbacks, depression and power struggles—challenges that build character. This Saturn insists that the native must learn form direct experience in the school of life. Having encountered restriction in childhood, and self-imposed austerity in adulthood, in elderhood the native appreciates the kind of conscious discipline it takes to overcome difficulties and achieve goals. The native's success is not defined by society, but by the inner teacher. Saturn is her favorite planet, because it is such a fundamental, crucial, and ultimately benevolent influence. Saturn, Master of Wisdom, is shown joyfully celebrating the Dance of Life in tarot Key 21, the final trump at the end of the major arcana.

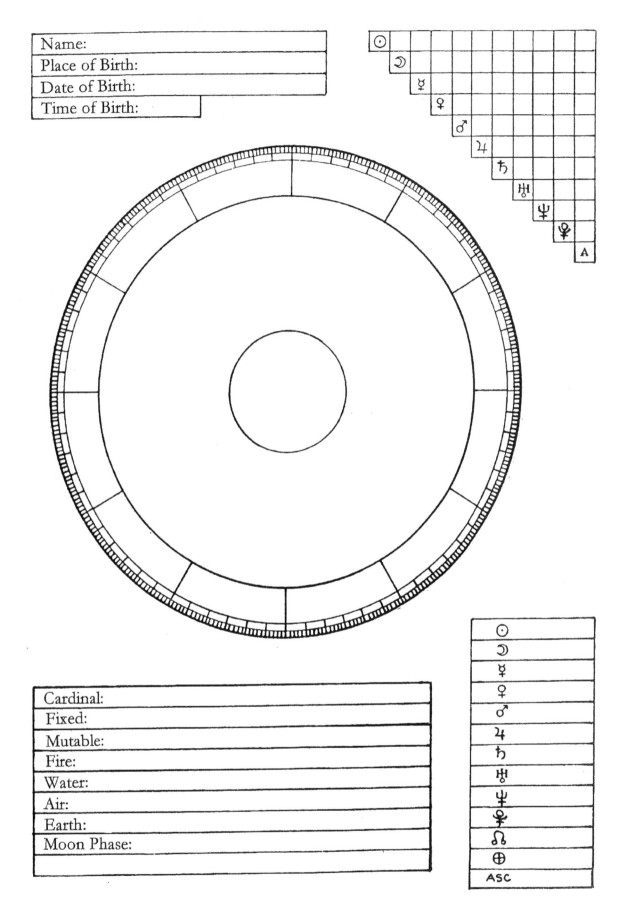

Name:

Place of Birth:

Date of Birth:

Time of Birth:

Cardinal:

Fixed:

Mutable:

Fire:

Water:

Air:

Earth:

Moon Phase:

CHART CHECKLIST

Planetary ruler of Sun sign, *no matter what sign the planet is in*
Ruling planet(s), *located in signs they rule*
Planet(s) ruling in house
Planet(s) in detriment, *in sign opposite rulership*
Exalted planet(s), *exalted in sign*
Fallen planet(s), *in sign opposite exaltation*
Dignified planet(s), exalted in house
Overall pattern of planets and aspects
Planetary formations(s):

> stellium
> t-square
> grand trine
> grand square
> other

Close applying aspect(s)
Close separating aspect(s)

Angular planet(s), *conjunct cardinal cusps (usual orb allowances)*
Retrograde or stationary planet(s)
Singleton planet, *stands out from the others*
Elevated planet, *closest to midheaven. All charts have one of these.*
Planet(s) above the horizon
Planet(s) below the horizon
Planet(s) in the "self" hemisphere
Planet(s) in the "others" hemisphere

Preponderance, a *lot more of one kind of mode, element, or aspect*
Absence, *none of one kind of mode, element, or major aspect*

Number of aspects between two planets, or a planet and the ASC

> conjunction
> sextile
> square
> trine
> opposition

PART 7.

THE CABALA

A combination of mystical insight and esoteric science,
the Universal Cabala encompasses
spiritual wisdom from every culture.
No matter what language we are speaking,
the sacred mysteries always deserve our utmost respect.

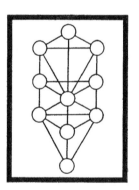

KARMA AND THE OCCULT

Occult means hidden, concealed. For example, when the Moon passes between the Earth and Sun, obstructing our view of the Sun, we can say that the Moon occults the Sun (thus creating a solar eclipse). Only ignorance and bad press—and the mistaken actions of some very unwise beings—connect the word "occult" with evil. Any knowledge can be used for unworthy purposes. To a thinking person, one word of caution is sufficient to stop any practice of misguided magic. That word is **karma**, *what you put out comes back to you, multiplied.* Karma is a law of Nature. Action causes reaction. Whatever energy you put into circulation will return in due course. Spiritual occultists have serious respect for karma.

Karma is never "bad." It is not punishment by God. Karma is life's way of balancing itself. Balance is extremely important to the soul. Unfortunate events that have nothing to do with your karma may occur in your life, due to another's abuse of free will. However, in the overall cosmic story, everything balances out and justice is done. Since we do not know each other's soul contracts, let us have forgiveness and compassion for each other's mistakes.

People who use occult or esoteric science in an unhealthy way are asking for trouble. They get lost in ego and forget the law of karma. Fear-based low magic tries to use the will to control circumstances or other people. For these confused individuals, life becomes like a battlefield when their own energy returns. Arrogance and greed throw them out of balance. Eventually, they fall.

Love-based high magic always aims for the highest good for all. As long as your intentions are altruistic, you will not get hurt. Quite the contrary; you are likely to discover whole worlds of beauty and majesty hidden just behind the surface appearances of people and things. But not everything occult can be revealed. There are mysteries within mysteries in this infinitely intelligent universe. While we are here in a human body with a physical brain, there is no way we can grasp it all. Sometimes God will lift a veil and give us a glimpse of splendor that makes all our effort worth the quest. The rewards of following the Path of Return are truly astonishing. They have nothing to do with evil in any way, except for the joy of seeing past it to the Primal-Will-to-Good.

The possibility of evil actually gives us a choice, an opportunity to use our free will. Nobody is stopping us from choosing the down side, except our own conscience and good sense. Egoic selfishness is caused by ignorance. The universe frequently sends messengers to awaken and re-educate us, and help us make the choice to step into the world of light, love, and unity.

If we keep choosing the Path, we are likely to find ourselves becoming more considerate, forgiving, and compassionate…more in love with life…aware of other realities and dimensions…closer to God. People often begin their inner journey from a stance of scientific investigation, and slowly come to realize the mystical side of their nature. Some have a sudden awakening, a major revelation that "blows their mind." Whatever happens on <u>your</u> journey into the occult mysteries, rest assured that your guardian angel walks with you every step of the way. Your own good intentions keep you safe.

The only real sin is interfering with the growth of a soul.

Voices of the Universe
Matthew

The Magic of Karma ☽ ✧ ☾ The Karma of Magic

A seed is sown.............Growth.................Many Fruits...................Harvest

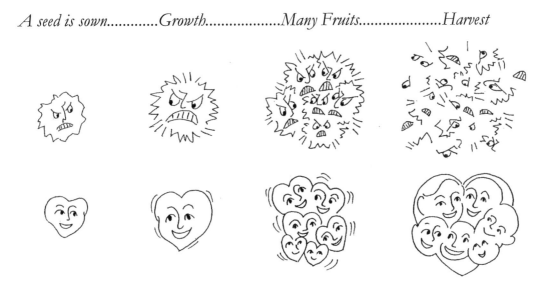

A plant grown from one seed can often produce 1,000 seeds. Thoughts are like seeds. Please be careful where you focus your mental powers. The energy of your every thought, feeling, word, and deed goes out and affects the whole universe. <u>Like attracts like</u> and returns.

As you sow, so shall you reap.

Jesus

A note on terminology: "Black magic" and "white magic" are inappropriate terms because they sound racist. Black and white are both beautiful. Black is equal to white, just as night is equal to day. Please do not use "black" and "white" in connection with "magic." Thank you for choosing wiser, more accurate vocabulary. For describing magic that does not aim for the highest good, try words like "low," "ego-driven," or "ignorant." For magic that honors the Golden Rule, some appropriate words are "high," "unselfish," or "enlightened." When **High Magic** is capitalized in the Cabala, it means *the transformation of personality into a conscious temple of the Holy Spirit.*

THE GREAT GLYPH

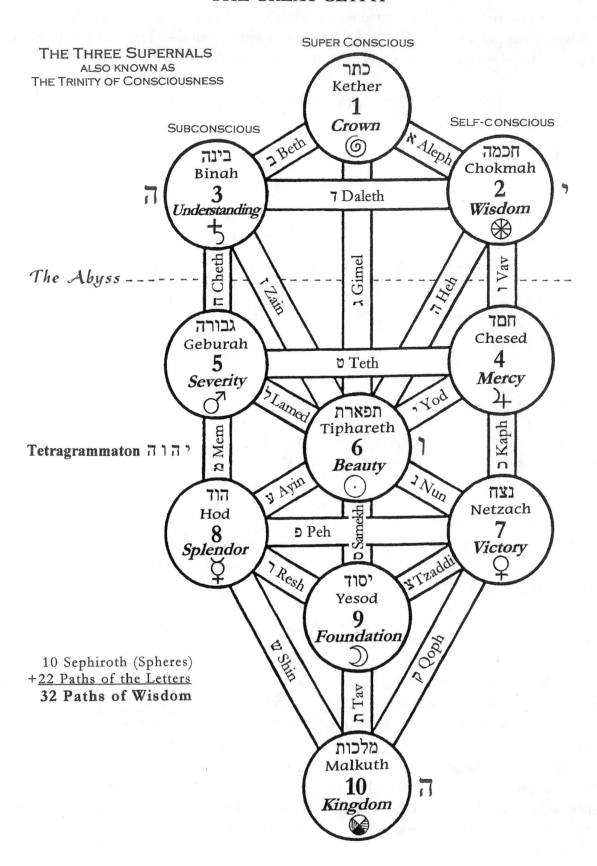

THE THREE SUPERNALS
ALSO KNOWN AS
THE TRINITY OF CONSCIOUSNESS

SUPER CONSCIOUS

SUBCONSCIOUS

SELF-CONSCIOUS

כתר
Kether
1
Crown

ב Beth

א Aleph

בינה
Binah
3
Understanding

ד Daleth

חכמה
Chokmah
2
Wisdom

ה

י

The Abyss

ח Cheth

ז Zain

ג Gimel

ה Heh

ו Vav

גבורה
Geburah
5
Severity

ט Teth

חסד
Chesed
4
Mercy

Tetragrammaton יהוה

ל Lamed

תפארת
Tiphareth
6
Beauty

י Yod

ו

מ Mem

ע Ayin

נ Nun

כ Kaph

הוד
Hod
8
Splendor

פ Peh

ס Samekh

נצח
Netzach
7
Victory

10 Sephiroth (Spheres)
+22 Paths of the Letters
32 Paths of Wisdom

ר Resh

צ Tzaddi

יסוד
Yesod
9
Foundation

ש Shin

ת Tav

ק Qoph

מלכות
Malkuth
10
Kingdom

ה

THE CABALA

*Cabala (ka-BA-la), from Egyptian **ka**, spirit, and **ba**, soul*
Literal meaning, reception. Spiritual meaning, inner guidance, inspiration.
A universal mystical philosophy, an esoteric science of symbols, and a spiritual practice
by which aspirants may attune to the infinite. The aim of the Cabala is Self-realization.

There are different spellings and presentations of this fascinating philosophy. **Qabalah** indicates the *Western Hermetic Mystery Tradition* of five occult sciences: Astrology, Tarot, Alchemy, High Magic, and Gematria (correspondences of numbers and letters). These disciplines are encoded in the great glyph known as the Tree of Life. **Kabbalah** is *Jewish Mysticism and Holy Magic.* It strongly emphasizes the Tree of Life and Gematria using the Hebrew alphabet. **Cabala** is the universal *"Everyman's version"* that partakes of Ageless Wisdom wherever it is found, especially in the Book of Nature. This is the spelling found in Webster's Dictionary, which calls Cabala t*he Secret Doctrine.* This doctrine, or set of guidelines, is an open secret for those who have "eyes to see" and "ears to hear," as Jesus so eloquently puts it in the ***New Testament.***

The Cabala in all its manifestations has always encouraged people to look, see, feel, and think for themselves. Exploration of truth, wisdom, and universal law outside the norm has been dangerous throughout much of humanity's history. Look at what happened to Galileo when he observed that the Earth rotates around the Sun. Under threat of torture, he had to recant (take back, disavow) his findings. Then he was placed under house arrest for the rest of his life. Since the Cabala leads people to discover the divinity of their Self, it had to be taught secretly. Cabala is still completely revolutionary.

As you know if you have read this book up this point, there is another way that the Secret Doctrine is secret. Life holds many mysteries that are hidden from the materialistic outer view. These occult realities are gradually revealed to those who attain the inner light of cosmic consciousness. Our Elder Brothers and Sisters have traveled the Path of Return, leaving many signposts for us. The adepts, "those who have gone before," are of every race and spiritual tradition. Some are famous and others are completely unknown. As more and more people awaken to the light of wisdom, it becomes easier for the rest of us to enter into peace also. The now-dawning Aquarian Age of Humanity holds the potential for <u>everyone</u> to wake up and embrace unity with all life. The Cabala enables us to study Ageless Wisdom and practice High Magic in order to transmute fear and separation into peace, love, and light. Mother Earth fervently wishes to take <u>all</u> her children into the Golden Age.

The Cabala section of this book introduces other branches of occult science, and some cross-cultural imagery with which astrology is interrelated. It is offered for further study, meditation, and inspiration, if you so desire.

THE TREE OF LIFE

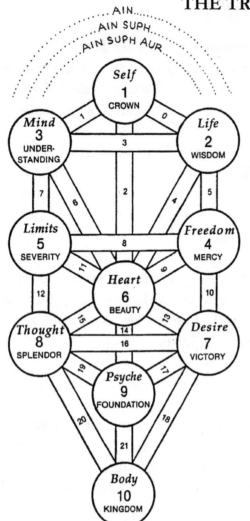

The Tree of Life

About the background of the Tree:

THAT which underlies all existence cannot be defined or described, so people invent poetic ways to refer to it. The ancient Chinese name it Tao, the Way. Buddhists call it Emptiness or the Void. Cabalists think of it as Limitless Light or Radiant Darkness. Within the unknowable mystery, the Cabala postulates three Veils of the Absolute known as

Ain, *no* or *no-thing,*
Ain Suph, *no limit,* and
Ain Suph Aur, *limitless light.*

Numbers on paths 0 to 21 indicate tarot major arcana Keys that correspond to the Hebrew letters, which are also assigned to the paths.

The Tree of Life is visualized as emanating from a point of super conscious light/dark that vibrates at infinite speed in number One. This Tree's "root" is said to be in "heaven," the highest vibration from which all other vibrations receive their energy. One, the Crown, is known as the Beginning of the Whirlings. This power may be called God, the Self, or any other name. No matter what we call it, it remains far beyond our mental comprehension. We cannot <u>know</u> it, but we can <u>be</u> it. The One Light is All That Is, including us.

The universe unfolds through successively lower and slower levels of density, symbolized by numbers Two through Ten. At the bottom, Ten represents this physical world that we inhabit, which is the "fruit" of the Tree of Life. Ten contains all the other numbers/centers. From the highest to the lowest, all centers on the Tree are manifestations of the <u>same consciousness</u>. All are constantly contributing to the whole. The universe is made to be this way, and so are we. As above, so below. Each human being is a whole Tree of Life.

THE FOUR WORLDS OF CABALA

When constructing the Tree of Life with a ruler and compass, first draw a straight line from Above to Below. This line stands for the endless "golden thread" that penetrates and connects all layers, levels, worlds, dimensions, and universes of the one Reality. Choose any point along the line to place your compass point, and draw a circle. Now put your compass where the circle touches the line, and draw another circle. Repeat until you have four circles lined up as shown. The Tree is located where the circles link together, and/or touch the central line.

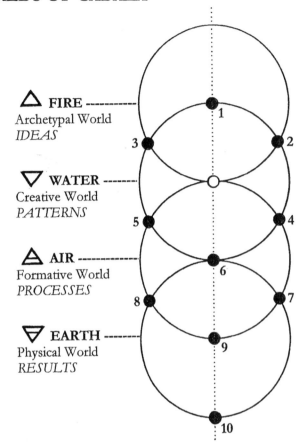

Basic Construction of the Tree of Life

The four circles signify the four worlds of Cabala. The Tree emanates from the center of the first world, where Limitless Light streams forth into the *holy trinity of consciousness* known as the **Three Supernals**, One, Two, and Three. These occur where the first world of fire joins the second world of water. The **trinity of consciousness** is composed of *super conscious, self-conscious, and subconscious.*

The white dot indicates the **Seat of Mystery** *where fire connects with air, making human intellect one with the light of God.* This point has no number and is not shown on the Tree because it is said to indicate an abyss, or chasm, that seems to separate the Three Supernals from the rest of the Tree. Crossing the abyss to join with the Supernals is accomplished through the mystery of grace.

The dot at the center of the third world of air (Six) indicates the Heart of the Tree, the heart of humanity. The center of the fourth world of earth (Nine) holds the genetic pattern of the body, and the last dot at the bottom (Ten) symbolizes the physical body. Ten stands alone; it becomes the One of another Tree of Life—and so on, creating an infinite Ladder of Lights.

For more on the four worlds, please cross-reference the four elements on page 53. Astrological/alchemical elements derive from the worlds of Cabala.

THE TETRAGRAMMATON

יהוה

Heh	Vav	Heh	Yod

26 = 5 + 6 + 5 + 10

Each Hebrew letter is also a number.

← Hebrew reads from right to left. ←

Tetragrammaton (Te-tra-GRAM-a-ton), *Name of Four Letters;*
All That Ever Was, Is, Or Ever Will Be

This ancient name for God is composed of four Hebrew letters: Yod-Heh-Vav-Heh. The original pronunciation has been lost, so it's anybody's guess as to how to say this name. Some believe it was always meant to be pronounced as four letters. In esoteric science, the Tetragrammaton is understood to be a code for the four worlds of Cabala—a reminder that divinity extends through fire, water, air, and earth. Divine Intelligence is infinite, eternal, and present everywhere. The Name of Four Letters is often translated as

THAT WHICH WAS, IS, AND SHALL BE.

Further deciphering the code, we may deduce the following:

☆ God is all things in time and space, and beyond.

☆ Everything is divine and sacred.

☆ You are holy, and so is everybody.

The Tetragrammaton is also called a formula of Divine Creation. For related topics, review the four elements on page 53, cardinal cusps on page 124, and astronomical symbol for Earth ⊕ on page 125. As a geometrical symbol of 26, this cross-in-a-circle also represents the Tetragrammaton, the sum of whose letters equals 26.

EXERCISE: Contemplate the Tetragrammaton. Let your inner teacher reveal other meanings or correspondences. Write them down. Write about how this ancient code/name applies to you, personally, today.

THE MEDICINE WHEEL

Native Americans go to the Medicine Wheel to pray and receive some "medicine," which is spiritual grace and healing for body, mind, and soul. All of Nature is sacred to the people who are indigenous to the land known as **Turtle Island,** *North America.* However, the Medicine Wheel is especially consecrated as hallowed ground. Each stone in the circle has been invited telepathically, and has accepted the honor and responsibility of being in the circle. Once it has been placed in the Wheel, a stone is never moved again. It forever holds all the prayers of the people. Spirits of ancestors, animals, elements, and directions gather in this holy place. The energy in a Medicine Wheel is inspiring, uplifting, and transforming.

The basic shape of the Medicine Wheel is always the same magical ⊕ circle and cross that is the basis of the astrological chart and a symbol of the Tetragrammaton. Different tribes have different ways of assigning colors, as well as elemental, animal, and other powers to the directions. Often, seven directions are honored in prayer: east, south, west, north, above, below, and center. The entrance always faces east, toward the rising Sun, and people always move sunwise (clockwise) inside the Wheel.

> *Every part of this Earth is sacred to my people. Every hillside, every valley, every clearing and wood, is holy in the memory and experience of my people. Even those unspeaking stones along the shore are loud with events and memories in the life of my people. The ground beneath our feet responds…lovingly to our steps…because it is the ashes of our grandfathers. Our bare feet know the kindred touch. The Earth is rich with the lives of our kin.*
>
> *Chief Seattle*

THE SHRI YANTRA

Shri (Sanskit), *a term of reverence and respect*
yantra (Sanskrit), *sacred symbolic diagram*

The Shri Yantra is the great glyph of Hindu tantric meditation. It has striking parallels to the Tree of Life. Instead of the Life Power extending downward, as it does in the Tree, the Shri Yantra shows the Life Power expanding outward. Both movements are happening at once in both glyphs, but this cannot be shown on a two-dimensional page. We have to use our imagination to see that these diagrams are approximations of something very alive and multi-dimensional. These wonderful meditation tools, designed by inspired adepts, have helped countless aspirants to greater awareness for thousands of years.

The Point of All Beginnings at the center of the Shri Yantra corresponds to the Cabalists' archetypal world of fire, number One on the Tree of Life, page 145. In the Yantra, this same fiery point is contained within a water triangle, which is downward-pointing, yin, and feminine. The meaning of this symbolism is exactly the same as the Cabalistic "fire in the water" discussed on page 55: The archetypal world of will operates within the creative world of possibilities. In other words, the initiating spirit of the Divine Father activates a reproductive process <u>from within</u> the receptive substance of the Divine Mother. Father and Mother are inseparable partners in one Self. Duality exists within unity, as the Tai Chi symbol ☯ reminds us.

The Shri Yantra's expanding, interpenetrating triangles represent the stages of development that occur in the creative world as a result of the fruitful union of yang and yin. The triangles are abstractions, but the growth pattern is similar to the way a baby grows in the womb. Lotus petals outside the triangles correspond to the formative world of air, where natural shapes are determined for whatever is being manifested. The outer boundary lines symbolize the physical world of earth—a graphic illustration of how the first three worlds are contained within the fourth.

Hindu spirituality is very ancient. Actually, "Hindu" is a western word given to people living in the Indus River Valley. These people call their tradition **Sanathana Dharma**, *the Eternal Truth*. This esteemed and highly respected philosophy is another manifestation of Ageless Wisdom, and therefore has many similarities with the Universal Cabala. Hindu gods and goddesses are comparable to the Intelligences pictured in our tarot cards. The most significant resemblance between these two philosophical systems is their teaching of the oneness of God and Self. Ralph Waldo Emerson and his fellow New England Transcendentalists introduced Hindu ideas to the United States around 1840. Emerson used to read the Bhagavad-Gita every morning.

Dare to love God without mediator or veil…Cast behind you all conformity, and acquaint [yourself] at first hand with Deity.

Man is made of the same atoms as the world is, he shares the same impressions, predispositions, and destiny. When his mind is illuminated, when his heart is kind, he throws himself joyfully into the sublime order.

Ralph Waldo Emerson

"The light of a lamp does not flicker in a windless place." This is the simile that describes a yogi of one-pointed mind who meditates upon the Self. When, through the practice of yoga, the mind ceases its restless movements and becomes still, he realizes the Self. It satisfies him entirely. Then he knows the infinite happiness that can be realized by the purified heart, but is beyond the grasp of the senses. He stands firm in this realization. Because of it, he can never again wander from the inmost truth of his being.

The Bhagavad-Gita, *Song of God*
written 5th - 2nd centuries BCE, in India

THE GREAT GODDESS

In India, all the goddesses in the Hindu **pantheon**, *family of gods and goddesses*, are expressions of one Great Goddess, Devi. In ancient Egypt she was called Almighty Isis. All ancient religions and Native traditions the world over have worshipped the Great Mother. Veneration of God, the Divine Father, was always included. There is no mother without a father, and vice-versa.

Obeisance to Her
who is pure Being-Consciousness-Bliss, as Power,
who exists in the form of Time and Space and all that is therein,
and who is the radiant Illuminatrix in all beings.

Vedic Scripture

The Great Goddess Giving Birth to the Universe
from 10ᵗʰ century Indian temple sculpture.
She corresponds to the Empress of tarot.

In whatever tradition we study, Ageless Wisdom declares that the actual working power of the universe is feminine. Thus we see, in the structure of atoms, it is the yin/feminine/negative electrons that spin and interact to form all the elements identified by modern science. Inspired from within by the Great Father's life force expressed in yang/masculine/positive protons, the Great Mother gives birth to all things in time and space. Creator and Creation are equal partners, neither pre-existing before the other.

THE MENTAL UNIVERSE

The Universe is mental, held in the mind of the ALL.

The Kybalion
Three Adepts

People often say, "It's all in your mind," meaning that "it" is not real. The Cabala says the whole universe is in your mind, and ultimately, it is not real either. Like all profound wisdom traditions, the Cabala defines the one true **Reality** as *That which is permanent and changeless.* Things that change are ephemeral, temporary, and passing, existing only briefly before shifting into a different form. The seeming permanence of the physical world is illusionary. How this magical holographic appearance occurs is Saturn's secret.

On the Tree of Life, number Three represents Divine Mind/ Divine Mother/ the Seat of Saturn. This book says a lot about the Divine Mother, because her function has been so generally misunderstood by the patriarchy. We delve only briefly into her designation as Divine Mind, because it is an advanced concept. If you are interested in this ancient teaching, you may ponder it to your heart's content. Meditation will gradually reveal what cannot be said in words. A hint: Cabala equates mind with water, and intellect with air.

In Hinduism, the enchantress goddess Maya weaves the web of material illusion by which we are hypnotized until we awaken to Reality. Then Maya's veils fall away and we behold the truth. Without veils there would be no revelation.

Buddhism teaches that all is consciousness, and emphasizes the fleeting nature of this world. Our attachment to ephemeral things causes suffering, because nothing lasts. The only everlasting thing is the consciousness from which all things arise and to which they return.

None of these teachings are saying the physical world is bad or wrong in any way. They are just explaining that things are not what they seem. When seekers realize the universe is mental, then they may truly enjoy the world. Consciousness is divine living Light, which is the nature of the Self. Illumined Cabalists, Hindu yogis, and Buddhist saints all tell us that true freedom lies in being able to <u>look</u> at the mind. We come to understand that mind is the tool with which we create our microcosm. We discover how to create a place of peace and harmony where every moment bestows a new perfection. Then we see why each immediate moment is called <u>the present</u>.

MAN

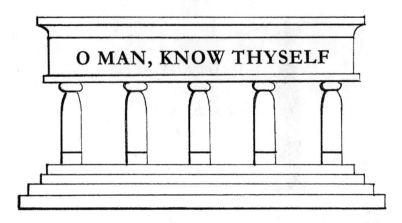

O MAN, KNOW THYSELF

Temple Inscription
We inherit a stirring challenge from antiquity.

manas, Indo-European, *mind*
Our word "man" is derived from this word that means "mind."

The word **Man** is *a very ancient, generic term for human beings.* Originally, this word meant all children, women, and men. In esoteric lore, Man still refers to all of us. The race of Man shapes its reality with the power of mind. We are children of the One Cosmic Mind, so by the Law of Correspondence, our minds are cosmic. In other words, we can do with our minds what God does with His-Her-Its-Their mind; we can create. The fact is, <u>we are constantly creating with the power of our minds</u>. Using Saturn's power to organize and structure atomic particles, Divine Mother Mind gives form to our thoughts.

We humans have gotten ourselves into lots of trouble because we have been unaware that the world is thought-created. We suppose God made it the way it is without any input from us, or it "just happened," or other people are somehow responsible. Usually we don't realize that our own thoughts are constantly taking form as so-called physical reality. This connection between Man, mind, and <u>manifestation</u> is a vitally important teaching of Ageless Wisdom. When we grasp how our minds work, we can take responsibility for our thoughts—and proceed to use atomic light and the Saturn Principle to co-create the world we really want. God <u>does</u> make the world, <u>with and through us</u>. Collectively, our free will can establish lasting peace on Earth.

We all belong to the race of Cosmic Man, whether we chose female or male bodies for this incarnation. To fulfill Man's potential to be "gods on Earth" is the high destiny of our race. Our greatest satisfaction will occur when, as one Self, we create the best scenario for everybody. Our task is to renew this planet, making it a happy home for our whole human family, and all of Earth's inhabitants.

MIND

The ultimate truth is the realization of one's own mind.

Buddha

You are not your mind; mind is your tool. **Mind** is *the seat of consciousness*. You are consciousness itself. Mind is often contrasted with **matter**, *substance, the physical world of form*, but we make a mistake when we separate mind and matter. They exist together in a single continuum. You may have heard the phrase, "mind over matter." According to Ageless Wisdom, mind actually does control matter. In fact, mind gives birth to matter.

In his deep trance state, Edgar Cayce often said, "Mind is the builder." Things and events exist in the mind before they manifest in the outer world. Within mind is a formative, structure-creating power known to alchemists as the Secret of Saturn. Once you imagine something as a concrete reality, its physical materialization becomes possible. For example, an architect's blueprints are "conceived" in his or her mind, and "born" onto paper. Of course, constructing the building with substantial materials requires a lot of physical work, but the building could not exist at all without the mental plan.

In the Cosmic Mind, the Divine Mother holds a blueprint for the highest expression of Man, and also for each individual. Cosmic Mind (manas) and Divine Mother (Ma in every language) are linked together through words. Look at the Latin word **mater**, *mother*. By materalizing matter, our Divine Mother Mind creates all the structures in the universe, both **incarnate**, *physical, low frequency forms* and **discarnate**, *etheric, high frequency forms*.

A mother—animal, human, or divine—gives birth to babies. She creates form, using the substance of her own body. According to Ageless Wisdom, mind has a very subtle substance. This essential matter has been called "mind-stuff." Alchemists refer to it as the First Matter. The new generation refers to the Field, or the Divine Matrix. At any rate, the mother principle organizes her/our mind-stuff into physical material, and causes us to experience it through our senses.

To hold an image in your mind is to energize that particular thing, to fill it with life. Whatever exists in the mind does truly exist, and if "your mind is made up," you can produce anything you want. All beings have intelligence, but Man is given a special conscious control. The extraordinary power of choice and change that we wield is mind-power. Our minds shape things according to our specifications. Occult science shows how we may master our minds, and consciously apply Saturn's magical secret to improving life for everyone.

EXERCISE: Ask yourself, "What is the blueprint for my highest expression?"

HUMAN EGO

The Devil is the unregenerate intellect.

Carl Jung

Ego literally means *I am*. There is a great divine I AM, and there seems to be a small human one, which is *our intellectual sense of separation in the third dimension*. The small ego is unregenerate when it sees itself as "better than" or "less than" others. The enlightened ego sees an underlying evenness, because in Reality, we are the same. Although we are One, we each have an ego. Even the most highly illumined master has a sense of separation while still in a body. A good example is Jesus, who as the Son of Man, was tempted by the Devil. He "put Satan behind him," which means he did not agree with his small ego or let it rule him. But he did not try to push it away or cut it off, because that is impossible. The ego is our shadow; it follows us everywhere. We can train it to become a helpful friend, a regenerated intellect that eventually gets absorbed into the divine I AM.

If there is an "enemy" it is ignorance.

Jason Lotterhand

Humanity is innocent. No one is to blame for the aspects of life that we do not like, that our ego might judge as "evil." Especially, there is nothing wrong with ego. It just has a limited viewpoint (ignorance), so it needs the loving support of our unlimited multi-dimensional Self. The ego fears that which it perceives as not-self. Anger and hatred arise from fear.

Each of us is part of humanity. When one part hates another part, it is like cancer growing in the body of humanity. "This is bad…wrong…should not be…has no right to exist. I will resist and push away this person, thing, circumstance, part of myself, etc." This judgmental way of thinking—prevalent on Earth for a very long time—creates tremendous pain in the psyche. **Judgment** is *the unregenerate intellect rebelling against the Law of Love, saying it has a right to judge self or others as good or bad*. This stance creates war in the psyche. Stay empty of judgment, and be full of peace.

When we oppose any part of life, we are listening to the voice of fear, and believing the lie of separation. This lie is the root of suffering. The Devil is called the Father of Lies. You could also call it the controlling, left-brain ego.

All hatred begins with self-hatred. When you don't like a certain energy in someone else, an honest look within will expose a similar energy in yourself. That which you resist in yourself gets projected onto others, and mirrored back to you. That which you do not resist in yourself will not bother you in others.

Resistance to life equals pain. All wisdom teachers down through the ages have asked us to accept and embrace whatever is arising. When it is dark on one side of the Earth, it is light on the other. Like God, we embrace both halves of the whole. When we let life flow easily, we are not helpless victims, but magical co-creators with Divine Intelligence as our partner.

MASTERS OF LIFE AND NATURE

All these things I do, you can do them too, and more.

Jesus

In the preface he kindly wrote for this book, what did Jason mean by "masters of life and nature?" Having known him for twenty-six years, the writer can guarantee he was not thinking of magicians who could conjure up gold and diamonds. More likely, he was referring to individuals who have learned to tame, and consciously direct, the natural forces within themselves, while keeping in mind the highest good for all. Masters have no ego attachments, because they no longer see themselves as separate from life. God works through such people. For example, here is a statement by a Nature genius, talking about drawing on the inexhaustible Source, and filtering that primal life force through his body.

**One can make a day of any size,
and regulate the rising and setting of his own sun
and the brightness of its shining.**

John Muir

Ageless Wisdom clearly states that we are all spiritual masters, because our God-Self is always alive and well. All human beings are born with God-awareness. As we develop ego-consciousness and are taught to identify with body and intellect, we forget our divine connection. When children are raised in an enlightened society, this amnesia will not happen. Until then let us attune to our inner master and faithfully follow spiritual guidance on the Path of Return.

The ancient masters were profound and subtle.
Their wisdom was unfathomable.
There is no way to describe it;
all we can describe is their appearance.
They were careful
as someone crossing an iced-over stream.
alert as a warrior in enemy territory.
Courteous as a guest.
Fluid as melting ice.
Shapeable as a block of wood.
Receptive as a valley.
Clear as a glass of water.

Tao Te Ching
Lao-Tzu
translated by Stephen Mitchell
*in **The Elightened Heart***

ALCHEMY

Alchemy is *the process of refining, or spiritualizing, one's own body and awareness.* Alchemists have existed in many countries, including Europe, India, China, and Arabia. This form of inquiry into the nature of matter was popular in medieval Europe. The alchemical laboratory is the body. As the practitioner becomes more conscious, the body becomes filled with light. The person vibrates at higher and higher levels. Eventually, spiritual alchemists emanate good will and healing energy to all beings in all situations. The **Great Work** of *Self-realization* has been accomplished on a personal level. Their energy, combined with that of other lightworkers, extends to help all people raise their awareness so that humanity may accomplish the Great Work on a global scale. **The Philosopher's Stone** is *an alchemical term for the Self.* **Philosopher** means *lover of wisdom,* and "stone" stands for stability and solidity. An awakened master is as strong, humble, and enduring as a rock, through being established in the Self.

Heaven is where thou standest.

Jacob Boehme, German alchemist, early 17th century

Alchemy was the parent of chemistry. Alchemical experiments consisted of combining various substances, and noting how they interacted. Researchers were of two kinds. Some experimenters were only interested in outer results. Those with spiritual consciousness probed the inner nature of things. They looked for physical and psychological correlations in themselves in relation to what they were observing. God was included in their practical applications of the Law of Correspondence: As above (Nature/macrocosm), so below (themselves, microcosm).

All alchemists were looking for a way to turn lead into gold. To spiritual alchemists, "lead" meant ignorance, and "gold" meant enlightenment. Ironically, modern chemistry has found a way to turn physical lead into gold, but the process costs more than the gold is worth. Meanwhile, true alchemists enjoy their heavenly riches such as peace, love, and wisdom. They have nothing against earthly riches, and are very grateful when blessed by financial abundance. Following the instruction of Jesus to "seek the kingdom of heaven first, and all else is added unto you," they do not force the issue with money. Enlightenment also fulfills alchemy's two other goals: the cure for all disease, and immortal life, both of which are experienced in super conscious states.

EXERCISE: Alchemists call their practice the Science of Sciences. What do you think is meant by this title? How would you personally proceed to turn your "lead" into alchemical "gold?" Write an essay of any length on these and/or related topics. For essay writing, see bottom of page 38.

CHAKRAS

Chakra is Sanskrit for *wheel*. In humans, **chakras** are *whirling centers of energy in the etheric brain and spinal column*. The **etheric body** is *a subtle field of energy patterns that permeates and surrounds the physical body*. (Sometimes people who have had a limb amputated can still feel the limb. They are feeling their etheric body.) There are seven major chakras. Energy in the body is regulated through these master switches. There are numerous minor chakras, as well. For instance, the palm chakras are active in healers. Many psychics can see chakras.

Alchemists perceive the heavens reflected within the human body and psyche. What Hindu seers called their "wheels," European alchemists called their "interior stars" (planets). Or they correlated the chakras to metals. Notice which chakra is associated with gold, an alchemical symbol of enlightenment.

Even though they had little or no physical contact during the Middle Ages, alchemists in Europe and India were seeing and experiencing the same inner awareness. Now east and west have met and mingled, and today almost everyone uses the Sanskrit word "chakra" to refer to an etheric energy vortex in the human body.

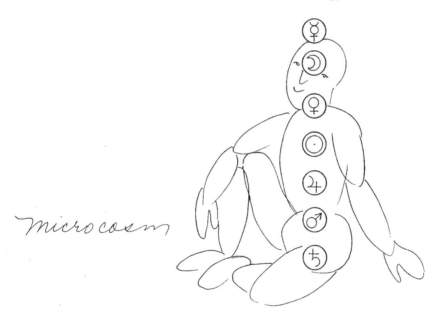

microcosm

CHAKRA	LOCATION	FUNCTION	PLANET	METAL	Rainbow Order of COLORS
7	crown of head	realization	Mercury	mercury	violet (purple)
6	third-eye	vision	Moon	silver	indigo
5	throat	expression	Venus	copper	blue
4	heart	love	Sun	gold	green
3	solar plexus	will	Jupiter	tin	yellow
2	gonads	creativity	Mars	iron	orange
1	base of spine	grounding	Saturn	lead	red

THE ZODIAC AND THE BODY

♈ head, face

♉ neck, throat

♊ lungs, arms, hands

♋ stomach, breast

♌ heart, spine

♍ intestines, abdomen

♎ kidneys, loins

♏ bladder, sex organs

♐ liver, hips, thighs

♑ spleen, knees

♒ calves, ankles

♓ feet, toes

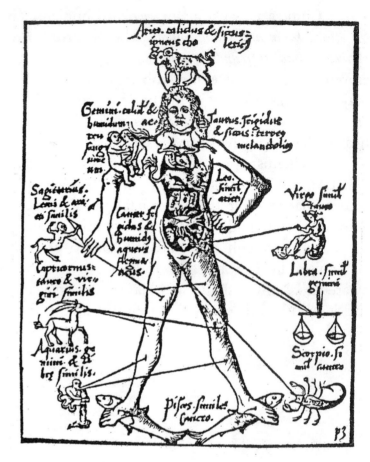

Medieval Portrayal of the Microcosm
*Each of the signs is represented by its symbol
and connected with the part of the body that it rules.*

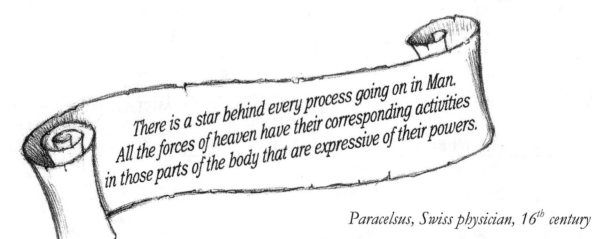

*There is a star behind every process going on in Man.
All the forces of heaven have their corresponding activities
in those parts of the body that are expressive of their powers.*

Paracelsus, Swiss physician, 16th century

*Thought to be a miraculous healer in his time,
today he is honored as the father of modern medicine.*

The Cabala

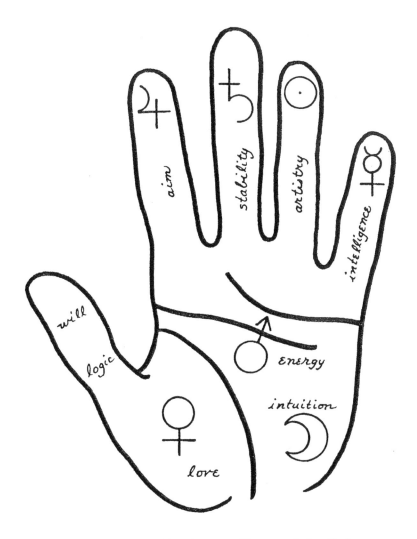

Planetary Attributions to Parts of the Palm

Spirit merges with matter to sanctify the universe. Matter transcends, to return to spirit. The interchangeability of matter and spirit means the starlit magic of the outermost life of our universe becomes the soul-light magic of the innermost life of our self. The energy of the stars becomes us. We become the energy of the stars. Stardust and spirit unite and we begin: One with the universe. Whole and holy. From one source, endless creative energy, bursting forth, kinetic, elemental. We, the earth, air, water, and fire-source of nearly fifteen billion years of cosmic spiraling...

Dennis Kucinich, USA politician, 21st century

THE TAROT

Tarot *(TARE-oh or tare-OH), a card deck of spiritually symbolic pictures,*
created to assist aspirants on the Path of Return. May be used for meditation and divination.

Tarot images were featured on the very first cards ever made. Modern playing cards descended from tarot. Although some people use tarot for fortune telling, these mysterious symbols have a much greater, more divine purpose. In Cabala lore, the tarot was given to humanity by angels. The word **Cabala** means *reception*. The Cabala is knowledge <u>received</u> from God, through divine messengers whom we may think of as angels. Tarot is a direct expression of Cabala.

A Tarot Angel Gives the Sacred Symbols to Humanity

There are a great many tarot decks available nowadays. Granny Rainbow recommends the tarot conceived by Arthur Edward Waite and drawn by Pamela Colman Smith, in any of its many colorings (especially the Albano version). The "Waite Deck" is the root deck, the first to have a different scene for every card. It has been the world's best-selling deck ever since it was published in 1910. The artist, "Pixie" Smith, was truly inspired. When she sat down to create the cards, each picture <u>appeared</u> on the canvas. All she had to do was trace what she saw, and paint in the colors. One could say she was instructed by tarot angels.

"Tarot" is an invented word, based on the following anagram:

ROTA	***THE WHEEL***
TARO	***OF TAROT***
ORAT	***SPEAKS***
TORA	***THE LAW***
ATOR	***OF NATURE***

TAROT AND THE TREE OF LIFE

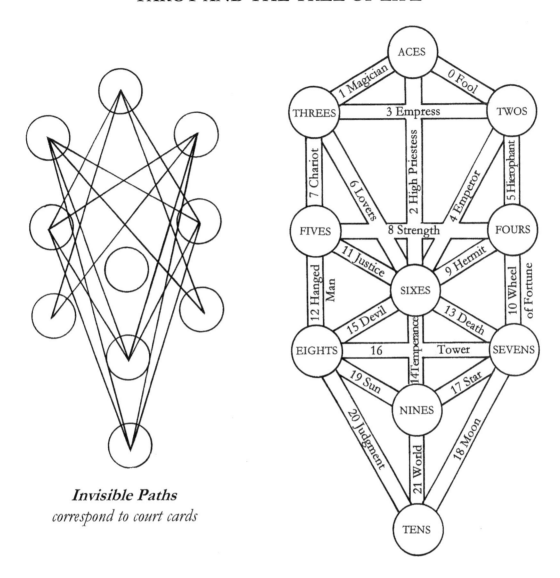

Invisible Paths
correspond to court cards

Tarot cards are organized according to the structure of the Tree of Life. There are a total of 78 cards in a tarot deck, derived from the Tree as follows:

*   22 major arcana cards correspond to the 22 visible paths that connect the 10 numbered centers.

*   16 court cards correspond to the 16 invisible paths between the 10 centers. (Connections not shown on the standard Tree of Life.)

*   40 minor arcana cards correspond to the 10 centers in each of the 4 Cabala worlds:

Ace to 10 of Wands	fire	archetypal world
Ace to 10 of Cups	water	creative world
Ace to 10 of Swords	air	formative world
Ace to 10 of Pentacles	earth	physical world

TAROT MAJOR ARCANA

Arcana means *secrets, essence, mysterious knowledge, hidden wisdom.*

Tarot and astrology are mirrors of each other. They help to define and explain each other. Tarot is more right-brain oriented, and astrology is more left-brained. All 78 tarot cards have astrological correlations. Meditation on tarot deepens our feeling for astrology, and vice-versa.

On the surface, some of the tarot images may be perceived as unpleasant, due to programmed reactivity in the viewer. For example, "Death is bad." Luckily, Cabala students are never fooled by surface appearances! For instance, in this example, we bravely philosophize thus: Ageless Wisdom tells us that we are immortal. Therefore, death cannot be the end of us. Rather, the Death Key signals major change, transition from one state to another. Without change, we really would be "goners." In order for us to stay healthy, transformations must keep happening spiritually, mentally, and physically throughout our lifetimes. At the end of this incarnation, we lay down the earthly body and take up a body of light.

The tarot major arcana cards are 22 sacred symbolic pictures, called Keys, which correspond to astrology's 22 planets and signs. They are like facets of a single jewel; sometimes they are called the Twenty-Two Faces of God.

☉	The Sun	♈	The Emperor
☽	The High Priestess	♉	The Hierophant
☿	The Magician	♊	The Lovers
♀	The Empress	♋	The Chariot
♂	The Tower	♌	Strength
♃	The Wheel of Fortune	♍	The Hermit
♄	The World	♎	Justice
♅	The Fool	♏	Death
♆	The Hanged Man	♐	Temperance
♇	Judgment	♑	The Devil
		♒	The Star
		♓	The Moon

EXERCISE: 1) Look at the tarot major arcana card that corresponds to your Sun sign, and examine your list of key words for your Sun sign (page 114). Write about where you see the meanings in your list reflected in the tarot symbols. 2) Repeat the previous exercise for the cards that illustrate your Moon and Ascendant. 3) Commit your ☉, ☽, and ASC major trumps to memory in connection with your chart, as part of your life-long tool kit of self-knowledge.

TAROT MINOR ARCANA

There are 56 cards in the minor arcana, comprised of 16 court cards and 40 pip cards. When playing cards were created from the minor arcana, the 4 Pages were left out, leaving 52 cards—plus one major arcana "wild card," the Fool/Joker.

Court Cards are *4 Kings, 4 Queens, 4 Knights, and 4 Pages.* Kings, Queens, and Knights rule the cusps between signs, from one decanate behind the cusp to two decanates ahead. A **decanate** is *10° (one third) of a zodiacal sign from 0-10°, 11-20°, or 21-30°.* In 360°, there are 36 decanates, 3 each for 12 signs. Example:

The King of Wands oversees the thirty degrees, or three decanates, from 20°♓ to 20°♈.

KINGS are cardinal. They rule cusps of cardinal signs.
QUEENS are fixed. They rule cusps of fixed signs.
KNIGHTS are mutable. They rule cusps of mutable signs.
PAGES are the power of the Fool embodied in the Child of God at the center of a chart, who receives all the blessings of the zodiac. All 4 Pages exist in every person. In a chart they align by element with the fixed signs, Queens, and Aces. Aces are root powers that stand in the "Four Corners of the Universe."

Pip cards are *Ace through 10 in each element.* Twos, threes and fours are cardinal. Fives, sixes, and sevens are fixed. Eights, nines, and tens are mutable. WANDS = fire, CUPS = water, SWORDS = air, PENTACLES = earth. Example:

Nine of Pentacles = mutable earth = middle decanate of ♍.

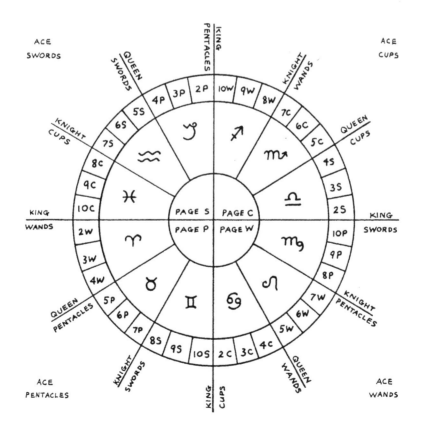

The Cabala

DIVINATION

Divination comes from the word "divine." It refers to *the discovery of hidden knowledge by the use of intuition through receptivity to the divine.* You do not need to have supernatural powers to read the cards. It is lovely if you have psychic talent, but all you really need is some grasp of symbols and numbers. The more you work with tarot, the more information it reveals, and the more intuitive you become. Astrology can also be used for divination. Study of Cabala can help keep students on the divine Path while working with these powerful divining tools.

People often want to know the future. However, thinking about the future takes us out of the present moment, which is actually here, and puts us in an imaginary place in our minds. The future is in our hands <u>now</u>, especially when we practice the teachings of Ageless Wisdom. Our thoughts are seeds that will grow, and our actions cause reactions. Awareness and free-will choices about our thoughts and actions always happen in the Now (page 172).

The same advice goes for thinking about the past, which only exists in the mind. When you are in the state of mind called "past," you are missing what is happening now. The Cosmic Now contains all past, present, and future—just as the Tetragrammaton is THAT which was, is, and shall be.

What lies behind us and what lies before us
are tiny matters compared to what lies within us.

Ralph Waldo Emerson

Living in the Now is a very healthy and effective lifestyle. Divination, receiving messages from the divine, can only happen Now. Often, trends and patterns viewed from the present do reveal events that have happened or are to come. That is fine, as long as the reader does not make big pronouncements and predictions that create self-fulfilling prophesies in the **querent**, *the questioner, seeker, person receiving the reading*. Every reader has a great responsibility to respect the querent, tell the truth, and avoid any power trips. Hold the intention that every tarot or astrology reading you give or receive will be an uplifting experience.

Tarot cards may be laid out in an infinite variety of patterns. Someone who understands symbolism, the language of the right brain, may read the many symbols of tarot to obtain a message. It is highly recommended that you always pray while shuffling the cards. Think of your message as coming from whatever Higher Power you pray to. This source may be your God-Self, a religious figure, a cosmic force, etc. It is up to you. Always ask for the highest good for all concerned in any situation that you explore through divination. Then you will receive the clearest, best information.

A good way to start working with tarot cards is to do the following meditation every morning: Shuffle your deck prayerfully, and without looking at the pictures, guided by your feelings, choose one card. Then look at it with open heart and mind. Trust whatever intuition (inner teaching) comes to you. Let this card symbolize your day. Recall the image during the day and again at bedtime, always asking your intuition how it correlates to what is happening. This practice will gently and gradually unlock the treasures of your subconscious mind.

When you first look at your card of the day, pay close attention to the very first signal from your inner Self. In response to the picture on the card, a feeling, sensation, or other awareness from your subconscious mind will emerge in your self-conscious mind. This first intuition is your clue to your message of the day. Let your insight continue to deepen throughout the day. Let your tarot deck teach you its secrets, its uses, and its healing powers.

There are no bad cards. The tarot covers all the experiences that life has to offer; none of these are bad, either. Challenging experiences are blessings in disguise, good for soul growth. Get used to all 78 cards. When you are ready to look at layouts, three are offered as templates, patterns that can guide you, on pages 166, 167, 169.

These are universal signs, and their fundamental significance is the same the world over, in all periods of history, in all forms of religion, in all varieties of philosophy. They are, in fact, drawn from that stock of images, common to all [people] everywhere, stored in what Dr. Carl Jung calls the "collective unconscious." … These pictorial images are those we weave into dreams. They are the symbols of poets, dramatists and novelists, as well as the substance of the visions of seers and prophets. Thinking in pictures is the fundamental activity of the human mind. We see before we say. Words are but labels for man's visual imagery.

The Tarot, A Key to the Wisdom of the Ages
Paul Foster Case

EXERCISE: This is an end-of-term type of project, "a big deal" that is also tremendous fun, if you like this sort of thing. Lay out your natal horoscope using the whole tarot deck, referring to the diagram on page 163. Use a big table or a clean space on the floor. Set out the 12 zodiacal Keys in order in a large circle, with your ASC Key at left center. Inside, make another circle of the 36 pips that represent the decanates. Place the Kings, Queens, and Knights outside on the cusps, and the Pages in the center. Beyond the Queens, the Aces form the corners of a square. Finally, inside of the circle of decanates, place the 10 planetary Keys so they touch their corresponding decanate cards. Meditate on this **mandala**, *sacred circular design.* Write whatever comes to you. If possible, take a photo of your Tarot Horoscope Mandala.

PLANETARY LAYOUT

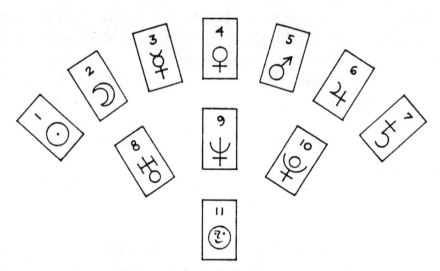

1. **SUN:** Life. Health. Spirit. Unity consciousness. Essence. Fire. Yang.
   How you are expressing Selfhood at the present moment.

2. **MOON:** Soul. Psyche. Subconsciousness. Emotion. Receptivity. Water. Yin.
   What you are feeling. Your intuition and right brain.

3. **MERCURY:** Intellect. Self-consciousness. Communication. Language.
   What you are thinking about and focusing on. Your mental state.

4. **VENUS:** Your love nature. Magnetism. Productivity. Artistry. Abundance.
   Your expression of art, love, and beauty. What you are birthing.

5. **MARS:** Power to act. Courage. Desire. Motivation. Excitement. Vitality.
   How you are using your energies to destroy the old and create the new.

6. **JUPITER:** Opportunities. Growth. Optimism. Blessings. Aspiration.
   How your consciousness is expanding. The state of your fortunes.

7. **SATURN:** Wisdom. Maturity. Organization. Self-discipline. Choice.
   How you are defining yourself. What you are teaching.

8. **URANUS:** Higher octave of Mercury. Freedom. Inspiration. Originality.
   How you are experiencing your individuality Now.

9. **NEPTUNE:** Higher octave of Moon. Sensitivity. Psychic development.
   Your inner world and connection to the collective unconscious.

10. **PLUTO:** Higher octave of Mars. Breakthrough. Magical power. Renewal.
    Transformation. Your spiritual work at present.

11. **YOU:** How you are experiencing the powers and faculties represented by the
    planets. You are the director of all planetary energies.

ZODIACAL LAYOUT

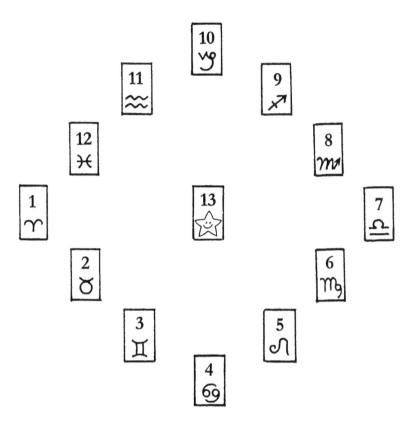

1. **ARIES:** Your basic energy. How life is reaching out through you.

2. **TAURUS:** Your body. Resources. Talents. Values. Finances.

3. **GEMINI:** Communication. Relationship to family, neighbors, environment.

4. **CANCER:** Your inner life and home base. Nurturing. Deep feelings.

5. **LEO:** Self-expression. Creativity. Where you shine. What you have to give.

6. **VIRGO:** Self-development and integration. Health. Work. Service.

7. **LIBRA:** Close relationships. Partnerships. Artistry. Peacemaking.

8. **SCORPIO:** Mystery. Sex. Death/Transformation. Magic. The Occult.

9. **SAGITTARIUS:** Your philosophy of life. Spiritual quest. Travel. Adventure.

10. **CAPRICORN:** Your influence. What you teach. Responsibility. Success.

11. **AQUARIUS:** Your relationship to society. Independence. Invention. Science.

12. **PISCES:** Your unity with all life. Compassion. Imagination. Mysticism.

13. **YOU:** Your experience of yourself at the center of these energies.

TREE OF LIFE LAYOUT

The Tree of Life provides a wonderful pattern for a reading. The power of the Great Glyph can create deep receptivity in a reader, and provide information on many levels. This layout is recommended for serious inquiry. Give the Tree plenty of time to speak its messages. To expand your ability to read this layout, study diagrams of the Tree in this and other books.

Start at the top. Name each position before laying a card there. Place each card in position one at a time, and say something about it before proceeding to the next card. One intelligent comment per card is good enough. As you go along, notice emerging themes and messages. As much as possible, see how the cards are interrelated. Always look for astrological input.

Once you have read all the way down, go up the seven levels to the top again. These levels correspond to the chakras (page 157). There are two cards on some chakra levels; just combine them in a single interpretation. After reading the chakras, place the summation card in position 11.

The querent may ask a specific question, but it is not necessary to do so. A person may simply ask for clarification, or say, "What do I need to know?" The most important thing the querent contributes to a reading is the prayer or attunement that happens during shuffling. And of course, their receptivity to the information that is given.

Some readers develop certain shuffling rituals, while others allow the querent to do whatever feels right to them. Avoid having too many rules, as regulations might interfere with the spontaneous flow of grace. Think of your readings as healings, and always ask the Powers That Be to help you help the querent. In other words, pray for people while they are shuffling and attuning. Conversation before the attunement, yes—during attunement, no.

Some people find it easier to read for others than for themselves. If this happens, just treat yourself as if you were reading for someone else. Do the same things you would do for another, and talk as honestly to yourself as you would to them. This is a way to activate the subjective/yin/querent within you as well as the objective/yang/reader. If you receive messages that seem especially meaningful, you may want to write them in a Notebook of Readings.

There is a fig tree
in ancient story
the giant Aswattha
the everlasting
rooted in heaven
its branches earthward.
Each of its leaves is a holy song.   **Bhavagad Gita**
                                              sages of ancient India

Tree of Life Reading

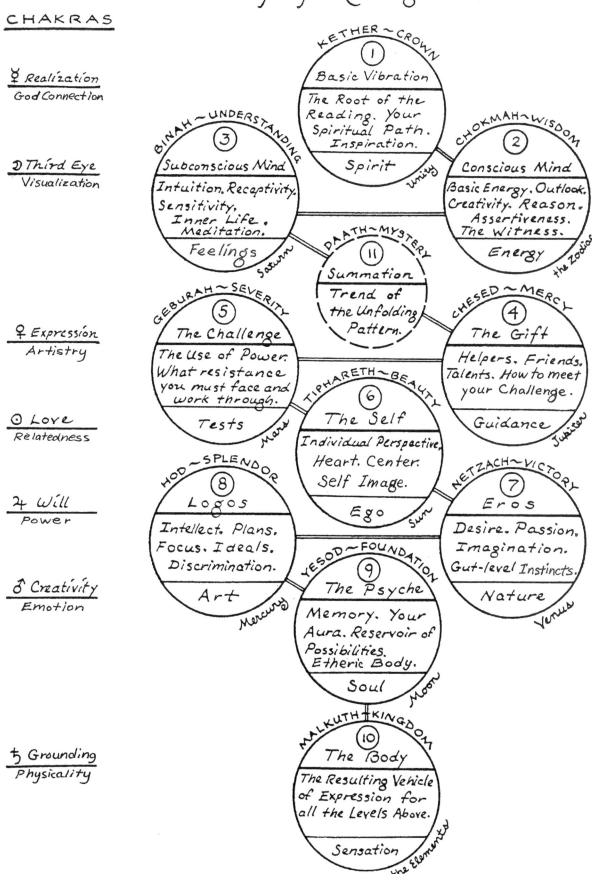

CHAKRAS

☿ Realization
God Connection

☽ Third Eye
Visualization

♀ Expression
Artistry

☉ Love
Relatedness

♃ Will
Power

♂ Creativity
Emotion

♄ Grounding
Physicality

KETHER ~ CROWN
① Basic Vibration
The Root of the Reading. Your Spiritual Path. Inspiration.
Spirit
Unity

BINAH ~ UNDERSTANDING
③ Subconscious Mind
Intuition. Receptivity. Sensitivity. Inner Life. Meditation.
Feelings
Saturn

CHOKMAH ~ WISDOM
② Conscious Mind
Basic Energy. Outlook. Creativity. Reason. Assertiveness. The Witness.
Energy
the Zodiac

DAATH ~ MYSTERY
⑪ Summation
Trend of the Unfolding Pattern.

GEBURAH ~ SEVERITY
⑤ The Challenge
The Use of Power. What resistance you must face and work through.
Tests
Mars

CHESED ~ MERCY
④ The Gift
Helpers. Friends. Talents. How to meet your Challenge.
Guidance
Jupiter

TIPHARETH ~ BEAUTY
⑥ The Self
Individual Perspective. Heart. Center. Self Image.
Ego
Sun

HOD ~ SPLENDOR
⑧ Logos
Intellect. Plans. Focus. Ideals. Discrimination.
Art
Mercury

NETZACH ~ VICTORY
⑦ Eros
Desire. Passion. Imagination. Gut-level Instincts.
Nature
Venus

YESOD ~ FOUNDATION
⑨ The Psyche
Memory. Your Aura. Reservoir of Possibilities. Etheric Body.
Soul
Moon

MALKUTH ~ KINGDOM
⑩ The Body
The Resulting Vehicle of Expression for all the Levels Above.
Sensation
the Elements

ESP

When I went to the moon I was as pragmatic a test pilot, engineer and scientist as any of my colleagues. But when I saw the planet Earth floating in the vastness of space, the presence of divinity became almost palpable and I knew that life in the universe was not just an accident based on random processes. That knowledge <u>came to me directly</u>—noetically.

As I looked beyond the Earth itself to the magnificence of the larger scene, there was a startling revelation that the nature of the universe was not as I had been taught. I was overwhelmed by the experience of physically and mentally extending out into the cosmos.

The Way of the Explorer: An Apollo Astronaut's Journey Through the Material and Mystical Worlds
Edgar Mitchell

ESP is short for *extra-sensory perception, knowledge that bypasses exterior senses and comes directly from our inner senses.* We have inner senses that correspond to our outer senses of sight, hearing, taste, touch, and smell. They are not really "extra." They were given to us for a reason. Inner perceptions provide information we cannot get any other way.

Messages from our inner senses simply arise in consciousness. We just <u>know</u>. Examples of common ESP experiences: we know a friend is going to call; a sudden sense of danger makes us change our course; plants and animals communicate their needs to us; we are aware of what someone is thinking or feeling. Then there are more exotic examples, such as psychic healer Edgar Cayce's unusual methods of study. He was failing his school subjects until he started sleeping with textbooks under his pillow, at which time he started getting high grades!

By means of a certain kind of ESP commonly called **telepathy**, it is possible *to communicate heart-to-heart or mind-to-mind* with another being. *Telepathy within a group of beings* is **pod mind**, such as dolphin families experience.

We all come into the world equipped with both inner and outer senses. Inner senses are known through feeling. Outer senses are recognized intellectually. When Edgar Mitchell wrote, "The presence of divinity became almost palpable (touchable)," he was describing "a startling revelation" that the universe was not what he had thought. In other words, extra-sensory perception showed him a greater reality beyond his thinking mind. The clarity of ESP erased his learned ideas, and replaced them with direct knowledge.

The Cabala

Mitchell used the word "noetic" to describe the knowledge that came to him directly. Another more common and familiar phrase would be "intuitive" knowledge. **Intuition** is *insight or instinct gained without the conscious use of reasoning.* Intuition or ESP happens in the right brain; reasoning happens in the left brain.

Just in case you are wondering if maybe you have to go to the Moon to experience a spiritual awakening, here is a very earthy example of profound realization. In this case, the gift of <u>knowing</u> came from a 2,000-year-old redwood tree.

> As I climbed in my bare feet—which I didn't wash so that the sap would help me stick to the limbs—I spoke with Luna. In return, she guided me to those branches that were safe and warned about those that were not. Without shoes, I could feel her underneath me and understand her messages.
>
> I made it to her lightning-hardened pinnacle, the most magical spot I'd ever visited. Luna is the tallest tree on the top of the ridge. Perched above everything and peering down, I felt as if I was standing on nothing at all, even though this massive, solid tree rose beneath me. I held on with my legs and reached my hands into the heavens. My feet could feel the power of the Earth coming through Luna, while my hands felt the power of the sky. It was magical. I felt perfectly balanced. I was one with Creation.

The Legacy of Luna
Julia Butterfly Hill

Now if you are thinking these grand experiences of cosmic consciousness only happen to special people, remember the teaching of Ageless Wisdom: Everybody is special. That means you have your very own unique way of experiencing your divinity and universal connectedness. You are perfectly equipped to know exactly what is right for you. Trust yourself, and trust your intuition. As well as inner senses, you also have an inner body, inner teacher, inner guide, inner Self, and inner universe. <u>Extra</u>-sensory perception could also be called <u>inner</u> sense perception. Note the similarity between "inner sense" and "innocence."

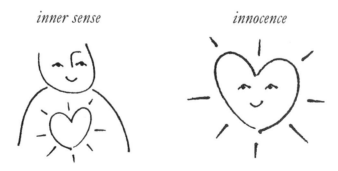

inner sense   *innocence*

Telepathic communication is every soul's birthright.

Matthew

THE NOW

The Now is *a timeless state of being experienced in super conscious awareness.* In other words, with God there is no past or future. People who experience God-consciousness report that past and future are mind-created states of awareness that do not exist in Reality. In the Now, there is only this present moment. We tend to think of eternity as infinite time, but it is more correct to say that **eternity** is *the absence of time.* And **infinity** is *the absence of space.* Moreover, **forever** exists *Here and Now.*

There is no beginning and no end in the Now. In our holographic universe every little piece contains the whole thing. All is One. In spite of our concepts about time and space, there is no real separation. While we live in a third-density body, we experience <u>apparent</u> separation, and we also have the ability to fully experience unity. In this connection, remember that the left brain analyzes (separates) while the right brain synthesizes (embraces).

When I say, "Time is an illusion," my intention is not to make a philosophical statement. I am just reminding you of a simple fact—a fact so obvious that you may find it hard to grasp and may even find it meaningless—but once fully realized, it can cut like a sword through all the mind-created layers of complexity and "problems." Let me say it again: the present moment is all you ever have. There is never a time when your life is not "this moment." Is this not a fact?

The Power of NOW: A Guide to Spiritual Enlightenment
Eckhart Tolle

NOW IS THE ONLY TIME THERE IS

EXERCISE: Pay attention to your mind. How long can you focus on the present moment without going mentally into past or future? What do you notice? What do you learn? What can increase your span of attention in the Now? This exercise can be practiced anytime, whether you are doing or not-doing actions. There is no right or wrong way to do this exercise. Do it as often as you like.

Astrology is a metaphysical language that can be used to understand what is happening Now. This book is not concerned with predictions of "what is to come." Desire to control what we think of as the future is based in fear. Notice how much pain and anxiety can be generated by thinking about the past or future. Happiness is ours when we are focused in the present, not wandering in unreality, but rather really living and welcoming without judgment whatever is occurring.

With positive thoughts and actions we can **co-create with the universe**, that is, *work cooperatively with the forces of Nature*. This conscious-choice approach to life is spontaneous and free. We enjoy the magic of each moment as it unfolds. We feel the presence of heavenly and elemental partners working with us for the highest good of all.

A divinely guided seer, dwelling in the Now, may be inspired to impart information about what our intellect perceives as the future (prophecies on pages 30, 178, 179, 185). But it is inefficient for us to dwell mentally in the past or future, because that makes us miss out on the present moment. Now is the point of power. Now is the only time there is. Now is joyous, blissful, and free!

Tarot image from BOTA School of Holy Qabalah and Sacred Tarot
5105 N. Figueroa St., Los Angeles, CA 90042
323-255-7141 ✳ www.bota.org

Key 0 symbolizes the joy and power of the Now.
The Fool is Uranus, ruler of Aquarius,
and patron of the Aquarian Age.

EXERCISE: The Fool card is a synthesis of the entire tarot, which makes it the most important card in the deck. Jot down some thoughts and feelings in response to this question: Can you identify with the tarot image of The Fool? Why and/or why not?

THE SPIRITUAL QUEST

quest (verb), *to seek*
quest (noun), *adventurous journey*
spiritual quest, *the Great Adventure into Selfhood*

The first quality of a seeker on the Path of Return must be **zeal**, *eager interest and enthusiasm*. You will never go on this journey unless you really want to. When you have a fired-up feeling, it means spirit is moving you. There are many trials on the Path; an aspirant soon learns its challenges. These tests stimulate strong spiritual growth. As you proceed, the rewards are incomparable in terms of self-awareness, freedom, and inner peace.

Taoists say that The Way is without moving, because it travels deep into the psyche. It is really a journey of awakening to what already lives inside: your super conscious God/dess Self, Buddha nature, Christ essence, Master of Life. You may think you have to get from "here" to "there," but no separation actually exists. How could you possibly be disconnected from your True Innermost Self?

What you are looking for is what is looking.

St. Francis of Assisi

The Self is the root of all desire. More than anything else, human beings want to experience and express Who They Are. In an infinite universe, the process of Self-discovery is aptly called the Great Adventure. If you do not feel called to the Path right now, that is fine, no problem. Humanity as a whole is evolving ever higher, either consciously or unconsciously. Whenever individuals consciously embrace a higher destiny, their zeal speeds up the process for everyone.

On the other hand, as with any endeavor, it is possible to overdo the spiritual path. A seeker may become too fervent, sort of "over-heated" and unbalanced. To be over-zealous is to become a zealot who believes that one specific way is the only "right" way, which makes all others "wrong." You might start trying to shove a particular ideology down somebody else's throat. This kind of proselytizing is useless. The Path is only explored by choice.

Ageless Wisdom teaches balance in all things. The middle way between extremes is recommended. As reminders, we have the middle pillar of the Tree of Life; the Tai Chi symbol ☯, and the Greek ideal of a healthy mind in a healthy body. The Path of Return is often pictured as a middle way between twin mountains that symbolize Wisdom and Understanding.

Equilibrium is the basis of the Great Work.

Alchemical Saying

REINCARNATION

Reincarnation means *again into body*. Most astrologers agree that an individual soul experiences many different lifetimes, in many different bodies. Ageless Wisdom says we are spiritual beings who can never really die. Physical **death** is viewed as *a soul's transition, a shift of dimensions, dropping the body*, or *going home to God*, but never as the final cessation of being. Even in one lifetime the outer form goes through major changes of state. For example, the baby's body you once lived in has been "dead and gone" for years.

All earthly bodies change and die but your real Self never changes and never dies. According to pre-birth agreements, your inner soul essence chooses bodies and **personages**, *incarnations*, somewhat as you choose clothes. The real YOU chose the body you live in, the moment of your birth, your horoscope, and even the moment of your passing from this outer level of existence to the Inner Planes.

You do not have to accept reincarnation in order to practice astrology. But before you decide against this ancient teaching, please take the time to explore it. Recommended reading: ***Life After Life***, by Dr. Raymond Moody, about near-death experiences, and ***Matthew, Tell Me About Heaven: A Firsthand Description of the Afterlife***, reviewed on page 182 of this book.

Ageless Wisdom says a human being who becomes a true master of life does not have to die physically, but may ascend in a body of light. An ascended master is not required to reincarnate, but may choose an Earth life in order to assist humanity's spiritual evolution.

> *Man, when he dies, only passes from one world into another.*
> *Emanuel Swedenborg*

From a linear left-brain perspective, it seems we live one life after another in sequence. From a holistic, right-brain perspective, our cumulative soul lives in the Now, experiencing many lifetimes simultaneously. Here is a metaphor for earth-life and spirit-life states: the left brain sees a series of of black and white beads strung upon a thread, while the right brain sees a circular necklace of black and white beads that has no beginning and no end. Both are valid viewpoints.

linear view

EXERCISE: Answer either or both of the following questions, if they are relevant to you. Give as much detail as you like. 1) Have you ever had a feeling about living in one or more other lifetimes in the past or future? 2) Have you ever believed you visited or lived on other planets or in other dimensions?

THE OUROBOROS

The Cosmic Serpent is an image bequeathed to us by our extremely ancient ancestors who lived many millennia ago. In the ages when Earthlings worshipped the Earth as their Great Mother—before Eve and the serpent were "framed" for a crime they did not commit—the snake was revered as the wisest creature because it lives so closely connected to earth. Today, snakes are still sacred to the Goddess. Serpent fire activates our chakras in spiritual awakening. Our DNA looks like snakes. Entwined snakes create the

caduceus, *symbol of healing.*

The **Ouroboros** *represents the Circle of Life.* It depicts *the whole universe as a Cosmic Serpent eating its own tail*—because there is nothing else to eat! Everything is constantly moving and changing, being absorbed by something that is being absorbed in turn. For example: we eat plants, which move through our snake-like digestive system. Waste from this process, and eventually our bodies as well, return to the ground and contribute to the growth of plants. Ouroboros contains the plants, our bodies, the Earth, and the cyclic process.

Life feeds on itself, for there is nothing outside of itself.
Energy and matter are eternally recycled.
Nothing is lost or wasted.
There is a use and
a reason for
everything.

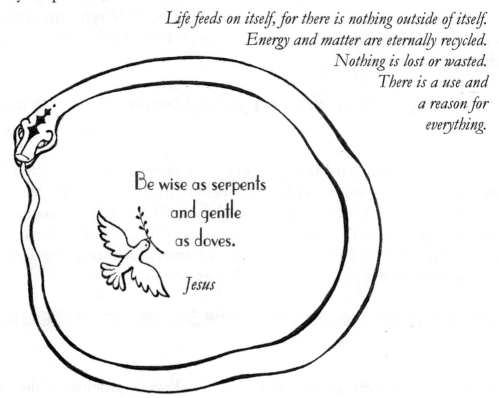

Be wise as serpents
and gentle
as doves.

Jesus

EVERY ENDING IS A NEW BEGINNING.

Ageless Wisdom

The Cabala

THE OCCULT ADMONITIONS

Admonish is a verb that means *to indicate duties, obligations, or required actions; to show a direction or give advice and encouragement, especially in friendly, earnest counsel.* The masters of wisdom who have gone before us offer four **occult admonitions** as *helpful suggestions for where we should focus in order to make progress.* Those who aspire to Self-realization through study and practice of Ageless Wisdom can use, as guides on the Path, this simple yet infinitely profound set of words: We are admonished to Will, to Know, to Dare, and to Be Silent.

Seeing a set of four, we know immediately that the admonitions are born of the four worlds and four elements of the Cabala. These admonitions are duties, obligations, required actions, directions, advice, encouragement, and friendly counsel. They deserve our utmost honor, respect, attention, and efforts at understanding. They are our inner magical implements, symbolized by the wand, cup, sword, and pentacle.

"The Force" has been known to occultists for millennia. This all-pervading, all-sustaining power that supports the universe also lovingly supports you. The occult admonitions help you to use the Force wisely, to create your greatest happiness and find your way home to the Self.

MAY THE FORCE BE WITH YOU.

*Obiwan Kenobi, beloved teacher of Jedi Knights
in the movie,* **Star Wars**, *by George Lucas*

FINAL EXERCISE: 1) Write an essay about how the occult admonitions can deepen your study and practice of Ageless Wisdom. 2) For the rest of your life, follow the occult admonitions to the best of your ability.

REVERSE OF THE GREAT SEAL OF THE U.S.

The founding fathers of the United States were inspired by the vision of a Golden Age of Enlightenment. In 1776, democracy was an experiment, an extremely revolutionary "idea whose time had come." George Washington, Thomas Jefferson, Benjamin Franklin and their friends foresaw a time of true democracy, or Global Brother-Sisterhood, resulting from **theocracy**, *government by God within (<u>not</u> by religious leaders)*. This means that all humans will evolve to a level where we are ruled by divine love, manifesting uniquely in each of our hearts. Then we will not want or need anyone telling us what to do. We will not need religion, police or armies. In the flowering of the Aquarian Age, we will honor each other as God/dess.

Anyone can help fulfill the vision of true theocracy by starting now to practice harmlessness. When you are incapable of harming yourself or another in thought, word, and deed, you have reached the pinnacle of human possibility. There are those who think that even true democracy is an impossible ideal, let alone real theocracy. Yet the torch of Ageless Wisdom never fails to extend the light of consciousness concerning humanity's divine destiny. When we stand in that light, we stand with the founding fathers and mothers of the Aquarian Age in a place of unmistakable revelation, un-shakable resolve, and immeasurable empowerment.

OUR UNDERTAKINGS ARE FAVORED.

THE NEW ORDER OF THE AGES NOW BEGINS.

There is much occult/hidden meaning in the symbols on both the obverse (front) and reverse (back) of the Great Seal of the United States. The reverse pictured above is important because it makes the statement that a new age is beginning, and our efforts in that direction are looked upon with favor by the Life Force. And of course the striking image of the 13-storey pyramid with the Eye of God as its capstone is worthy of contemplation. Remember that Uranus, ruler of Aquarius, was discovered shortly after the American Revolution.

AMERICA'S DESTINY

The following prophecy has always inspired the writer of this book, who wishes to pass on the inspiration to her readers, insofar as it may resonate with them. Notice the references in the fourth paragraph to <u>seeming</u> darkness. An occultist always looks deeper. If you like the prophecy, you are probably here to serve its unfoldment.

✳ ✳ ✳ ✳ ✳ ✳ ✳ ✳ ✳ ✳ ✳ ✳ ✳ ✳ ✳

The divine plan for the future of North America is a condition of intense activity in the greatest peace, beauty, success, prosperity, spiritual illumination, and dominion. She is to carry the Christ Light and be the Guide for the rest of the earth, because America is to be the heart center of the Golden Age that is now dimly touching our horizon...

In your beloved America, in the not so far distant future, will come forth a recognition of the Real Inner Self, and this her people will express in high attainment. She is a Land of Light, and her Light shall blaze forth, brilliant as the sun at noonday, among the nations of the earth. She was a Land of Great Light, ages ago, and will again come into her spiritual heritage, for nothing can prevent it. She is strong within her own mind and body— stronger than you think—and that strength she will exert to rise out of, and throw off from border to border, all that weighs heavily upon her at the present time.

America has a destiny of great import to the other nations of the earth, and Those who have watched over her for centuries still watch. Through their protection and love, she shall fulfill that destiny. America! We, the Ascended Host of Light, love and guard you. America! We love you...

A form of perfect government will come at a later period, when you have cast off certain fetters within that hang like fungi, and sap your strength as a vampire. Beloved ones in America, be not discouraged when the seeming dark clouds hang low. Every one of them shall show you its golden lining. Back of the cloud that seems to threaten is the Pure Light of God and His Messengers, the Ascended Masters of Love and Perfection, watching over America, the government, and her people. Again I say, America, we love you.

One by one, great awakened souls are coming forth who will become clearly conscious of their own mighty, inherent God-Power, and such as these will be placed in all official positions of the government. They will be more interested in the welfare of America than in their own personal ambitions and private fortunes. Thus will another Golden Age reign upon earth, and be maintained for an aeon.

The Count of Saint-Germaine
quoted in **Unveiled Mysteries**
by Godfre Ray King, 1939

Granny Rainbow's Theme Song

Arisa Victor

There are countless living beings in the Cosmos. Can you identify these 30 beings?

The Cabala

PART 8.

CONCLUSION

Inspiration is built into life.
Look around.
Astrology is one of your tools
for enjoying a wholesome
and creative existence.

HEAVEN

Matthew's high school graduation photo

Most people's idea of heaven is quite fuzzy. Even if we have happy thoughts about being with angels and God or the religious figure of our choice, we don't have much notion of what happens there. For a wonderful big boost in understanding where we go when we make our transition, read ***Matthew, Tell Me About Heaven: A Firsthand Description of the Afterlife*** by Suzanne Ward. Whatever idea you hold of heaven, it is sure to be upgraded. Real knowledge and certainty will replace speculation and dogma.

Matthew Ward departed this world in a single-car accident at age seventeen, to fulfill a pre-birth agreement between his soul and the soul of his mother, Suzanne. The agreement was that he would contact her telepathically from the other side, and she would write down what he told her about the afterlife. After fourteen years, her grief abated enough for him to get through to her. So far, four books have been produced, each full of very clear information that rings true and makes one's soul sing with inspiration and guidance. Here is a very brief sampling.

All inhabited planets have sanctuary realms where souls go when a physical lifetime is complete. Earth's haven (heaven) is called Nirvana by its residents. A cumulative soul—the sum of all its incarnations, or personages—reviews the lifeprint of the personage who has just made the transition from a physical to a spirit lifetime. In this review, the group soul experiences the results of all free will choices made throughout the most recent incarnation. The purpose of a planetary lifetime is for a soul to experience what was chosen and agreed upon by all principal participants before reincarnation. Lessons are chosen that will bring balance to the soul. Perfect balance is enlightenment.

Nirvana is a multi-layered realm encompassing both what we think of as heaven and hell. A soul will go to the level with which its lifetime free-will choices resonate. Lower levels are dense; higher levels are filled with light. Creator's and God's love permeates every particle of every level. Although some souls choose to reject the light, they are deeply loved, with hope that they will return to the love from which they came.

Souls have etheric bodies, homes, and scenery in Nirvana. A quote from Matthew: "Life is meaningful, Mother! We have important work, almost limitless studies, visits to Earth families, glorious music, astounding travel, and incomparable beauty." Matthew assures us that Earth is ascending into fourth density, aided by our benevolent universal family from many other worlds.

LOVE

What is love? In simplest terms, love is God's sharing of Himself with all of His creations. Love is the healing force of the universe. Love is within the soul and needs only your allowance of those innate sensations of loving others and receiving their love for you. Love has no limitations, no boundaries to its capacity.

In expression, love is treating others with kindness, fairness, honesty, compassion, helpfulness, caring. If love can be said to have "ingredients," then those are some of the ingredients of godly expression in action.

Knowing that you are God and every other of God's creations are inseparable is love. Knowing that Earth is a sentient, conscious life herself and respecting all of her life forms is love. Realizing that no one can know others at soul level and therefore does not judge them but rather does not condone an action seen as injurious, is love.

Listening to one's godself is love. Living the kind of life that engenders loving self is love. Feeling joy yourself when you see it in others is love. Doing something that brings joy to another is love. Forgiveness of self and others is love. Sharing your resources with full heart is love. Doing good deeds without attaching expectations is love.

Feeling peace of heart and mind is love. The quiet thrill of seeing a sunset or hearing a songbird is love, and a smile is one of the simplest and most radiating expressions of love. In any or all of these instances, and many others that you instinctively know are love in action, you are manifesting your love for God.

Mother, I don't think I've told you anything at all surprising. But perhaps it is good to have some references as a guiding light in these times when darkness may seem to be overshadowing the magnificent abundance of love that is in your world.

Illuminations for a New Era:
Understanding These Turbulent Times
A Matthew Book with Suzanne Ward

Be unto others as you would have God be unto you.

In Death We Do Not Part:
An Alternative Guide to Grieving
Marshall and Gail Kent

SERVICE

The desire to serve usually arises when some progress has been made on the Path. At first, one desires freedom. Further up the road, we come to realize that true freedom is the result of inner peace. Saints and sages tell us that service brings peace. In helping others, we help our Self. Sufis say that God's favorite name for God is the Servant of Servants. **Service** is *lovingly helping others, in the spirit of giving.* True service does not make you a menial or lesser being in any way. When you work from your heart, you are God's assistant. According to the masters, God's service is perfect freedom. Life will always send you people to serve, and when you help them you are doing God's work. In fact, all work and all activity can be joyfully done for love's sake.

> *Maharajji, how can I know God?*
> *"Serve people."*
>
> *Maharajji, how can I get enlightened?*
> *"Feed people."*
>
> *Maharajji, how can I raise kundalini?"*
> *"Serve and feed people."*

These questions were asked of Neem Karoli Baba, by different people at different times.

The Miracle of Love
Compiled by Ram Dass

We serve God in order to become free, and we become free in order to serve.

Ram Dass
Be Here Now

Mother Teresa of Calcutta

PHOTO BY RAGHU RAI COURTESY ELEMENT BOOKS LTD.

The fruit of silence is prayer.
The fruit of prayer is faith.
The fruit of faith is love.
The fruit of love is service.
The fruit of service is peace.

Mother Teresa's "business card"

FOND FAREWELL

When the iron eagle flies and horses run on wheels,
the Tibetan people will be scattered over the earth
and the dharma will go to the Land of the Red Man.

ancient Tibetan lore

Obviously, this prophecy has come to pass. The Land of the Red Man—Turtle Island, North America—has been a gathering place for every spiritual tradition on the planet. This land has embraced all paths to God, including Tibet's liberating version of the **dharma**, *spiritual truth and law/The Way It Is/Ageless Wisdom/Cabala.* A "soul soup" has been concocted in America's "melting pot," on soil that has very magical energies, spiritual powers that are known and honored by her indigenous inhabitants. This magical mixture can feed the hungry souls of this world. No one owns Ageless Wisdom, because it belongs to all of us. No one owns any particular religious teaching, either. These are the times when the dharma can be grasped in whatever form or forms appeal to us personally, and shared with the whole human family.

True morality consists,
not in following the beaten track,
but in finding out the true path for ourselves
and fearlessly following it.

Gandhi

All who love the light are on the same journey. The Path of Return is just one name for countless roads leading homeward. All paths, ways, and methods meet at the top of the Mountain of Aspiration, where the Torch of Truth stands as a beacon to guide our steps. Ageless Wisdom promises that everyone will get to the top eventually, in a grand ascension process that spans eons. There we merge into Creator's One Light. After a while we decide to go down the other side for another "ride" through the realms of appearance. The trick is to remember who we are, beings of light, as we surf the dimensions. The universe is a very big place. We, humanity, God's children, can explore it to our heart's content forever.

All humans are born free, and equal in rights and dignity.

Article 1, Universal Declaration of Human Rights

Intellectual freedom and religious liberty are necessary to the
unfolding spirit in [humanity]. Whatever is true is free to all alike.
God has no favorites and knows no privileged class.

Ernest Holmes, founder, **Science of Mind**

There is no need for temples;
no need for complicated philosophy.
Our own brain, our own heart, is our temple.

Fourteenth Dalai Lama

It is only with the heart that one can see rightly;
what is essential is invisible to the eye.

The Little Prince
Antoine de Saint-Exupery

Here come the Children of Light, of whom you are one.

Aquarian Gospel of Jesus the Christ
Levi

My heart has become capable of every form.
It is a pasture for gazelles,
and a convent for Christian monks,
and a temple for idols,
and the pilgrim's Ka'ba,
and the tables of the Tora,
and the book of the Qur'an.
I follow the religion of Love.
Whatever way Love's camels take,
this is my religion and faith.

Ibn 'Arabi, Sufi poet

SINCERELY YOURS

Dear Friends,

It has been a great pleasure to write this book. Not only did I feel assisted by my favorite masters of Cabala and some helpful angels, I also felt your presence, dear readers. Your courage and enthusiasm, your spirituality, intelligence, and creativity have inspired every page. Thank you.

I hope that **High School Astrology** has helped you get solidly grounded in the basics of Ageless Wisdom. You can use what you have learned as a jumping-off point for further exploration on the Paths of the Great Adventure. Books, teachers, fellow travelers, intuitive information, spiritual guidance, and direct magical/mystical experiences will come to you as the journey unfolds.

Whatever you learn on your inner quest, always try to put it to use in your everyday life. The whole point of esoteric science is to help you know yourself and express yourself, and thereby improve the quality of your life. As you absorb more light, your vibratory rate goes up, healing energy emanates from you, and the whole world benefits. Flowers spring up wherever you walk in peace and beauty. Life is magical, and so are we.

As for astrology, remember the old saying, "The stars incline; they do not compel." In other words, your chart indicates tendencies. Where you take it from there is up to you and your free will. Your horoscope is a dwelling place for your consciousness, a framework that supports you. Every part of your chart is exactly right for you. If it were any different, you wouldn't be you.

In any occult study, there are always some pitfalls, thorny patches, and swamps along the Path. We humans need challenges because they make us access our inner strength. If spiritual life were too easy, we would not feel as though we are winning a great prize. According to Ageless Wisdom, Self-realization is the greatest reward life has to offer. We must be willing to "give our all," joyfully sacrificing the lesser (ignorance) for the greater (illumination).

From the perspective of our separate self, the goal of the Cabala is to lead a guided life. Each of us has an inner guide who is with us every moment of our lives. Feeling a connection with our divine Friend is one of the happiest results of this work. The Western Occult Tradition suggests that if you are drawn to the Path, it is because your True Self is calling you Home.

Have fun! See you around the cosmos!

With great love and respect,
Sincerely yours,

Granny Rainbow

Rest in the unborn nature of mind:
Like space, no center, no limit,
Like the sun and moon, bright and clear,
Like a mountain, unmoving, unshakable,
Like the ocean, deep, unfathomable.

Milarepa

A Vision

PART 9.

INSPIRING PEOPLE

We all grasp Ageless Wisdom intuitively.
People have amazing ways of expressing
the inner sense that we all share.
This includes you.
Here are the people quoted or mentioned in this book.

Peace is the highest happiness.

Buddha

INSPIRING PEOPLE

Baal Shem Tov (1698-1760) Ukrainian. "Master of the Good Word," Rabbi Yisrael ben Eliezer, founder of Chasidic Judaism (named for Chesed/Mercy on the Tree of Life).

Black Elk, Nicholas (1863-1950) Oglala Sioux holy man. Had an amazing vision at the age of 9 that went on for days; it was thought that he was dying. He was shown a Great Tree of Life, and a Great Hoop that contained the hoops of all the Nations.

Braden, Gregg (double ♋19-) Scientist, author, New Age teacher who bridges wisdom of the past and science of the future. Many books, such as *The Divine Matrix*.

Browne, Sir Thomas (♎1605-1682) British physician and mystical author.

Boehme, Jacob (1575-1624) German alchemist-mystic of the Hermetic Tradition. Shoemaker and family man, always in trouble with the church. A major influence on the thought of Carl G. Jung. Boehme's dying words: "Now I go hence into Paradise."

Budapest, Zsuzanna ("Z") (≈1940-) Hungarian. Grandmother of feminist Earth-religion in America. Wrote *Holy Book of Women's Mysteries*. www.zbudapest.com

Buddha, Siddhartha Gautama (♉ 563-483 BCE) Born a prince in India, as a young man he left worldly wealth behind. Compassion for suffering humanity drove him to find enlightenment. His discovery: "The ultimate truth is the realization of one's own mind."

Caddy, Eileen (♏1917-2006) One of the original founders of Findhorn Gardens in Scotland. Angels and Nature Spirits spoke to her daily, offering advice on how to grow a garden in a seemingly hostile environment. Roses grew in the snow!

Carson, David (♊1937-) Choctaw Indian Nation writer who, with Jamie Sams, created *The Medicine Cards: Discovery of Power Through the Ways of Animals*. Accompanying book is a standard reference of animal lore. "We extend our humanity when we recognize our kinship with animals." www.medicinecards.com

Case, Paul Foster (♎1884-1954) Devoted his life to spiritual science by researching old alchemical and scriptural texts, and writing about the Qabalah, which he called the yoga of the west. Expressed ancient wisdom in modern psychological terms. First to place the Tarot on the Tree of Life. One of the Three Adepts who wrote *The Kybalion*. Founded Builders of the Adytum Mystery School of Sacred Tarot and Holy Qabalah, 1505 North Figueroa St., Los Angeles, CA 90042. 213-255-7141. www.bota.org

Casey, Caroline (♎1952-) Shamanic astrologer, wrote *Making the Gods Work for You*. Founded the Center for Visionary Activism.

Cayce, Edgar (♓1877-1845) The Sleeping Prophet who delivered accurate diagnoses and treatment for health and other problems while in deep trance. To his own amazement, these readings included past life details and information about Atlantis. "Good and only good thoughts should be projected into the subconscious…The body becomes that upon which it feeds…Any condition ever becoming a reality is first dreamed."

Chang Chu Ling (673-740) Chinese poet.

Chief Joseph (1840-1904) Indigenous name: Hinmatan Yalatkit. Great Chief of the peaceful Nez Perce tribe in Oregon. Tried all his life to reason with white government men, to no avail. "All men were made brothers. The Earth is the mother of all people, and all people should have equal rights upon it."

Chief Seattle (1786-1866) Great Chief of Suquamish Indians. In 1854 he made an oration to the U.S. government that is a stirring document of humanity's true connection with, and responsibility to, Nature. "The Earth does not belong to Man, Man belongs to the Earth."

Clarke, Arthur C. (♐1917-2008) World-renowned British science fiction writer. In 1968, he wrote *2001: A Space Odyssey*, a major ground-breaking movie.

Dalai Lama, Tenzin Gyatso (Ocean of Wisdom), **Kundun** (The Presence) (♋ 1935-) Born in Tibet, escaped into exile because of Chinese invasion when he was 15. His Holiness is the 14th incarnation of the Buddha of Compassion. Won Nobel Peace Prize.

Da Vinci, Leonardo (♈1452-1519) Italian artistic and scientific genius; painted *Mona Lisa*, the world's most famous painting.

Dickenson, Emily (♐1830-1886) Shy poet with great depth of feeling. She never left home, but her soul sailed the universe.

Einstein, Albert (♓1879-1955) Genius German-Jewish physicist/mystic; gave the world the Theory of Relativity, $E=mc^2$. He played the violin and loved peace.

Emerson, Ralph Waldo (♊1803-1882) Quit being a clergyman because he disagreed with dogma. Encouraged intuitive spiritual experience. With Henry Thoreau and Walt Whitman, was one of the New England Transcendentalists.

Fatunmbi, Awo Fa'lokun (double ♐1946-) American priest of the ancient African Yoruba religion. "Astrology in Ifa is called *gede. Ge* is the Yoruban word for 'female power of reproduction' and *de* means 'stand up or come into manifestation.' So the word for astrology means 'the hidden coming into manifestation.'" www.awostudycenter.com

Franklin, Benjamin (♑1706-1790) Genius American statesman and inventor. Never patented his inventions, saying that God gave him the ideas to share with others.

Fuller, Buckminster (♋1895-1983) Amazing visionary, far ahead of his time; invented the geodesic dome. "We can do more and more with less and less."

Gandhi, Mohandas (♎1869-1948) Known as **Mahatma**, *great soul*, he led India to throw off British domination through the greatest non-violent actions ever to happen in recorded Earth history. "It is possible to live in peace."

Gibran, Kahlil (♑1883-1931) Lebanese. One of the most important Arabic authors of the 20th century. Beloved for his book, *The Prophet*, result of 20 years of meditation.

Gladstone, William Ewart (1809-1898) Liberal British politician.

Greer, Mary K. (double ♎1947-) Cabalist magician, author of tarot books and more.

Hakuin (1686-1769) Japanese Zen Buddhist monk, poet, author.

Harrison, George (♓1943-2001) British guitarist known as "the spiritual Beatle."

Hermes Trismegistus Greek name for Thoth, the Egyptian god of magic and science.

Hill, Julia Butterfly (♒1974-) Set off to travel the world in search of her mission. First stop was a redwood forest. Had mystical experience, fell in love with the trees, lived over two years in Luna without ever touching the ground. Works tirelessly for ecological sanity. Wrote *The Legacy of Luna*. www.circleoflife.com

Holmes, Ernest (♑-♒cusp 1887-1960) Founder, Science of Mind, "A correlation of laws of science, opinions of philosophy, and revelations of religion applied to human needs and the aspirations of Man." www.scienceofmind.com

Homer (800 BCE) Ancient Greek author of epic stories *The Odyssey* and *The Iliad*.

Hugo, Victor (≈1802-1885) French novelist and human rights activist who championed "common" humanity in *Les Miserables*,. published in 1862.

Ibn 'Arabi, Muhyiddin (1165-1240) Philosopher-sage of Moorish culture in Spanish Andalusian Spain, the center of a merger of Jewish, Christian, and Islamic thought.

Isaiah (700 BCE) Hebrew, Yeshayah. Prophet who wrote the *Tanakh* Book of Isaiah.

Isis Almighty Isis, Queen Mother of the Universe, was worshipped in ancient Egypt by the name Auset. Isis is a Greek word; her worship extended around the Mediterranean, rivaling early Christianity. There are modern temples of Isis at www.isisoasis.org and www.fellowshipofisis.org.

Jefferson, Thomas (♈1743-1826) Wrote *Declaration of Independence*. Third U.S. President, a populist (man of the people).

Jesus of Nazareth (?) A completely Self-realized ascended master from the cosmic Christed realm who taught that we are all sons and daughters of God. His birthday is celebrated in ♑ but many think Jesus/Emmanuel/Sananda was a ♓ or perhaps born on 08-08-08. The truth will probably be revealed soon.

Jung, Dr. Carl Gustav (♌1875-1961) Swiss psychiatrist, first modern doctor to treat the soul as well as the mind. Introduced concepts of psychological shadow, archetypes, introvert and extrovert, persona, individuation, and collective unconscious. Also an artist, spiritual occultist, and gourmet cook.

Kabir (early 1400s) Arabic-Indian poet-saint of the Sufi and Bhakti devotional traditions.

Keller, Helen (♋1880-1968) Became blind and deaf at 19 months old due to illness. Overcame alienation with the help of teacher Anne Sullivan. Became a writer and philosopher. Recommended: movie with Anne Bancroft as *The Miracle Worker*.

Kenobi, Obiwan Ben Fictional Jedi Master, inspiration to a generation, played by Alec Guinness and Ewan McGregor in the *Star Wars* movies by George Lucas.

Kenyon, Tom: (≈1949-) Healer-channel for the Hathors, Masters of Love and Sound.

King David: Composed the Hebrew Psalms (songs for God) in his teens, when he was a shepherd; ancestor of Jesus.

King, Dr. Martin Luther, Jr. (♑1929-1968) African-American civil rights leader, teacher of non-violence. Won Nobel Peace Prize. His "I Have a Dream" speech inspired visions of a world beyond racism. "Violence begets more violence. Only love creates love."

King, Godfre Ray (1887-1959) Pen name of Guy Ballard. He met ascended master St. Germaine in person in 1930, then wrote *The I AM Discourses*.

Kubler-Ross, Dr. Elizabeth (♋1926-2004) Compassionate Swiss psychiatrist who helped people transition to heaven. She wrote *On Death and Dying*.

Kucinich, Dennis (♎1946-) Born in a ghetto, grew up on the streets, went into politics to truly serve people, never took bribes, created the USA Department of Peace.

Lao Tsu: (6th century) Chinese Taoist sage, authored the Tao Te Ching, an all-time worldwide best seller. Translations in this book, Stephen Mitchell in *The Enlightened Heart*..

Levi (♉1844-1911) Pen name of Levi H. Dowling. Devout, free-thinking author of *The Aquarian Gospel of Jesus the Christ*, very inspiring to the Flower Children (the hippies).

Levine, Stephen: (1937-) Compassionate Buddhist, sees beyond the appearance of death.

Lewis, C.S. (♐ 1898-1963) British author of Narnia children's books.

Lincoln, Abraham (≈1809-1865) 16th U.S. President. Guided USA through Civil War, signed the Emancipation Proclamation that freed the slaves. He was a mystic who held séances in the White House, and dreamed of his own death.

Lotterhand, Jason (triple ♈1911-1997) Friend and student of Paul Foster Case. Author of *The Spoken Cabala: Tarot Explorations of the One Self,* based on a class he taught every Thursday night for 42 years. Granny's teacher. "There is nothing wrong with people."

Lucas, George: (♉1944-) Creator of mythic *Star Wars*, cinematic epic of good and evil.

Lusseyran, Jacques (♏1924-1971) French. Completely blinded at age 8, he could see by an inner light. At 16, hero of the French Resistance against the Nazis. Survived concentration camp. Became a college professor. Autobiography: *And There Was Light.*

Matthew (♏1962-1980) Matthew Ward left his Earth life at age 17. His soul knew he would telepathically commune with his mother, Suzanne, from the other side. Together they wrote four Matthew Books, beginning with *Matthew, Tell Me About Heaven: A Firsthand Account of the Afterlife*. "Spiritual growth is what life on Earth is all about." www.matthewbooks.com .

Maynard, Jim (♊1949-) Publishes the highly recommended *Celestial Guide* calendars, which include moon phases, daily movement of planets, and an ephemeris for the year. Quicksilver Productions, PO Box 340, Ashland, OR 97520 www.CelestialCalendars.com

Milarepa (1052 CE) A great Tibetan meditation master. Born into a wealthy family, he and his mother and sister were enslaved by his wicked uncle when his father died. Mother made him vow to get revenge, so he studied unholy magic and killed most of the family by incantation. Became afraid for his soul, sought redemption. Did backbreaking work for years under guru Marpa. Finally won complete enlightenment.

Millman, Dan (♓1946-) World champion athlete who became a spiritual teacher. His books have inspired millions of readers in 22 languages. He wrote *Way of the Peaceful Warrior*, which he made into a terrific movie.

Mitchell, Edgar (♏1930-) Sixth man to walk on the Moon, a spiritual experience that inspired him to create the Institute for Noetic Science, dedicated to expanding science beyond conventional paradigms.

Mohammed ibnu Abdillah (569-632 CE) Messenger of Allah, Prophet of Islam, created the *Qur'an* scriptures.

Moody, Dr. Raymond (♋1944-) First to interview people who had been pronounced clinically dead, and had visited the "other side." Wrote *Life After Life* in 1975, sold over 13 million copies. Created the term "near death experience," sometimes said NDE.

Mother Teresa (♏1910-1997) Catholic nun who won Nobel Prize for her work with the poorest of the poor. Had to disobey the Church in order to follow her heart.

Muir, John (♈-♉ cusp 1838-1940) Born in Scotland, fell in love with the California Sierra Nevada mountains. His writings helped awaken people to see God in Nature. Started the Sierra Club to protect environment; helped make Yosemite a U.S. National Park.

Neihardt, John Called Flaming Rainbow by Lakota Indians. Poet and writer who interviewed Nicholas Black Elk. Wrote the great spiritual classic, *Black Elk Speaks*, 1932.

Newton, Sir Isaa: (≈1642-1727) British genius mathematician, astronomer, astrologer, and alchemist. He created calculus and discovered the Laws of Gravity.

O'Keeffe, Georgia (♍1887-1986) A truly independent and innovative American woman who followed her inner vision and became a huge success as a painter.

Paine, Thomas (1737-1809) American revolutionary who urged independence in the famous pamphlet, *Common Sense*. "These are the times that try men's souls."

Paracelsus (1493-1541) Swiss Cabalist/alchemist/physician, considered a miracle-worker, the greatest healer in Europe, hailed today as the first modern medical scientist. "The main reason for healing is love."

Ramakrishna (♒1836-1886) Indian yogi, considered "out of it" until someone recognized his very advanced state of **Samadhi**, *super consciousness*. Devoted to the Divine Mother. His student, Vivekananda, was the first yogi to visit the USA, at the Parliament of World Religions, held in Chicago in 1893.

Ram Dass (♈1931-) "Servant of God." Richard Alpert, Ph.D., as a young Harvard psychology professor, experimented with psychedelics in the 1960s. Met his enlightened guru, Neem Karoli Baba, on a pilgrimage to India. Wrote *Be Here Now*, spiritual guidebook to Granny's generation.

Roosevelt, Eleanor (♎1884-1962) A shy child who, as First Lady, (wife of Franklin D. Roosevelt) became a champion of underprivileged people all over the world.

Rudhyar, Dane (♈1895-1985) Born in France, became an American pioneer of modern astrology. "The first known attempt to discover a consistent and dependable order in existence produced the earliest and most basic forms of what is today called astrology. As such, astrology can truly be said to be the 'mother of all sciences' and the original core of all culture and religions."

Rumi, Mevlana Jalaluddin (♏1207-1273) Tajikistanian master poet of Sufism, the Religion of Love. He started the Mevlana Sufi Order (whirling dervishes).

Saint Francis (1182-1226) of Assisi, Italy. Gave up wealth to love and serve all of God's creation, including animals. Wrote canticle, *Brother Sun, Sister Moon*. Taught that we must give what we want to receive. "Where there is hatred, let me bring love."

Sams, Jamie (♎19-) With David Carson, created the Native American *Medicine Cards* (not a tarot deck) of animal totems. Also *The Sacred Path* cards and teachings.

Santana, Carlos (♋1947-) World-renowned Mexican guitarist. Humanitarian. Familiar with angels. His music touches body, mind, and spirit. Over 50 million albums sold.

Shakespeare, William (♈-♉ cusp 1564-1616) Oft acknowledged as the world's greatest poet, playwright. Themes of peace, love, and justice. Wildly popular for 400+ years.

Smith, Pamela Colman (♒1878-1951) British artist, set designer, and story teller. Painted the Waite Tarot Deck, first tarot to have scenic paintings for all 78 cards. It was first published by Rider in 1910, and is still the world's best-selling tarot deck.

Solomae Sananda (♐1959-) As a housewife, she was enlightened by a spontaneous kundalini awakening. Now she is a spiritual teacher at the Living Spirit Foundation. www.cherylstoycoff.com .

Stevenson, Robert Louis (♏1850-1894) Scottish. Sickly as a child, developed imagination, became famous novelist: *Treasure Island*, *Dr. Jekyll and Mr. Hyde*.

St. Exupery, Antoine de (♋1900-1944) French writer, early aviation pioneer. *The Little Prince* is one of Granny Rainbow's favorite children's classics, right alongside *Alice*.

in Wonderland, The Wizard of Oz, and *The Princess and Curdie*

St. Germaine An ascended master. Incarnated as a French Count in a place called St. Germaine. Has been instrumental in the cause of freedom, especially democracy in America, and the Aquarian Age. Known as Lord of the Violet Flame of Transmutation.

Swedenborg, Emanuel (1688-1772) Swedish scientist who had a near death experience and thereafter communicated with angels.

Thoreau, Henry David (♋1817-1862) New England Transcendentalist and naturalist; practiced civil disobedience to unjust law and authority; wrote *Walden Pond.*

Three Adepts Three Qabalists who wrote *The Kybalion* anonymously. Recently it was revealed that they were Paul Foster Case, Ramacharaka, and possibly St. Germaine.

Tolle, Eckhart (♒1965-) Swiss. In the middle of a suicidal depression during his first Saturn Return, he realized his true Self. His book, *The Power of NOW* is "straight from the horse's mouth" by one who knows.

Twyman, James (♓1962-) Peace Troubadour who sings his peace songs in war-torn areas while millions focus peaceful energy there. Telepathic contact for the Mystic Children. Author of *Emissary of Light* and *Emissary of Love* and many more books. Co-author of movies, including *Indigo.* www.emissaryoflight.com .

Victor, Arisa (♈1939-) Priestess, artist, writer, Cabalist, spiritual occultist. Became Granny Rainbow on her second Saturn Return. Compiled and edited *The Spoken Cabala*, by Jason Lotterhand. He taught the class for 42 years; Arisa attended for 22 years.

Vissell, Rami (♈19 -) Barry and Joyce Vissell fell in love in high school, married in 1968, became teachers of how to have good partnerships. Wrote *The Shared Heart*. Raised three sensitive children in accord with Ageless Wisdom. Rami is one of their daughters.

Walsch, Neale Donald (♏1943-) In the depths of despair, he wrote an angry letter to God. God used Neale's hand and pen to answer him! Together they created *Conversations with God, Books 1, 2,* and *3*, full of wisdom, inspiration, and comfort. Starred in movie, *Indigo*; created movie, *Conversations With God.*

Ward, Suzanne (♈1933-) Channel for her departed son, many inter-galactic beings, and God, whose uplifting messages for Earthlings she recorded in *The Matthew Books*. www.matthewbooks.com.

Washington, George (♓1732-1799) Accomplished the super-human feat of shepherding a democratic nation into existence. Was asked to be king, but opted for president. "First in the hearts of his countrymen," he was also famous for how much his dogs loved him.

Watts, Alan: (♑1915-1973) Popularized Zen Buddhism in the western world.

Werneke, Angela C. (19 -) Artist of the Medicine Cards, a Native American deck of beautiful animal portraits. Discovery of Power Through the Ways of Animals.

White Buffalo Woman A Christ-like woman who brought the peace pipe to the Lakota Indians, and taught them sacred rituals and practices.

Wright, Frank Lloyd (♊1867-1959) Genius architect, caused a revolution in thinking.

Wonder, Stevie (♉1950-) Born poor and blind, became a star composer and performer of *wonder*ful popular music.

Yogananda (♑1893-1953) Brought Kriya Yoga to the West. Wrote spiritual classic, *Autobiography of a Yogi.* Founded Self Realization Fellowship in Los Angeles.

PART 10.

GLOSSARY

All the words
defined in this book
are collected here
in alphabetical order:
a beginner's dictionary of Ageless Wisdom

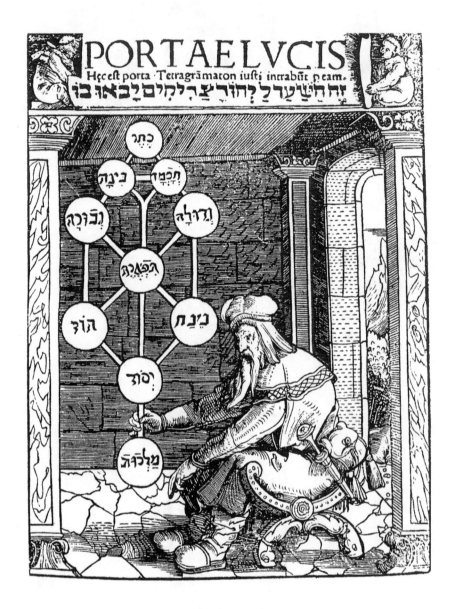

The Old Philosopher

Tree of Life from **Portae Lucis** *(Gate of Light)*
by Ricius, 1516

Glossary

GLOSSARY

Abyss - on the Tree of Life, a separation that seems to exist between the Three Supernals and the rest of the Tree below. The Abyss is a state of consciousness across which, by the miracle of grace, the soul learns to fly.

adept - a person who has realized the Self, a master of life. The power wielded by adepts is as far beyond that of ordinary humans as the ordinary human is given power beyond the animal kingdom.

Age - an astronomical Age is one twelfth of a Great Year: 2,160 years in one zodiacal sign.

Age of Aquarius - the Humanitarian Age we are entering now, due to Precession of the Equinoxes, a cycle of 25,920 years, often rounded to 26,000. page 30

Ain Suph Aur - Hebrew, "No Limit Light"; the three Veils of the Absolute existing before the Tree of Life; also called Limitless Light and Radiant Darkness.

air - symbol of intellect; third alchemical element, third world of Cabala, where division occurs.

alchemy - the process of refining, or spiritualizing, one's own body and awareness, turning one's "lead" or lower nature into the "gold" of higher awareness. page 156

androgyne - a being that combines both sexes; symbolizes the human psyche, which has both female and male characteristics, arising from right and left brain. page 51

anima - yin, feminine aspect of the soul; a Latin term used in Jungian psychology.

animus - yang, male aspect of the soul; a Latin term used in Jungian psychology.

arcana - Latin, secrets, mysteries, hidden wisdom. page 164
    major arcana - in tarot, 22 faces/facets of God that outline the spiritual path.
    minor arcana - 16 court cards and 40 pip cards of tarot.

archetype - original energy/idea/awareness. Archetypes are pure spirit, and inhabit the collective unconscious of humanity; symbolized in the tarot major arcana cards.

art - expressing how you feel, a function of the right brain; the conscious use of skill, taste, and creative imagination in the production of beauty.

Ascendant, ASC - in a horoscope, the degree of the zodiacal sign rising over the horizon at the time of birth; defines 1st house cusp; symbolic sunrise. page 123

aspects - in astrology, angular relationships between the planets, measured in degrees. Example: Planets that are 90° apart are in square aspect, symbolized ☉☐☽. page 127
    applying aspects - moving toward exact degree; dynamic may be intense.
    separating aspects - moving away from exact degree; dynamic is relaxed.

astrological chart - see **horoscope**

astrology - language of the stars; a science of correspondences between the macrocosm and the microcosm: As Above (the heavens), So Below (the native).

awo - Yoruba, secret and invisible forces applied in Ifa divination. page 104

Cabala - Hebrew, "reception." A Cabalist is open to receive God's grace. page 143, 160

caduceus - two serpents entwined around a winged staff; symbol of healing; also symbolizes yin and yang aspects of kundalini rising up the spinal column.

cardinal - yang initiating quality of the astrological signs ♈ ♋ ♎ ♑.

cardinal points - 1st, 4th, 7th, and 10th house cusps, also known as ascendant, nadir, descendant, and mid-heaven; key points of activation in the horoscope. page 124

centered - in touch with your innermost Self. page 50

centrifugal force - Jupiter's outward-spiraling thrust. page 79

centripetal force - Saturn's inward-spiraling pull.

chakras - Sanskrit, "wheels"; whirling energy centers in the etheric body.

Christ - state of being one with God; pure love-light essence in every human heart. The Christed realm is Creator's first emanation, made completely of highest light.

co-creation - conscious cooperation between humanity and Nature.

collective unconscious - the great ocean of all human psyches joined together beyond time and space; a term invented by Dr. Carl Gustav Jung. page 83

conscience - according to Matthew: the voice of truth in one's mind that guides the consciousness in line with the soul's chosen missions. A function of Saturn.

color - visual effect caused by light vibrating at different frequencies. page 58

court cards - Kings, Queens, Knights, and Pages of tarot. page 163

Creator - according to Matthew: Supreme Being of the entire cosmos (all universes). Source of all life throughout the cosmos. Its first creations were the Christed realm and highest souls, including the archangels. Together these highest souls co-created the gods and goddesses, some of whom went forth to rule the universes they co-created with Creator. The ruler of our universe, called God and other names, is *in effect* Creator for this universe. Creator is still and unchanging; God is active in our behalf. "The ultimate power of the cosmos (the omnipotent, omniscient essence, the Totality, I AM, or any other designations you have for God) actually is Creator. Whether we say "God" or "Creator," no problem; our intention is understood.

crop circle - mysterious, huge designs that appear instantaneously in fields of grain. Real crop circles are geometrically perfect. The grain continues to grow. page 33

cumulative soul - Matthew: the collective memory, wisdom, knowledge, and spiritual growth of all personage lifetimes. Reviews the lifeprint, a record of every thought, word, and deed of a physical lifetime, while feeling their effects on others.

cusp - the point where one sign, house, or Age ends, and another begins. page 122

death - not a cessation, because life never stops; transition, change of state, shift of densities/dimensions, entry to new life in Nirvana/heaven. page 175

degree - geometry, 1/360th of a circle. There are 30 degrees (30°) in each sign.

density - according to Matthew: a more accurate word than "dimension" because it refers to natural laws of vibratory rates. Bodies and forms do exist in higher densities, but we cannot see them with our 3rd density eyes and brain. Density refers not only to amount of mass, but also to light frequencies of spiritual evolution.

descendant - the degree of the zodiacal sign that was setting below the horizon at the time of birth; 7th house cusp; symbolic sunset.

dharma - Sanskrit, "spiritual truth, law, and duty;" the Way of Life; Ageless Wisdom.

dignity - each planet is dignified, raised to highest activation, in the house corresponding to the sign of its exaltation: ♃ is exalted in ♋ and dignified in 4th house.

direct motion - when a planet appears to be moving forward relative to Earth.

divination - process of receiving divine guidance through using astrology, tarot, etc.; discovery of hidden knowledge by using intuition. page 146

dualism - unwillingness to embrace opposites in their underlying unity; either-or thinking.

earth - symbolic of body, form, the physical world; fourth alchemical element; fourth world of Cabala that contains, embodies, and gives form to fire, water, and air.

ego - the sense of separate self which, without spiritual understanding, gives rise to fear. An enlightened, regenerated ego experiences individual self and God-Self as One. page 154

elements - in occultism: fire, water, air, and earth. page 53

Emissary Wheel - also called Prayer Wheel; given by Emissaries of Light through James Twyman to assist the awakening of Christ consciousness, page 33

empirical evidence - direct experience that proves something to you, personally.

enlightenment - being able to see or sense the light (divinity) in everything; a state of unity consciousness; heart rules head; the "gold" of alchemy.

enneagram - classification of nine different types of energy through which human souls find physical expression. Each body focuses one type of energy per lifetime. Diagram on page 56.

ephemeris - a table showing planets' daily positions relative to the Prime Meridian. page 60

Equal House - astrology's original system of dividing a chart into 12 houses of 30 degrees (30°) each. To honor the wisdom of the ancients, Granny uses the Equal House system.

equinox - Latin, "equal night;" happens twice a year in spring and fall when day and night hours are exactly equal.

eros - Greek, "love, pleasure, desire;" the right-brain balance to logos. page 47

esoteric science - study of metaphysical realities; the balance for exoteric study of physical realities. "Eso" is inner, right-brained. "Exo" is outer, left-brained. pages 24, 25

ESP - extra-sensory perception. page 170

essay - see bottom of page 38.

eternity - the absence of time.

ether (or ethers) - poetic word for "the heavens" or "atmosphere." Visible to the inner eye.

etheric - denotes substance vibrating at a higher-than-third-density frequency (not visible in 3rd density, but still forming bodies, buildings, etc. made of light).

etheric body - in humans, the subtle field of energies that surround and permeate the physical body. Etheric patterns precede, and also sustain, our 3rd density forms. Souls in heaven, fairies, and ghosts have etheric bodies.

exalted - the 7 original planets are raised to highest expression in one zodiacal sign each. 63

exoteric science - study of the physical world, the balance for esoteric metaphysical studies. The two forms of science are not really separate.

fire - symbol of spirit; first alchemical element; first Cabala world, where everything begins.

First Matter - alchemical name for very fine substance of Mother Matrix/Quantum Field.

fixed - steady quality of the astrological signs ♉ ♌ ♏ ♒.

fixed stars - As Earth turns on her axis, the distant constellations of stars seem to wheel through the sky, but they never change in relation to each other. Planets, on the other hand, are always changing position because they orbit our Sun.

Flower of Life - All life grows in this pattern, found carved in a wall of Egypt's most ancient temple. The Tree of Life is contained in this diagram. page 33

forever - eternity, the absence of time. All that ever was or will be is here, now. page 172

frequency - rate of vibration. More light means higher/faster frequency.

glyphs - symbolic writing. Example: This glyph ♀ stands for Venus.

God - Our Divine Mother/Father Parent, who, with Creator and the archangels, co-created this universe in pure love and light. Every part of the universe is made of God; nothing is separate; all is divine. All souls combined = One God.

Golden Rule - One law of life is all we need to live happily together forever. Do unto others as you would have them do unto you. Treat others the way you want to be treated. Give what you want to get.

Great Work - alchemical term for the inner process of turning "lead" to "gold," applicable to individuals and to humanity as a whole. page 156

Great Year - one rotation of Earth's axis backward through the zodiac, a period of 25,920 years; often rounded off to 26,000 years. page 18

heliocosm - Greek, "body of the Sun;" Sun's cohesive force-field holds the solar system.

hermaphrodite - see **androgyne** page 51

hermetic - magical, from Hermes, Greek god of magic. Sealed, hidden from outer view.

hermetic androgyne - the union or "marriage" of opposites in a person's psyche; represents balance in the soul. page 51

hieroglyphs - Greek, sacred texts written with pictorial glyphs; may be quite elaborate.

High Magic - working with the lower aspects of human personality and consciousness to transmute them into a Temple of the Holy Spirit.

horoscope - astrological chart; symbolic representation of a cross section through the universe at a specific time and place of an event, such as a birth; a portrait in the stars. Shows the 10 astrological planets' positions in the 12 zodiacal signs.

houses - areas or fields of daily life where the astrological planets and signs operate; there are 12 in every chart; houses correspond to the signs of the zodiac; pages. 118-121

Hunab Ku - Mayan, "Giver of Movement and Measure." The divine intelligence at the center of our galaxy. Diagram is similar to Tai Chi symbol. page 33.

Ifa - an African divination system of the Yoruba tradition; page 104

indigenous - that which is natural and native to the land; original tribes, plants, stories, etc. Indigenous wisdom arises from inner knowing and feeling, has cosmic, holistic, magical energies. Indigenous tribal people have much to teach the technocratic world.

infinity - the absence of space.

intellect - our ability to perceive, think, reason, and analyze, personally localized within the One Cosmic Mind; intellect may become enlightened or "endarkened." To avoid the trap of darkness, let conscience guide your free-will choices.

intuition - the inner power of direct knowing that is inherent in everyone.

judgment - dualistic thinking, in terms of good or bad, right or wrong. Instead, there is "what works." God is love. God does not judge. When we arrive in heaven, it is we ourselves who evaluate our recent incarnation.

Kabbalah - Jewish mysticism based on the Hebrew language and the Tree of Life.

karma - the cyclical law of cause and effect. As you sow, so shall you reap. The thoughts and actions that emanate from you create energy that will return to you multiplied. The purpose of karma is to balance all experiences of the soul. pages 77, 140

kundalini - Sanskrit, "serpent fire." Spiritual energy rising up the spine to awaken the chakras; stored in the first chakra; in India, said to be a goddess. page 85

Law of Correspondence - As Above, So Below. page 34

light - Conscious, living, and divine, light is both a wave (energy) and a particle (substance). Light is manifested love, the great healer and up-lifter. For Earth, light is the gift of life from the Sun; we are made of light. page 16

Lights - in astrology, the Sun and Moon.

logos - Greek, "word, reason, logic;" the left-brain balance to eros. page 47

love - the most powerful energy in the Universe; the original creating material; God.

Lux Occulta - Latin, "Hidden Light;" Creator's holy light/life/love in all things. page 58

macrocosm - "great world;" the above in As Above, So Below. page 34

magic - spiritual control of vibration; creation and transformation brought about by cooperation with divine forces. According to the Cabala, life itself is magical. Magic exists in the creative interaction between spirit and matter. page 22

Man - "born of mind/consciousness;" when capitalized, a term including all human children, women, and men. The race of Man co-creates with Cosmic Mind. page 152

manas - Indo-European, "mind;" root of the word "Man."

mandala - circular picture with symbols designed to be meditated upon for spiritual deepening. The horoscope is a kind of mandala.

manifestation - the process by which spirit creates form. pages 46-48, 152-153

masters - beings who have awakened to super consciousness, realized their divinity, and conquered death. They are always aware of the presence of God Within. page 155

mater - Latin, "mother," found in the words: matter, materialize. page 153

matter - substance, the physical world of form. page 153

maturity - expertise and wisdom developed from experience; responsible; self-aware. pg. 79

Medicine Wheel – sacred diagram made of stones by North America's indigenous people, its cross-within-a-circle construction corresponds to the Tetragrammaton. page 147

meditation - continued thought, holding a focus in mind; solemn reflection; a way to explore your inner Self and receive spiritual guidance. page 40

mercurial - ever-changing, like the mutable planet Mercury, named for the Greek messenger of the gods.

meridian - in a horoscope, the vertical line between mid-heaven and nadir; divides chart into hemisphere of the self (left) and hemisphere of the other (right). page 125

metaphysical - above the physical; in higher frequencies than the third dimension.

microcosm - "small world;" the below in As Above, So Below. page 34

mid-heaven - highest point of a horoscope; 10th house cusp; symbolic high noon and point of highest consciousness. page 125

mind - the seat of consciousness. pages 151-153

modes - in astrology, cardinal, fixed, and mutable. page 52

mutable - changeable quality of the astrological signs ♊ ♍ ♐ ♓ .

nadir - the lowest point of a horoscope; 4th house cusp; symbolic midnight. pages 124, 125

natal chart - horoscope drawn for the moment of birth (nativity).

native - in astrology, the person for whom a horoscope is drawn/created.

Nature - all things in time and space, the entire manifested universe; a multi-dimensional, conscious, creative matrix; Web of Life connecting all things. pages 20, 73

Nirvana - heaven; proper name of Earth's sanctuary realm; where souls go after a physical lifetime to prepare for the next incarnation. The higher dimensions of this multi-layered world are in a very loving, healing environment with opportunities for learning and spiritual growth. Also a Buddhist term for a heavenly state of mind.

Nodes of the Moon - points where the ☽ goes north or south of equator. pg. 131

Now - a timeless state of awareness experienced in super consciousness. page 172

occult - hidden, subtle, etheric, concealed behind surface appearances.

Occult Admonitions - suggestions from the Hermetic masters: to will, to know, to dare, and to be silent. page 177

octaves - repetitions of pattern in the spectrum of vibration. Example: ♅ (super conscious) is the higher octave of ☿ (self-conscious). page 130

orb allowance - a few degrees on either side of an exact aspect. page 126

original planets - Those known in antiquity, before outer planets were discovered. page 63

Ouroboros - the universe as a cosmic serpent eating its own tail; Circle of Life; page 176.

pantheon - family of gods and goddesses. Example: The Grecian divinities Apollo, Artemis, Hermes, Aphrodite, Aries, Zeus, Chronos – correspond to Sun, Moon, Mercury, Venus, Mars, Jupiter, Saturn.

Part of Fortune - important integration point for Sun, Moon, and Ascendant; where the Moon would be if the Sun were rising; from Arabic astrology. pages 125, 131, 134

Path of Return - the trail left by Those Who Have Gone Before (to Self-realization).

Paths of Wisdom - 10 Centers plus 22 connections (corresponding to 22 Hebrew letters, the planets and signs, and tarot major arcana) = 32 Paths on Tree of Life, page 124.

permutations - 3 modes and 4 elements combined in a given order create a coherent set of 12 signs. page 88

personage - in each physical lifetime, the distinct/unique essence of a soul having that physical experience. All a soul's personages add up to a cumulative soul.

philosopher - lover of wisdom.

Philosopher's Stone - in alchemy, the One Self; spirit grounded in the physical body.

pip cards - Ace through 10 of Wands, Cups, Swords, and Pentacles in tarot.

plane of the ecliptic - a force field extending in space from the Sun's equator, in which the planets orbit.

planetary formations - stellium, T-square, grand trine, grand square. page 128

planetary patterns - bundle, bowl, basket, see-saw, open angle, splash. page 128

planets - Greek, "wanderers;" in astrology, all ten heavenly bodies that "wander" across the sky: Sun, Moon, Mercury, Venus, Mars, Jupiter, Saturn, Uranus, Neptune, Pluto. Planets have souls; they are living, conscious, and intelligent. They correspond to forces in us.

    personal planets - inside Saturn's orbit. ☉ ☽ ☿ ♀ ♂ ♃ ♄

    transpersonal planets - beyond Saturn's orbit. ♅ ♆ ♇

pod mind - dolphin pods are families of up to 50 individuals who communicate telepathically, so the pod can act as one being. Humans are capable of pod mind with each other and with animals, angels, planets, and all other beings, including God.

polarity - interaction of opposites; the dance of yin and yang.

precession of the equinoxes - Earth's slowly spinning axis moves backwards through the signs of the zodiac .042 degree per year, creating a different point for the spring equinox each year; a 26,000 year cycle page 28

Prima Materia - Latin, "First Matter"; alchemical term for the facet of cosmic mind that materializes into physical forms, utilizing the Secret of Saturn.

Prime Meridian - the point of zero degrees longitude, Greenwich, England.

psyche - the reasoning mind of a soul; the collective unconscious.

psychology - scientific study of the psyche.

Qabalah - this spelling of Cabala refers to the Western Hermetic Mystery Tradition.

quadruplicities - signs that belong in sets of four, sorted by mode. page 88

querent - a person seeking information through divination.

quest - the zealous and adventurous journey toward Selfhood; the Path of Return. page 174

Radiant Darkness - a name for the mysterious Source of Life; a beautiful combination of sparkling light and inky darkness sometimes seen by mystics.

rainbow - harmonious collection of countless multi-colored particles; symbol of God's promise of fulfillment and of humanity's unification. 6 basic, 6 tertiary colors in progressive order. page 59

Reality - with a capital "R," that which is permanent, changeless, birthless, and deathless.

rectification - calculation of birth time from examination of events in a life.

reincarnation - rebirth of the soul in a different body. page 175

regeneration - "beginning again;" stimulation of new life; a power of Pluto.

retrograde - a planet appears to be in reverse motion, due to orbiting more slowly than Earth around our Sun. The outer planets appear to retrograde frequently. page 129

Rising Sign - in a horoscope, the zodiacal sign rising over the horizon at birth. Ascendant is a certain degree of the Rising Sign. Example: 22°♒ on 1st house cusp. page 123

Sanathana Dharma - Sanskrit, "Eternal Truth;" eastern version of Ageless Wisdom; Hinduism; oldest (8,000 years) continually-practiced faith in the world.

Saturn Return - one orbit of ♄ through the zodiac, a 29½ year cycle; time of personal reassessment. ♄ pulls you to the center of yourself, asks you to release what is not-self.

science - systemized knowledge derived from observation, study, and experimentation. There are two basic kinds: esoteric/inner/metaphysical, and exoteric/outer/physical.

Seat of Mystery - invisible center on the Tree of Life, in the Abyss between the Three Supernals and lower centers; in Hebrew, Da'ath, "Knowledge." page 145

Self - spelled with a capital "S," your inner divinity; in Cabala, a name of God as the One Self from which all small selves emerge and to which they return. page 12

Self-mastery - expert knowledge of one's True Being; skillful directing of one's motives and behavior through graceful command of the ego. pages 79, 155

Self-realization - awakening to the fact that God dwells within you as your Self.

service - lovingly helping others, in the spirit of giving. page 184

shadow - in psychology, the denied parts of our psyche. Dr. Carl Jung discovered that, when denied, the shadow is then projected onto others. To be consciously whole, we must face and embrace our shadow; sometimes called "the dark side."

shaman - a medicine person who heals by using Nature's magic in the spirit world.

Shield of Love - 6-pointed star combining fire and water triangles. page 55

Shri Yantra - Hindu meditation diagram, corresponds to the Tree of Life. page 148

sidereal astrology - eastern/Vedic/Indian system. Not used in this book . page 29

signs - in astrology, 12 zodiacal constellations that act as channels or doorways through which cosmic energies flow to Earth. Signs influence planet's behavior, and imprint the houses in a horoscope.

sin - usually, what is called sin is just a mistake due to ignorance, or missing the mark (as in archery). The only real sin is interfering with the growth of a soul.

singleton - in a horoscope, any one planet positioned away from all the others; often "pulls a lot of weight" in the chart.

soul - eternal divine God-essence of each individual; forever connected with souls of all other life forms; each individual soul makes pre-birth agreements to learn chosen lessons with some other souls; see also **cumulative soul**.

spirit - the divine, intelligent life-essence within a person, place, or thing.

spring equinox - the point of equal day and night occurring March 19, 20, 21, or 22 in the northern hemisphere; ushers in the spring season and the sign of Aries. pages 28-29

stationary - when a planet appears to be changing from direct to retrograde motion, or back again. page 129

Sufism - the Religion of Love; mystical branch of Islam.

sunlight - conveys life, consciousness and love to all planets in the solar system.

symbiotic - beneficial interdependence. Example: Human breath creates carbon dioxide, absorbed by trees; trees create oxygen, absorbed by humans.

symbol - a visual image that stands for something invisible (an idea, quality, or feeling).

symbolism - the language of the right brain/psyche/subconscious/intuition/soul.

Tai Chi symbol - ☯ a study aid to help us understand that light and dark are partners; each contains the seed of the opposite; also called the yin-yang symbol.

tarot - card deck of 78 spiritually symbolic, encoded pictures; the first cards, page 160

telepathy - direct heart-to-heart and/or mind-to-mind communication; every soul's birthright; possible between any two or more conscious beings.

Tetragrammaton - Greek, "Name of Four Letters;" That which was, is, and shall be; a primary name of God in Qabalah/Kabbalah. page 146

Three Supernals - trinity of consciousness: 1, 2, and 3 on Tree of Life. page 142

transformation/transmutation - major change from one state or form to another, a specialty of Pluto and Scorpio.

transpersonal - extending or going beyond the personal or individual.

Tree of Life - in Cabala, a diagram of unfolding universal consciousness; pages 144-145

trinity - a set of three things that belong together and define each other. page 52

trinity of consciousness - super conscious, self-conscious, and subconscious.

triplicities - signs that belong in sets of 3, sorted by element. page 162

tropical astrology - uses the yearly spring equinox as the starting point for the zodiac by calling that moment (of equal day and night) zero degree Aries 0; this book is about the tropical system. page 29

Turtle Island - indigenous name for North America. pages 147, 185

unity - love consciousness that embraces opposites and celebrates diversity.

water - symbol of psyche, mind, soul; second alchemical element; second world of Cabala, where sensitivity, feeling, intuition, and instinct are experienced.

weight - in astrology, the powerful influence that some things may have in a chart.

yang - assertive, outgoing, masculine energy. page 18

yin - receptive, magnetic, feminine energy. page. 18

yoga - Sanskrit, "union;" refers to conscious joining of small self and the One Self.

zeal - eager interest and enthusiasm; necessary for the spiritual quest. page 174

zenith - see **mid-heaven**

zodiac - Greek, "circle of animals;" many of the astrological signs are named for animals, a hint that astrology had shamanic, indigenous beginnings. page 43

ACKNOWLEDGEMENTS

Paul Foster Case (♎), kind, modest, brilliant, awesome teacher of my teacher; you have done more than most people will ever know for the Great Work. Thank you from the bottom of my heart for giving me a reason to live, to travel the Path of Return.

Jason C. Lotterhand (♑), beloved friend and teacher, thanks for 22 years of blissful immersion in Tarot and Cabala classes every Thursday night. And for nudging me, even from beyond the grave, to write *High School Astrology*.

Paul A. Clark (♒), Steward of the Fraternity of the Hidden Light, my magical publisher, profound gratitude for bringing my books "to earth."

Tony DeLuce (♏), for calling me out of the blue and for all your insightful coaching.

The Jelinsky Family: Sharon (♎), Patrick (♏), Sarah (♓), and Benjamin (♊) Jelinsky, infinite and undying thanks to my beloved family for your immense patience, generosity, and goodness to Granny. You are THE BEST. I love you!

Silma Pamela Smith (♑), sweet Cabala sister, my heart overflows with gratitude for all your invaluable proofreading and typing and moral support.

Don Nicodemus, Jr. (♓), your impressive computer wizardry saved the manuscript. Your supportive friendship for so many years is deeply appreciated.

Rob Calef (♒) of the Open Secret Bookstore (♊), my home away from home, BIG thanks for your encouragement over the years, and for giving me a place to teach.

Mary Adya Garner (♊), profuse thanks for being the first to invest money in this project. Your bright visions and generous heart are blessings to the world.

Tanya M. Joyce (♏), you are an endless fountain of helpful suggestions and creative gifts. Thanks for your dedication in sharing Cabala with the world.

Mike Weiner (♌), loving thanks for all your bright ideas, encouragement, and backing for this book and also *The Spoken Cabala*.

Ilona Marshall (♏), Priestess of Isis, bless you for taking me into your heart and home when all other doors were closed.

Mark R. Price (♒), you were da Superscanner Man! We all love you, angel.

Sarah Shockley (♏) and Connor Jensen (♎), thanks for the tip-top Photoshop assistance.

Wonderful, helpful friends: Crista Mercuria Artos (♒), Peter Burchard (♊), Brad Burton-Smith (♉), Vivek Chaturvedi (♌), Ira Fabricant (♓), Angela Ford (♌), Jean Garrett (♈), Aeon Karris (♏), Dan (♎) and Yvonne (♉) Klitsner, my brother Rodger Larson (♏), Jan Martino (♏), Niranjan Mehta (♋), Cathy Devorah Meyer (♉), Letha Moore (♊), Janet Isabel Murphy (♐), Kevin Parker (♎), Suzanne Richards (♊), Dan Reiter (♏), Uma Schaef (♏), Joelle St. James (♓), Da Vid Rafael (♋) of the Light Party (♒), Shirley Ronkowski (♓), (Lynn Scheurell (♋) of MyCreativeCatalyst.com, Suzy Ward (♈) of matthewbooks.com, Ruah Wild (♐), Loreon Vigne (♊) of IsisOasis.org. All your caring contributions and encouragements have helped tremendously.

Spiritual friends: Creator, God, Angels, Masters, Guides, Ancestors, Mother Earth, Nature Spirits, and beings in our Space Family, eternal thanks for guiding me on the Path.

♥♪ 🕊 ☼♪❀ ♥♪ 🕊 ☼♪❀ ♥♪ 🕊 ☼♪❀ ♥♪ 🕊 ☼♪❀ ♥♪

GRANNY RAINBOW'S GUIDELINES

FOR ASSISTING CHILDREN'S SPIRITUALITY

1. In Rainbow Land, we believe all children are holy.

2. Since children have recently emerged from the Divine Source, they are wise and full of blessings for the world.

3. All children deserve unconditional love, with no "good" or "bad" judgments about them.

4. All children deserve unconditional support for who they are as unique individuals.

5. Children are born of Nature. They have a natural affinity for Nature, and should be assisted to establish deep communion with Nature on their own terms.

6. Collectively, today's children are here to heal the Earth, and lead humanity into the Light.

7. The most important pursuit for any child is to find out why he or she is here – to discover and act upon their specific purpose in this life.

8. Children have the right to express themselves openly, spontaneously, and honestly – and have their communications received with respect.

9. All children deserve good role models, adults who are honest, wise, and compassionate.

10. In all we do, let us keep in mind the welfare of our children's children, unto the seventh generation.

⋛✶⁂ HOW TO ORDER ⁂✶⋚

⋛✶⁂✶⁂✶⁂✶⋚

THIS BOOK
High School Astrology: A Textbook of Ageless Wisdom
by Arisa Victor

All you need to know to be intelligent about astrology.

⋛✶⁂✶⁂✶⁂✶⋚

THE COMPANION VOLUME TO THIS BOOK
The Spoken Cabala: Tarot Explorations of the One Self
by Jason Lotterhand
Edited by Arisa Victor

(formerly The Thursday Night Tarot)

Words of truth that go to the heart. - Mary K. Greer

⋛✶⁂✶⁂✶⁂✶⋚

OTHER BOOKS BY THIS PUBLISHER
Featuring the early work of Paul Foster Case,
Jason's Teacher
and Arisa's Teacher through written Lessons

⋛✶⁂✶⁂✶⁂✶⋚

Please go to

The Fraternity of the Hidden Light
Fraternitas Lux Occulta

www.lvx.org

⋛✶⁂✶⁂✶⁂✶⋚

CPSIA information can be obtained
at www.ICGtesting.com
Printed in the USA
BVHW050613120720
583417BV00006B/550